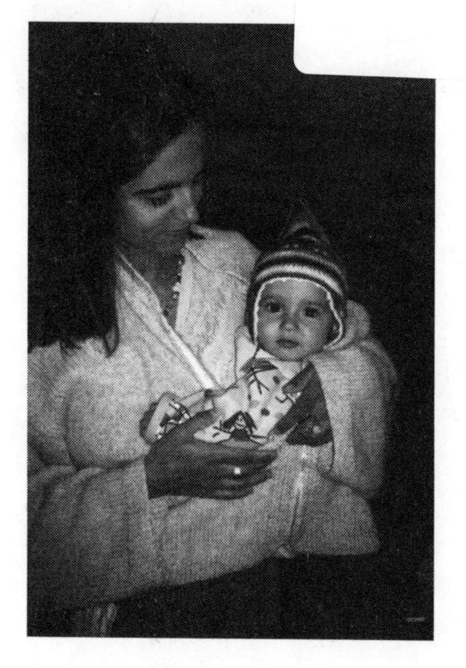

An extraordinary tale of courage, hope, determination and love

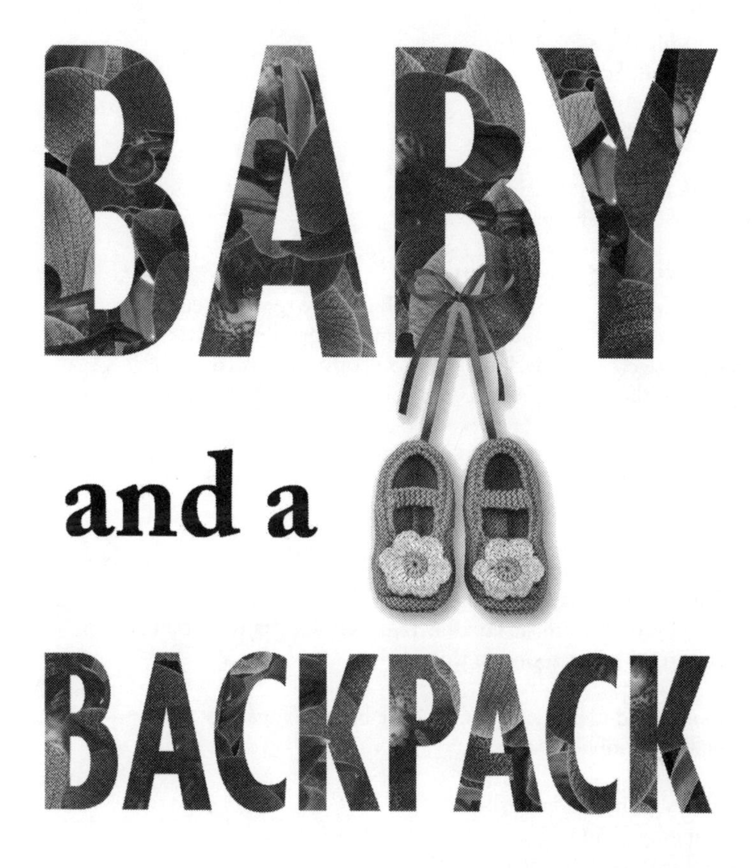

BABY and a BACKPACK

Jane Cornelius

The Five Mile Press Pty Ltd
1 Centre Road, Scoresby
Victoria 3179 Australia
www.fivemile.com.au

Part of the Bonnier Publishing Group
www.bonnierpublishing.com

First published 2014

Printed in Australia at Griffin Press.
Only wood grown from sustainable regrowth forests is used in the manufacture of paper found in this book.

Some names and identifying details have been changed to protect the privacy of individuals.

Internal design by Nada Backovic
Typesetting by Shaun Jury
Internal illustrations by Shafei Xia
Front cover texture © Shutterstock
Front cover image by Jane Cornelius

National Library of Australia Cataloguing-in-Publication entry
Cornelius, Jane, author.
Baby and a backpack
Jane Cornelius.
ISBN: 9781760060244 (paperback)
Cornelius, Jane—Travel.
Mother and child—Anecdotes.
voyages and travels—Anecdotes.
910.4

To my mum

For being the best mum you could be

Contents

Chapter 1
Magic Carpet

I had two hours to wait. I was at a London airport with a 12-week-old baby strapped to my chest, a backpack at my feet and a round-the-world ticket in my hand. I handed over the ticket at the check-in counter. It was the cheapest ticket I could buy and I smiled at the lady. My baby was feeding under a thin blanket draped over my shoulder and I hoped she wouldn't notice. It was the wrong time and place to feed but the queue was long and I didn't want to miss my turn. I wanted to be up in the air. I wanted to be as far away as possible. I wanted a different life.

I didn't want to be a single mother living on the dole in England. I had no family support. I had no money to start up a business and no bank would ever lend me any. As a struggling parent living in the countryside the same way my mother had, my life was doomed. I wanted to give my child the possibility of a different future and so, despite the huge risk, I'd chosen to travel and live rather than stay and die where I was.

People always dream of a shinier future. Little girls dream of being princesses; little boys, supermen. Little girls dream that a prince will come along one day and, with a single kiss, make their lives perfect. Sadly, the prince who kissed me had turned my life into a landslide of epic proportions. I knew no knight in shining armour was ever going to come and save me: I had to save myself. So I grabbed at every fluffy, floating thread of thought that came into my head and I wove it all together into a carpet strong enough to fly away on.

I said goodbye to the friend who had driven me to the airport. She wished me good luck and told me to be strong, but she trembled. She told me she believed in me and together we held back tears as she kissed my baby's head.

'I know your life will work out for you, Jane. Go or we'll cry too much.'

She took me to the Customs gate, the point of no return, and I let go of her hand and walked through. I was the one trembling now.

Once through Customs, I bought a cup of tea and found a table with an empty plastic chair. I had one more hour to wait before my plane departed. I sat down and took a sip from the hot polystyrene cup. I stared out at the planes on the other side of the window and adjusted my sitting position so my baby could feed again. I felt weary. I shook a brown sugar packet, ripped the corner off and poured it into my tea for extra energy. I stirred and stared at the planes until I felt the plastic stick wilt.

It was in the quiet moments that memories of him returned. Memories of him abandoning me. They would make me feel as though I was drowning in overwhelming anxiety, and thoughts of my mum's life as a single mother would push me further into the water. I'd catch myself. I'd stop breathing. I'd shake my head to make the feelings go away. I never understood how people meditated quietly and found inner peace; I had a nightmare constantly playing in my head. I tried to focus on something else and sipped my tea, but he returned again.

I hated quiet moments; they kept revealing a broken heart. I shook my head again and sighed; how had I fallen so in love with him? It was easier to keep busy. I looked up at the departure board, put the tea bag and serviette inside my cup and fussed with my baby's clothes. An announcement was made: our plane to Bali was now boarding.

Relieved, I stood up with my boarding pass in my hand, my baby strapped to my chest and my hand luggage on my forearm and started walking. I was about to find a new life for the two of us.

Chapter 2
A Twinkle

As we flew through the night, I looked out the window at the stars. My mum used to call me a little star. She said the stars you can see in the night sky are actually angels waiting to be born. They peek and blink through little holes, looking down at life. She said angels look at all the people on earth and decide which ones will be their parents. She said when she met my dad she could see a twinkle in his eye and she knew that twinkle would be me.

I'd always believed I started out as a star, an angel who chose my parents, and now my baby had chosen me. I felt the responsibility. I wanted to give her the best life I could. A tear plopped out and fell on her head. I looked out at the stars again.

When I was a little girl I used to think my mum was a star as well. She would tell me stories of how she used to dance and laugh with a famous woman called Eartha Kitt who had a singing voice like the purr of a pussycat in heat. My mum wore beautiful clothes then, all her own designs. My dad was a star, too. He was a famous British wrestler and a mutual gangster-friend had introduced them to each other. One night on the dance floor, Dad held Mum close and asked her, 'Do you want to come and live with me and have my baby?'

'Yes,' she instantly replied. She was in love with him and desperately wanted to get away from her gypsy family. When she arrived on his doorstep with her suitcases, he took the cases out of her hands and gave her my baby brother George. Dad had already been married, but his wife had run off and left baby George behind. She thought George could have a better life with my dad. My mum accepted her fate on that doorstep and walked over the threshold into a new life. Mum then filled Dad's home with two more children: my older sister Kay and me.

'To love well you have to keep working at it. Don't ever give up,' Mum would say to me.

Mum always said she came from gypsy blood, but when I was a little girl she looked nothing like one. She was beautiful and had style and grace. She said, 'All women have the choice to enhance their features and make the best of themselves,' and everyone said my mother was inspiring because of the way she looked and the way she loved her man.

'You will never find the perfect person to love,' Mum would say, and my dad definitely wasn't perfect.

He was a lover and a wrestler and I thought he was superman. He'd fly all over the world from London to Japan, thrilling people with his skills and making them scream in delight. He wore a sequined cape, shiny wrestling knickers and high lace-up boots. His wrestling name was 'The Dazzler'.

He was a regular on television and every Saturday afternoon everyone all over England would watch my dad fight.

Mum and Dad also owned a pub, which we all lived in, and Mum had a hairdressing salon, too. It was her cut-and-blow-dry specialist who turned our lives upside down: Dad slept with her and I remember the day he left the pub to go and live with her. I was about three years old.

He told me, 'Everything will always be all right in your life, Jane. Remember this.'

I was sitting at the top of the stairs outside the apartment above the pub where we all used to live. Dad took my face in his hands and told me I was beautiful. He told me how much he loved me and how I had been made absolutely perfect. He told me he had to leave and he wouldn't be living with us any more, but he promised me again, 'Everything will always be all right, Jane,' and he turned and walked down the steps.

I slipped down the few stairs on my bottom to the first landing and walked into the toilets that the staff used. I stood with my back against the cold white tiles. This was where I normally sang and pooed. I'd finish pooing and then scream for my dad, '*Come and wipe my bum!*' He'd come rushing up from the office below and find me sitting on the toilet with my feet dangling because they were too short to reach the floor. He'd place my face in his hands and tell me how clever I was. He'd pull out sheets of rough, hard toilet paper and he'd say to me, 'This hard toilet paper is not appropriate for my princess.' He'd scrunch it up and make a soft nest and would lean me forward to wipe my bum. 'Oooo,' he'd always say, 'Your poo smells like roses.'

For years I never thought my shit stank: until now.

I shook my head and tried to get more comfortable in my aeroplane seat. I badly needed to sleep.

Chapter 3

Curdled Affair

It didn't take long before Dad moved back into the pub and moved us out.

Dad bought a house for us to live in and as soon as my brother George was old enough, he left home. We girls were left to live by ourselves and Mum found it all highly embarrassing: her marriage had failed and now she was looked down on as a woman who couldn't keep her man. She stopped going to the pub, because the blow-dry specialist had moved in. Dad's family – Nana, Grandpa, our aunts, uncles and cousins – all stopped visiting us. It was like everyone forgot about us. Mum felt her whole life had gone to shit; it was over. But she was only 34.

Mum became sad and she went to the doctor. He gave her pills for depression and she said they made her head foggy. The mornings were also foggy when the milkman started to come and visit. The milkman drove a float that went 15 miles per hour and I'd get to ride on it. Mum started making him some of her delicious food.

'The way to a man's heart is through his stomach,' she'd say, and our milkman fell in love with her.

Dad became sad, too. Somebody was trying to kill him. An evil, sinister voice kept calling him telling him he was going to die. For weeks, Dad borrowed a gun from his gangster friends and carried it around. He asked the gangsters if there were any contracts out on him. They said, 'No, Joe.' So the police tapped Dad's phones and they discovered who the caller was and in the middle of the night they came around to our house to arrest Mum.

We all sobbed as Mum was dragged away in handcuffs and charged with conspiracy to murder. Mum said she knew nothing about the calls, and Kay called Dad to ask him to bail Mum out of jail because we were alone in the house. Dad refused to help her. Kay was the only one who still visited the pub. She was 15, ten years older than me, and with the separation of our parents, she had had to grow up fast and become very serious and sensible. She was the one who used to stand outside the pub, because we weren't allowed in it, and ask Dad for money so we could survive. In winter, she even had to go and ask for a winter coat. Kay always told me, 'When you grow up, Jane, make sure you study hard, go to college and get a proper job. Never grow up and be a housewife.' George was now working out of the country and Kay phoned my mum's brother (who we didn't like) for help instead. There was no one else who could help us and he bailed our mum out of jail so she could come back to us. The milkman stayed locked up.

Mum and the milkman's court case continued for a year at the Old Bailey. It made headlines in London: *Milkman Falls in Love with Wrestler's Wife and Threatens to Kill 'The Dazzler'*. Eventually Dad believed that Mum had nothing to do with the calls. He dropped his court case against her and filed divorce papers instead, and the milkman went to prison.

I didn't get to ride on a milk float any more, and Mum discovered Miss Valium. The doctor said lots of women my mum's age took Miss Valium to make them happy. I'd be playing with my dollies when she'd pop the pills in her mouth and take sleeping pills too. She'd put pillows over her head to try and block out the world and I'd try to wake her up. I couldn't. I'd go and see my sister Kay to see if she would play with me instead, but she was always too busy studying, trying to make her life better, so I'd return to Mum's side. I'd shake her and end up picking up her pill bottles and shaking them instead. I'd play by myself, pretending the bottles were rattles for my dolls. I never wanted my mum to be sad about her life.

Maybe it was the pills that made her drive into a brick wall. I was in the front seat of her big maroon car and we were driving down the hill really fast. Normally we slowed down at the bottom, but this time we didn't. I looked at Mum.

She was staring straight ahead at the ugly brick wall in front of us and said: 'We're going to die.'

I told her, 'I can't, I'm too young,' and I reached over and pulled the keys out of the wooden dashboard.

She looked at me and time froze. She spun the wheel. The car swerved. Mum flung her arm across my chest and I slid right under it. The car stopped. On my knees on the floor, I stared up at her. I was happy we hadn't hit any bricks. She reached out her hand and pulled me back onto the seat. She said she was very sorry for her bad driving. That night she disappeared and returned with tickets for the circus.

An airhostess offered me a plastic glass of water and woke me up; I accepted it. Flying and breastfeeding was very dehydrating.

I never wanted to be a single mum like my mum, left all alone to look after a family. This was never my life plan. My plan when I was a little girl was to have a great life, travel the world like my dad, be famous and get to stand on a stage and entertain people. I rested my head against the window frame and the corners of my mouth lifted as I felt a bubble of pride pop in me. At least I'd got away from living on the dole in the English countryside.

Chapter 4

A Fairy Tale

As I got off the plane I sniffed at the Bali air. It had flowers in it, and the smell of the ocean, and its humidity kissed my face hello. My baby was now awake and she timidly looked out from the sling on my chest.

'This used to be our home, Poppy,' I whispered into the top of her head; I didn't want other people to know our secret. At Customs I watched tourists looking anxious as they moved along in the queue and then dashed to the conveyor belt for their luggage. They looked hot and bothered and I wanted to tell them, 'Relax, you've entered paradise,' but instead I told myself, *You can relax now – at least for a little while.*

Kadek, my first Bali friend, was slumped over the barricade waiting to greet us. When he saw me he jumped up and waved.

I loved seeing his toothy grin and enthusiasm for life. We grabbed each other, but it was difficult to hug with Poppy between us. She made squawks of disapproval and he pulled her out of her sling and held her up for inspection.

'So this is Poppy!' he said, showing her his teeth – and she stopped squawking. He pulled her close to him and safely tucked her under one arm and picked up my bag with the other. We looked at each other and couldn't speak. No words could describe what had happened to me in these past few months.

'You okay?' Kadek asked with kind eyes. I nodded.

In the jeep, relieved to be together again, we chugged into Seminyak. But as I looked out at the ocean from the road, I remembered the same drive I had taken with Poppy's father when I first met him. I'd picked him up from the airport, too.

He had been travelling with a friend of mine. I was slumped over the barricade waiting and I noticed a stranger's golden skin and hair so blond sunlight bounced off it. My daughter's was the same colour. I'd watched the man haul a large black tin trunk off the baggage carousel and I was mesmerised by him. He wore an expensive linen suit and his shirt was hanging out. I knew an expensive label lay at the back of his neck and I wondered what his neck would be like to touch. I looked down at his shoes. My mum always taught me you can tell a lot about a man by looking at his shoes. They were leather, smart, well designed – and he made me tingle. My knees gave way on the barricade and I leaned onto the metal rail for support and it began to give way too.

Embarrassed, I realised I should be looking for my friend, not gazing at this stranger. It was my friend who found me. He had a European swagger and as he came close I couldn't understand why he was wearing grubby fisherman's pants from Thailand. He grabbed me by my shoulders and kissed me on both cheeks. Over his shoulder I saw the angelic vision I'd been staring at earlier. The vision was walking towards me and smiling. I thought I was having a fantastic day back then.

'Jane, I hope you don't mind. I've brought a friend with me,' my European buddy said. 'If there's not enough room in your house, we can easily rent somewhere else.'

'Welcome to Bali,' I said quickly, not wanting anyone to leave, and in polite English fashion I held out my hand to the Blond. He took hold of me instead and kissed me on both cheeks and looked into my eyes and said 'Hello.' He had a strong London accent and this was another pleasant surprise. I'd missed hearing English voices in Bali and here was an English hottie with the most stunning indigo-blue eyes I'd ever seen, about to come home with me.

We all piled into my old jeep and drove along the beach road to my house. I watched surfers in the ocean pretending to be fish food and birds swirling above them waiting for their dinner. Men with long hair played frisbee on the Kuta sand, and tourists lay on sarongs, imitating red lobsters.

Today, the sun was dazzling on the beach. Green palms swayed in the breeze and I looked at Kadek and pulled the blanket higher over Poppy's head to protect her from the wind. I looked behind me. My jeep was from the Second World War and welded on to the back of it was the original radiophone. It was still there. I had thought many times that instead of driving the Blond back to my house that day, I should have stopped the car and called for help then and there. But I didn't. Instead, deliriously smitten, I kept driving over all the Bali potholes and took him home.

My jeep coughed and spluttered and squeezed down a thin alleyway. Kadek's wife Elu heard the noise and came running out to greet us. I wanted to sob as I fell into her arms, and I held her tightly as Kadek took Poppy from me again, but I had no more tears. I'd cried so much since I had left Bali, I had no more salty water left in me. Holding each other, we all stumbled up the uneven, pebbly path. Elu ran ahead to push open the door in the wall. It opened and revealed my old fairy tale existence.

I used to love Bali so much, but like Poppy's father, it hadn't protected me and kept me safe. I knew I had to be strong; I took a deep breath and stepped through the doorway into my old life.

An emerald garden awaited me and I brushed away rubbery banana leaves and held Poppy closer. I wasn't sure how I was going to feel or what I was going to find. My eyes were fresh, like a tourist's. It was as if I was experiencing Bali for the very first time. I stopped. I was in awe of the magical life I used to live.

A house rose from the garden. It was open-plan, with minimal walls. Thick coconut poles held up a mammoth straw roof and bamboo blinds hung, ready to pull down for protection from the monsoon rains. The house looked more like a luxurious five-star camping facility than an actual home. Elu came closer and asked to take Poppy. Elu used to be my maid and she had made my life here even more heavenly. It was so unfair I had had to leave back then. I carefully gave Poppy to Elu. She turned, and she and Kadek ran to the end of the garden. Under the mango tree I watched them squabbling. They both wanted to hold Poppy and it made me giggle; nobody had fought to take Poppy out of my arms since she had been born. I watched Elu pick flowers and let Poppy sniff them and then she ran towards me and hugged me again, sniffing me. In Bali when you greet good friends, you often sniff their faces. You not only take in how good it is to see, feel and hear that person again, you also take in how good it is to smell them. Bali can heighten your senses.

'You like shower?' Elu asked. 'We keep Poppy and you have papaya juice?' I nodded yes and forced myself to move so

I wouldn't stay stuck on the white stepping-stones. I stepped up into my house and looked at the teak dining table. It had fresh flowers on it, and the Buddha painting done by my girlfriend gazed down on it. Bamboo day beds and a hammock overlooked the garden. In front of me stretched an expanse of clean white tiles. I used to teach yoga classes on this floor. Elu was now busy in the open-plan kitchen and dashed around making my juice. I walked to the back of the house. The bedroom door was open and the mosquito net had already been taken down and tucked carefully around the bottom of the bed. I stepped back and looked up at the spiral staircase and walked up to the second floor. A few years ago, I'd built a platform up here so I could put a mattress on it. I wanted to be higher so I could lie in bed and watch the sunrise and see the paddy fields. The mattress was huge, big enough for four people, and a princess mosquito net hung over it with puffs of iridescent cushions underneath. Before I used to work in this spot as well as sleep; it was so perfect. I imagined doing the same again, with Poppy by my side.

'I made you food in fridge. If you hungry.' I heard Elu calling from downstairs. I returned to her and she handed me a fresh juice as Kadek swung in the hammock singing to Poppy. 'You have shower,' Elu said, pointing me to the bathroom. I nodded. Maybe I smelled? Elu disappeared into the downstairs bedroom and started unpacking my bag. I walked into the bathroom and shut the door.

I took off my clothes and dropped them into a basket. Elu would collect them the next day. She'd wash, iron and fold them and I would find them neatly back in my wardrobe. *Why do I plan to leave here again?* I stepped into my oversized, shell-shaped terracotta bathtub. The bathroom opened onto a small garden. I turned on the hot water and tried to wash off the past year of bad memories. Geckos sang on the bathroom walls and stomped their feet. The sky was becoming darker and fruit bats had taken the place of birds. They were flapping and feeding as the banana trees shook a primeval beat in the breeze. I could hear waves crashing nearby.

I came out of the bathroom wrapped in a towel and Elu slipped in by my side with Poppy in her arms.

'I wash Poppy and get her ready for bed. You eat food.' She waved me away and I smiled at Kadek. I felt so much love being around them both again.

They both finally got ready to leave and we hugged and sniffed each other goodbye.

'You rest,' Kadek said as they walked over the stepping-stones away from me. 'We see you in the morning.'

They walked through the door in the garden wall and locked it behind them, and I was left holding a clean Poppy in a thin cotton nightdress and a clean nappy. I looked into Poppy's face. She was tired and her cheeks were red. She had been such a good girl for the whole journey, but now it was time to feed her and let her go to sleep. I climbed up the spiral staircase to my little bit of heaven and clambered onto the bed's platform. I pulled back the mosquito net and climbed inside. I lay Poppy down and made a pile of cushions around her for protection. I then held her close as she fed and drifted off to sleep. I stroked her blonde hair and looked out at the sky. It was covered in pomegranate colours and I remembered I'd never given this house a name, but I now knew what it should be called: Villa Poppy.

Chapter 5
Made with Love

With jet lag, the heat and the new environment, we both kept waking up in the night. Poppy would want to feed and I stroked her head, watching the geckos stuck to the wall like baby dragons guarding us, my mind drifting off to the time I spent with the Blond in this house.

We had become stuck to each other back then in the beginning, like the pads of gecko feet to my walls, but we never kissed or made love. I didn't want a relationship with a passing tourist, simply getting to taste something sweet and knowing they would be leaving soon. I wanted something more.

In Bali I had a business designing homewares for the UK. I had been 19 when I first discovered the island. I was crazy then, travelling all over the world and scared of nothing. I'd been looking after myself since I was 15 when I had run away from a revolting home life. Back then, I clunked my heart closed to my family. It was self-preservation and it gave me strength to get away from them and go to college. I got myself a skill, and then travelled with it and didn't stop. Some travellers get worms, but I grew wings, and by the age of 18 I'd been to many different places: Thailand, Africa, Russia, India. I'd find things to buy in one country and sell them in another. 'How do you have the balls to do what you do, Jane?' friends would ask me, and I'd answer, 'I don't feel any fear.' My business grew and made me lots of money and when I was 24 I built a house for myself in Bali.

When I was 27, the Blond came into my life and I knew I was ready for things to change. I wanted to open my heart, and even though I didn't want to fall in love with a tourist, passion got the better of me. Followed by what I thought was love. The time had come: the time to love, to fully open my heart to another, and I made a choice to trust the Blond with it. Too soon I became pregnant, and overwhelming vulnerability flooded me. I looked to him to be my family. I hoped he would keep me safe. But instead, he took everything he could, helped to spend everything I had, and then left me stranded, pregnant, with no money.

He used to work as an offshore diver before he came to Bali. He'd work for months, make lots of money, go on long holidays until he spent it all, and then he would go back to work. But when he met me he didn't want to leave me or Bali. He had another idea. If he changed his diving qualifications, he could be a diving instructor and teach the tourists how to dive instead of leaving Bali to work somewhere else. All he needed to do was go to New Zealand, do a few crash courses and get re-qualified. The only problem with his idea was that he was already broke and living off his gold credit cards.

We were both young and carefree then and I didn't want to focus on his silly money issues, so I ignored them. I had a good job in Bali. I was still making homewares for a company in London and life was cheap. It didn't bother me to pay for his day-to-day living expenses until he worked things out, and we were very happy together for a year.

My sister Kay even came to Bali on a holiday and we told her our good news: 'We're getting married!'

'When?' she asked.

'We have no idea, whenever the moment takes us,' we both replied.

Kay thought it was simply a phase I was going through; she'd been through many before. She told me the Blond was nice, but she said no more and I knew she didn't like him.

I went on a road trip with Kay and her family around the island and when I returned the Blond was sitting on my bamboo couch. He dragged me onto it. There, in a wild love-making session with no time to run upstairs and get supplies, he blew.

'What the fuck have you done?' I asked, sweaty and shocked.

'You said you wanted a child, and I want to make you happy.'

'Are you fucking mad?' I said. 'I didn't mean I wanted one with you now!'

The two of us forgot about that little incident. We thought there was no way we could make a baby with only one little mistake, but destiny had a different plan for us. And when we discovered I was pregnant, neither of us questioned whether we should keep the baby. We were in love; we were going to get married; we'd already spoken about spending the rest of our lives together. We thought life was simply speeding up that process.

In tranquil Bali there are often earthquake tremors, but now our lives began to rock and roll.

With our baby coming into the world, I wanted to start afresh. I didn't want debts hanging over our heads, so I did what I thought was the right thing to do: I paid off all his credit cards. Then I bought us tickets to New Zealand so he could re-qualify as a diving instructor. I felt my life was on a conveyor belt and I was doing the right things to make a successful start for us as a new family.

Travelling in New Zealand wasn't easy, though. I hired a Maui camper van for a couple of months and while the Blond went to school I went windsurfing. In the evenings when I picked him up he was always quiet and I'd ask him what was wrong, but he'd say, 'Nothing – just school,' and then ignore me. He'd say, 'You're hormonal. Chill out. I just have to concentrate on my studies.' I felt I had to trust him because maybe he was right, maybe my feelings of insecurity were simply hormonal. So I practised being more caring and tried to ignore his behaviour and when he qualified we travelled around New Zealand for a holiday before returning to Bali. We cooked organic food, camped on beautiful sites, and swam naked on long white sandy beaches, but he was like the fish, he stayed so distant. When I tried to confront him about the change in his behaviour, he'd slip out of my hands, saying: 'Stop worrying. Relax. It's the pregnancy.'

I knew I was hormonal and I was trying to chill out, but something in me felt very wrong and I knew it wasn't my baby. I didn't know what to do about it.

When we arrived back in Bali I had very little money left, but I didn't worry as I was about to receive my biannual order from London. It would bring in enough money to finance my life for another year. I looked forward to working again. I thought it would take my mind off our relationship, but then a cyclone blew into town and it smashed up the idyllic world I was trying to hold onto.

I didn't receive my order from London.

That meant I was now officially broke.

And pregnant!

Fucking hailstones started coming out of my mouth in torrential storms and they all flew in his direction. He was now re-qualified, but he wasn't looking for work. Instead I'd watch him lying in my hammock reading spiritual books. Or he'd go for a surf or a puff of happy baccy at our neighbour's house. 'You're not fucking on holiday now!' I'd say, disbelieving. I'd walk away from him to the end of my garden. I felt if I was any closer I'd kill him, and I'd pace around with hormonal cricket balls for eyes.

'Everything will work out,' he'd call out to me from his hammock.

'How the fuck do you work that out?' I'd shout back at him. He'd wave the Osho spiritual book he was reading up in the air. 'You have to trust in life.'

I felt like a cricket player. I wanted to spin the balls of my eyes and knock him out of his hammock. *Trust in life!* Up until now I'd only trusted in myself.

How was I going to live in Bali with no money? How was I going to pay for food, the house and a hospital in case anything went wrong? I didn't have parents who could support me; I knew he didn't either. Where was the man I thought I had fallen in love with? My husband-to-be? Wasn't this the man I was meant to trust with my life? How could I trust him to look after my child and me?

I was angry. Childhood feelings of not being cared for returned and swirled inside me. I had a three-and-half-month-old baby in my tummy. It was too big to give back to existence. I couldn't ask, 'Could you please send it back when my life is more organised?' I kept looking at him reading his spiritual books and I knew I had to do something drastic. I felt like vomiting again.

I still had a ticket back to the UK. He still had an onward ticket to Australia. I decided to make some new samples of work and we would go back to those countries and hopefully sell them. Then we could both return to Bali. He'd help me with production and we could have our baby together. The Blond brightened up like a sunflower when I told him my new plan. A Bali heatwave arrived, caused by the El Niño effect. Everything heated up.

Chapter 6
Bali Hell

For the next six weeks the Blond became my driver. We bounced all over Bali on a motorbike making new samples. My jeep was too slow and clunky to manoeuvre down the small Bali lanes. It kept overheating in the traffic. A Yamaha bike was quicker. We went to all the factories I'd ever worked with, seeing what they were up to and what I could be inspired to make. I showed the Blond how Bali businesses worked: sampling, placing orders, delivery times and quality control. We flew over broken roads, paddy fields and dirt tracks. I strapped my belly with bandages to stop the motorbike vibrations affecting the baby and I'd often have to shout 'Stop!' He'd screech to a halt by the side of the road and I'd jump off and rush to a paddy field and heave. No vomit would ever come up, but the retching and waves of nausea would take me off balance. I'd grab hold of blades of grass to stop myself falling into the drainage ditches and he'd shout at me, 'Are you all right?'

I'd be bent over double, sweat pouring down my ever-enlarging breasts. I'd heave, 'I'm okayyyy.' I'd look at the thin blades of grass through watery vision and my knuckles would be white, holding on to my knees for support. The wave of nausea would pass and I'd stagger back to our bike. I'd wipe the sweat off my face with my sarong, get on the bike and rest my head on his back. I'd strap the sarong around the two of us and he would tie it tightly in front of him so if I fell asleep, he could feel if I started to slip off the bike.

El Niño was against us, and so were the Bali gods. Bali was a great place for being creative, which is why so many artists lived there, but you had to give it time and we were in a race against it. Our samples never got made, or turned up too late, or were simply crap. The rice offerings my staff made to the gods in the little temples around my house looked better than what we came up with.

Our passion also died. The Blond no longer wanted to make love to a stressed-out fat lady and, exhausted at the end of a day, I would want to feel close to him. I wanted to feel everything was still all right in my life. I wanted to feel he still loved me and I wanted him to make love to me. But he would roll over and say he was tired and I would stay awake and look at his back.

They say Bali sits on powerful earth energy lines called lay lines. They say you have to be careful when you're on them because they will enhance your every emotion. Balinese constantly go to temples to give thanks and have cleansing ceremonies to change their energy if they find themselves moving towards the dark. During this time, I too lit lots of candles and incense. I had regular flower baths to cleanse myself and instructed my staff to put more food and flowers on the altars inside and outside my house. But the only beings the offerings made happy were the packs of wild dogs that started living outside my door. I'd hear their barking at night-time as I looked at the Blond's back and the sound seemed to confirm that my paradise was fucked up.

I was five months pregnant when I sat in an aeroplane seat and clicked my seatbelt closed. I was ready to fly out of Bali to London. I rented out my house and gave money to Kadek to look after his family. The Blond flew off the island, too, and we each had bags full of crap samples.

In London I stayed at a friend's house and tried to sell the samples. It didn't take long before I received a fax from the Blond saying:

> I don't want to return to Bali any more. Australia is a good place to live. I like it here. Maybe you would like it too?

I faxed back:

> How are we going to survive there, work, make money and have the baby?

He didn't fax back for a long time. Then I got another fax:

> I will make surfboards.

I faxed back:

> How do you know how to make surfboards? You come from Southall in London.

He replied:

> I don't know, I'll learn.

I couldn't help myself. I faxed back:

> **Like you learned how to be a diving instructor and then worked at that?**

Tears fell in London. They fell through holes in the wicker trunks I leaned against for support. I kept re-reading his faxes. He never mentioned his baby. Did he forget he had made a little soul? Another fax then arrived with a clear statement:

> **I don't want to be with you any more.**

I replied:

> **What about the baby?**

He wrote:

> **We can co-parent.**

He'd moved on – obviously to live in Australia. The Blond had no idea how we were going to co-parent. He had no idea how he was going to help me in London. His answer to everything was 'I'm sorry.'

But I had to take responsibility for this mess I was in. I'd fallen in love and made a baby with the wrong man, and I too said sorry often to my ever-growing belly. I hoped my child would forgive me one day – at least I could tell her she had been made with love.

Chapter 7
A Friend

When I received the fax from the Blond saying he didn't want to be with me any more, my heart broke into a million pieces. I packed up my bag. I wanted my dad. I got in a taxi to go and stay with him, and while I was there another wife of his, the Bunny, went loony.

Dad said to me, 'I think it would be best if you leave, Jane.'

I asked him, 'Leave and go where exactly? I have no money, no home, I'm pregnant and have just been abandoned by the father of my child. Where do you expect me to go?'

'Go and stay at your friend's house again,' he said. 'You like it there and you'll be happy.'

Distraught, I went to Raymond and Dee's. I instantly fell asleep and didn't wake up until the following morning. I'd slept for nearly 20 hours.

Nobody was awake, not even London, when I made myself a cup of tea. British tea can heal all sorts of wounds and I looked out of the window over the London mews and felt strangely calm and still. I couldn't remember the last time I felt this way. It felt like a massive storm had passed. I sipped my drink and made some toast and noticed the stillness wasn't only in me. It was everywhere. Nothing was moving in the apartment or on the streets and there were no pigeons in the air. The smell of toast was the only indication there was life in the world at all. The toaster popped. I stared blankly out of the window. I knew what I had to do. That's what had brought the calm in me – just like the morning stillness. My baby fluttered inside my stomach and I placed a hand on my belly. Something banged against it.

I ate the toast, ran a hot bath, made another mug of tea and wallowed in the steaming water. The heat soothed me and took away the pains from the previous day. I sipped my tea and watched my bloated breasts float. I felt my baby fluttering. I stayed in the bath water until my fingers became wrinkled and then hauled myself out. I opened the small bathroom window to let the steam out and noticed gentle snowflakes falling. They were pretty and delicate and I wanted to watch them, but I left the room so I wouldn't get cold. I dried and dressed hunched over the small heater. Once I was complete with my Converse sneakers, dungarees and beanie on, I packed a bag and wrote a note for Raymond and Dee. I washed up my cup and plate and left them on the drying rack next to the sink.

Snowflakes were still lightly falling but the sky was glowing brighter, telling me it was a more acceptable hour to call my father. The phone kept ringing and ringing. I didn't put it down. I kept waiting and eventually he answered. I asked him if I could borrow his car.

'Yes,' he said.

'I'll come over to get it now.'

In the snow, I walked to his pub and tried to catch odd snowflakes in my mouth. He met me outside and gave me the keys, but then insisted on driving me to the petrol station. We didn't speak about the day before, and in the petrol station I sat in the car watching him as he changed a tyre, filled the tank with petrol and filled the water tank with anti-freeze. I drove him back to the pub and he put some cash in my hand. He wished me good luck as I drove off to the sounds of the radio.

The music cheered me, the heater warmed me, and the windscreen wipers were good at taking the snow away. I drove out of London, west into the countryside. It was going to take me about four hours to get to where I was going.

I enjoyed the freedom of letting go of all the thoughts about how my life should be. It made me feel as light as the snowflakes. I was open to new possibilities and there was no point getting stuck on old ideas. They were painful, fruitless and made me feel I was bashing my head against a rotten apple. All I was getting was maggots. I had to do something and the only person that could help me was me. I jiggled in my seat to the music and it made me giggle. I used to do this with my mum when I was little and we would wave our arms out of the windows like wings, laughing at each other, pretending we were making the car fly.

I had no good reason to drive to Glastonbury. I only knew I couldn't survive and find cheap lodgings in London. I knew life in the countryside was cheaper and I was now five months pregnant with no money to get back to Bali. Even if I did get there, I had no job or money to survive with. I had to find a safe place to settle down and give birth. I couldn't stay on the mattress at my friend's house. Every year I used to drive to Glastonbury; I used to go to the festival there and always had a good time – and I didn't know where else to go. So that's where I headed.

I stayed in a B&B outside Glastonbury for the first night. In the morning, starving, eating eggs and bacon, I read the local newspaper and circled cheap accommodation in thick red pen. I used the B&B's phone to call a number and the woman at the other end of the line gave me directions.

I drove along country lanes, towards Somerset's Mendip Hills. The English village I was looking for came into view and it looked like the picture on a box of traditional English fudge. It had a stone church and a stately manor house with a few cottages scattered around it. The cottages all had smoke coming from their chimneys. I drove through the village and up towards the open fields the woman had described, and there on the left was the car park she had told me about. An L-shaped cottage sat in front of me with white snow lying on its old tiled roof. Crystal covered fields sat all around and fat cows blew steam from their noses like dragons. I heard a lock turn in the cottage door. A smiling lady appeared and called out across the car park.

'Hello! Please come in out of the cold.'

The lady's name was Rosemary and she had a Labrador dog that smacked her legs with its tail. I stepped into the cottage and found myself in a country kitchen with thick wooden beams overhead, and in the middle of it stood a wooden table that could sit ten people.

'Your home is so pretty,' I said, feeling stunned by everything that had happened to me over the past few days.

'It really is,' said Rosemary. 'Come and have a look at my garden before you sit down. You would like that too.' And Rosemary waved me over to the window by the deep kitchen sink with its brass taps and together we gazed out. Rosemary was a qualified gardener and deeply in love with her garden.

She described to me how I could only see a hint of the glory that would emerge later on in the year.

'Sometimes you have to be very patient for good things to happen in your life, my dear,' she said.

Over tea at her kitchen table we chatted and got to know each other. Rosemary would be my landlady if I rented the accommodation she was offering and she told me about her children who were about the same age as me. They had moved away from home too. I told her I used to live in Bali, but had now decided to come back and live in England. Rosemary never questioned why I was returning but she did ask, 'Will it be just you renting the cottage?'

'Yes,' I replied. *Kind of*, I thought. I didn't want to tell her about the baby in my tummy just yet.

'Let me show you the little cottage I have to rent,' she said. 'Come on, Gwellar old girl.' I followed Rosemary as she limped through her kitchen and into the lounge room with her dog. She told me she had a bad knee and had had many operations to fix it, but it was still bad. The lounge room was full of too many upright antique chairs and she told me they'd all come from her mother's house. 'I hardly ever sit in this lounge,' she said as we slowly passed all the chairs. 'It's too cold in winter and I don't want to pay the electricity bills to heat it. I spend most of my time in the kitchen anyway.' We came to a door and she unlocked it. It was the connecting door to the accommodation she was renting. She looked back and smiled at me, 'It's up to us whether we keep this door locked,' she said and I felt like we were about to discover a secret place together.

Down a corridor we went. We passed four rooms to the left and it looked like the cottage extension may have been set up as a B&B at one time. I liked the slow pace at which we moved together. A separate front door from the main cottage opened onto the car park and Rosemary told me she had run the cottage as a B&B, but it proved too much with her knee. That's why she now wanted to lease the whole thing. The cottage was adorable. The kitchen, bedroom, bathroom and lounge each had a window overlooking an apple orchard, and beyond that you could see the Mendip Hills and Glastonbury Tor. We gazed out the windows together.

'I never tire of the views here,' Rosemary said. 'And Gwellar loves going for walks, but I'm afraid I'm not up to it nowadays.'

'I'll take her,' I said, but then realised I didn't even live in the cottage. 'I mean, I'd take her if I lived here.' I paused again. 'Sorry – I don't mean to be so rude – I really mean to say, I'd love to live here and be your tenant, if you want me. I could help you with Gwellar and your garden and we could have more tea and talks. I'd like that ...'

'That would be lovely,' Rosemary said. 'Let's have another cup of tea to discuss this further.'

'That's a good idea,' I said, 'because there are other things I need to tell you before you actually say yes to me.'

Back in the kitchen I sat down and watched Rosemary make tea in a teapot on her Aga stove. She covered the teapot in a hand-knitted cosy and then asked me, 'So what else do you have to tell me?'

I gulped. 'I'm pregnant.'

'I know, my dear.'

'How do you know?'

'You're too little to have a tummy like that,' Rosemary said. I looked down and relaxed, finally letting it out.

'Rosemary. I'm also doing this alone.'

She sat down now with her teapot and two china mugs. Her voice went soft. 'I love children. I miss mine very much. I have grandchildren, but they all live in New Zealand. Having you and a baby around would be fun. We'd like it, wouldn't we, Gwellar old girl?' Gwellar's ears stood up and she started wagging her bum and bashing her tail on the edge of her wicker dog basket.

'Rosemary, you're so sweet, but I need to tell you something else.'

'What, my dear?'

'Sometimes, you fall on hard times, and that's what's happened to me.' I went quiet. Trying to get my words out was difficult. They were pebbles lodged in my throat. Gwellar lay quietly looking at me and Rosemary put her hands on mine.

'We've all had hard times, my dear,' Rosemary said. 'The man I had my children with and gave all my good years to left me and now I'm too old to move on and change my life. I also don't have the energy any more and my knees won't take me anywhere ... My children have grown up and left me too and now it's just Gwellar and me. I know what hard times are, my dear. I think you are very brave, Jane.' Her kind words moved the pebbles in my throat and they made my eyes water. She took the tea cosy off her teapot and poured us both some tea.

'Rosemary, I want to be honest with you. I think honesty is always the best thing, then you can't let anybody down because they've always known the truth.' I swallowed hard. 'As well as being pregnant, Rosemary, I also have no money. My bank balances are empty and that's why I'm back in England. I'm not telling you this for you to worry, because I will always pay your rent on time, I promise you that! But I am telling you because I have to go to the Social Security and go on the dole until I can sort my finances out again.' I quickly grabbed at my teacup and took a big mouthful. My heart was beating. I thought, I should have stopped talking a while ago. I couldn't look her in the eye. I was too worried about what I might see. I couldn't bear

any more rejection. I continued talking because of nerves, and because the silence was deafening.

'If you rent the cottage to me, Rosemary, you will probably have to sign forms from the Social Services. But I promise you, on my child's life, I'll always pay your rent somehow and you will always have your money on time.' I took another mouthful of my tea. I swallowed and finally had the courage to look her in the face for some indication of her feelings. She looked numb. I knew landlords didn't like to rent their properties to people on the dole, because they could be unreliable, and I had nothing apart from my words to prove otherwise to Rosemary. But then her face broke into a smile.

'My dear, that's no problem at all,' she said and she put both her hands on top of mine again and my eyes dropped bubbles of water.

'I'm sorry,' I said. 'Everything has been very difficult lately and I'm overwhelmed.' Rosemary moved her chair closer to mine and put her arms around me so my tears could drip all over her hand-knitted woolly jumper.

'I'm going to be next door,' Rosemary said. 'I'll be happy to help you and your baby. We should be celebrating now, not crying. I've found a tenant I like very much and we have a baby to bring into this world.'

I felt I needed to tell her everything – however bizarre it was.

'There's one more thing, Rosemary.'

'Yes, my dear,' and she pulled her chair back, looking utterly fascinated as she took hold of her tea mug.

'I want to give birth underwater.'

She started to laugh, spitting out her tea, and then excused herself for being so rude. She told me she didn't know if her laughter was out of nervousness or sheer joy.

'How absolutely wonderful,' she said, 'I've heard about it, but please tell me more.'

'You give birth in a tank of water and it looks like a large children's paddling pool.'

'Really?'

'Yes.'

'But the thing is ...'

'What?'

'I want to give birth at home.' Rosemary sat back again. How much more could this poor woman take? Why can't I simply shut up?

'Rosemary, I'll be giving birth in four months' time and I want to get a birthing pool to give birth in. The lounge in the cottage you have for rent has a little sink and taps and it would be the perfect position for a birthing pool. It has such a magical view. That is of course if you still want to rent the cottage to me and I completely understand if, knowing everything now, you don't want to.' I gulped and waited for an answer. The kitchen went very quiet. 'I won't get your carpet wet,' I said hopefully.

'It all sounds wonderful to me! Doesn't it, Gwellar?' she said, beaming. 'I would love for you to live here. It would bring some fun and energy back to the old place and blow out some cobwebs, and we all need that.'

Chapter 8

Making a Nest

I spent the rest of the day sitting in the Social Services office in Glastonbury, and it was a demoralising process. The only upside was that I was in a town where no one knew me. In between discovering what I was entitled to, how I could get it and filling out the endless forms, my mind would bash me up. How could you be so fucking stupid? How could you get yourself in this mess? The words in my head overwhelmed me and made me feel sick, so I tried other words to calm myself. You've done really well, you've just got to get over this hurdle of the Social and you're safe.

I was now responsible for another person's life as well as my own. I wasn't doing a very good job of looking after myself, how was I meant to look after a child? A flicker of sanity returned as my name was called. I stood up and walked towards the window and was given more forms to fill in.

The baby books I'd read in Bali said you pass on what you think and feel to the baby. My thoughts were destructive so I had to start changing them. Dad always said to me, 'Jane, fake it till you make it.' But what was I supposed to do? Fake I had a supportive man by my side helping me through this? I had to keep focusing on what was happening right now, step by step; focus on gratitude instead of all the shit in my life. I felt grateful I was English and paid taxes. It felt good to know I was born into a country that helped its people when they were down.

I wanted to sleep again. Fuck – I needed a car. The cottage was in the middle of nowhere. I needed washing powder too. I had less than a hundred pounds left. How was I going to pay the deposit on the cottage? Crash. Bang. Breathe. I needed to calm down. *I was going to have to call everyone and tell them what had happened and ask for help. I couldn't do this alone.* I'd never asked for help before. I fell asleep and was awoken by my name being called repeatedly.

In the darkness, I drove back to London. The cold in the office had seeped into my bones, but I'd found a home and the Social said it would pay the rent and also give me a small amount of money each week to live on. What I had achieved gave me the energy to keep driving. I couldn't afford to pay for another night in the B&B.

Maybe I could become like Rosemary and learn how to garden. Maybe she would let me have a little bit of her garden so I could grow vegetables and save money. I'd have to find a way to make some money.

Back in London, I called Helen, the mother of an old boyfriend. I'd met her years before when I had been dating her son, and we'd stayed friends ever since. I got on so well with her I once asked her jokingly, 'Helen, if I ever have a baby would you be my baby's adopted grandmother?' Now, not having my own mother around, I hoped Helen would help me out.

'Of course!' she replied happily, 'It would be an honour.' I felt touched, and wished I'd made a baby with her son instead of the Blond, but I hadn't. Mark and I had remained best friends too, because we still adored each other. Like me, he worked between London and Bali, so over the years we would see each other, and when I was having problems in Bali, it was Mark I'd run crying to. He would tell me to pull it together and to go back and try to work at my relationships. 'You are not young and stupid any more,' he would say.

'Before we drive down to the cottage,' Helen said on the phone, 'I'll drive you around town and help you pick up anything you need. I have extra towels, pots, pans and crockery, so you won't need to buy much.'

'You're going to be a great Nana, Helen,' I told her.

A couple of days later, with two cars crammed full of baby stuff, Nana Helen and I drove to Glastonbury in convoy. I couldn't believe I needed all this for a baby. When I visited my brother and he kept piling the kid's stuff he didn't want any more into my car, it made me feel uncomfortable and very environmentally unfriendly. In Africa I had noticed babies only needed a few cloths, but now I had plastic prams, cots, changing tables and bouncy things; plastic seats for cars, tables and the floor; colourful designer plastic to hold stinky nappies; bottles; bottle sterilisers; cutlery; blankets to wrap her in; plastic toys to rattle, chew and ding; and a whole designer wardrobe of midget clothing. I could have melted all the plastic down and re-built it into a boat to live on. Happily, though, also squeezed in my car were my faithful organic wicker trunks from Raymond and Dee's.

Rosemary and Gwellar were there to greet us as our cars arrived, and Helen made friends with the two of them as quickly as I did. We were like a little gathering of goddesses brought together to provide a safe haven for another one to come into the world.

It was partly because of Guru Johnny that I'd first come to Glastonbury. As yoga and meditation teachers, every year we applied for free tickets to the Glastonbury Festival and in exchange we'd teach workshops. Johnny liked to call himself Guru de Lux and he'd set up camp with a fully kitted-out Winnebago van and build a fence around it. It was the only Winnebago on site then. 'This fence is to keep those fucking hippy nutters out,' he'd say. During the day we would teach our practices and at night Johnny would make us gourmet dinners and open up a bottle of red. We'd have hot showers and even our own sit-down toilet. We would sit on chairs around a roaring campfire he'd made and happily watch the lunacy revolving around us. A dirty grungy would run by with a chainsaw, offering us acid, and Johnny would say, 'Love you mate, but fuck off we don't need anything – we're high on life – come to class tomorrow.' Others would run by holding flowers and we would raise our glasses to them. Then the Hare Krishna mob would pass, singing and dancing and banging their tambourines. I only knew the festival fields and had never been to actual Glastonbury town, but every year I'd always had a good time there. So on that calm snowy morning, that is where I drove to.

The work to prepare the cottage commenced. Nana Helen started scrubbing the kitchen. Rosemary provided us with cups of tea and biscuits. I cleaned the bathrooms and prepared the beds. At one point, exhausted, I noticed my ankles were swelling, so I sat sideways in an armchair opposite Helen with my legs up the wall and my head dangling down off the seat. Upside-down I watched Helen with her frilly piny and bright yellow rubber gloves, her head popping in and out of my oven and fridge as she scrubbed them clean. My heart swelled with her kind-heartedness and my head started to swell with blood as she began to speak to me about making a list and doing more shopping tomorrow. She wanted to fill my fridge and freezer with food before she left.

'You don't have to do that,' I told her.

'I want to,' she replied as her head disappeared again into my fridge.

Helen settled me into the cottage and had fun with Rosemary and me for one more day before she left. I even took her walking over the fields with Gwellar, and got her to hug a tree. 'Oooo I've never done this before,' she said, excited.

Raymond and Dee arrived the next weekend with more food and a present for me: larger knickers from Marks & Spencer's.

Then there came a blur of sleeping, resting and eating as the last few months came crashing down on me and a large lump started poking out of my body. Rosemary was always around for support. We never once locked the connecting door and ate most of our meals together, constantly chatting. It always amazed me we had so much to talk about even though we had only just met.

Rosemary became my best friend in that cottage. She also became like a surrogate mother. She cooked me meals, we drank cups of tea, and when I fell in a heap on the carpet in floods of tears thinking life was too hard to handle, it was Rosemary who'd find me. She would pick me up off the carpet and take me into her kitchen. She would hug me, Gwellar would lick my hand, and she'd make more cups of tea until my world was all right again.

Nana Helen would visit a lot, too, and call me. It warmed my heart to experience such simple and uncomplicated mother's love.

Chapter 9
Moment by Moment

Glastonbury Festival happens every year on the last weekend of June. Because Rosemary's cottage was so close to the festival, they gave us free tickets to make up for the noise and inconvenience of the weekend. Kay and her daughter Ellie were staying with me at this stage. Kay was determined I should not be alone when I gave birth, and had flown over from her home in Australia. The three of us decided to go and see the festival preparations.

Crews were building stages and sets, volunteers were seeping in from all directions and some homeless people were crawling out of bushes to help. Vendors were arriving early with their vans to set up shop. Hoping to shake the baby into movement, we drove around the bumpy festival site, watching it all out of our car windows. Men and women were busy working.

Children ran about wildly and colourful flags flew in the air. You could smell food cooking on wood fires.

We bounced out of the festival gates and continued around the small winding country lanes. Kay, being the sensible one in the family, stuck to speed limits. At one point I counted 25 cars behind us.

'Look in your rear-view mirror, Kay, you're torturing people.'

'It's good for them,' she laughed. 'Look at the speed limit,' and she'd tap the dashboard. I begged her to let the people behind us pass but she refused. Ellie sat in the back seat of the car wailing out Wiggles songs and Kay also had a favourite song that she played and sang over and over again. I realised we all came from a tone-deaf gene pool.

The baby was overdue and I was to be induced on 28 June. If my pregnancy went any later it would be dangerous for the baby. Kay and I discussed the birthing situation. We still had about a week before the 28th and at this stage neither of us cared how the baby came out, just as long as it did. Kay had been living with me for three weeks, as we thought the baby would come earlier, and we were all getting impatient.

It was at this moment that the Blond reappeared. I got a phone call from him saying that he was in London and coming to Glastonbury. He had a stall at the festival and was going to sell a new range of clothing he had made in Bali. A friend of his had put up the money for his new business. He had people working for him so he'd be able to come and visit me, but he had to go back to Bali in a few days. Kay said she would go and visit a friend and give us some time alone. If I needed her all I had to do was call.

I was apprehensive but went to the station to meet him, and looked for a designer suit, slicked golden hair and the shoes that I had adored. But he was almost unrecognisable. He wore psychedelic-printed leggings, a psychedelic-printed swirly waistcoat and, underneath the waistcoat, a multi-coloured sloppy joe. His soft golden hair was greasy and dreadlocked. There was a silver bolt underneath his bottom lip and another one through his right eyebrow. I was in shock.

I took him to the cottage and showed him the garden I'd made from seeds Rosemary had given me. I was proud of it and told him how it was feeding me because the money I got from the Social wasn't enough to live on. We walked across the fields and I told him about my sister arriving to help me at the birth and about Rosemary and all the help I'd got from my English friends. Telling him what I was grateful for in my life made me feel better about his successes. I told him about the baby's stubbornness, not wanting to come into the world, but how I'd definitely be giving birth by 28 June.

'Maybe you could be here?' I said. 'It's only in a few days time.'

'I can't, I have to go back to Bali,' he replied.

I walked faster towards the house and grabbed at a tree for support. Life was supporting me now, I had to trust in that. Moment by moment. That's what I had to practise. Guru Johnny had taught me to do it. Moment by fucking moment. Don't think of the future, the pain is too overwhelming. Don't think of the past, it's just as bad there. Only stay in the present. That's how you get through childbirth, or so I'd read in a natural childbirth book.

The Blond hadn't come to save me: he was never going to save me or help me in any way.

Chapter 10
Push

Three days later I was admitted to hospital with Kay by my side. The Blond had returned to Bali and told me to call him so he could know if he had a daughter or a son. Kay held my hand for my 36 hours of labour. The birthing pool I had hired never got used except as a dirty laundry basket, and Rosemary took care of Ellie while we were in hospital. We had called our dad to see if he could come and look after Ellie, but he said he was busy.

It was a long and arduous task, like trying to shit out a watermelon. The baby wouldn't put her head down and my cervix wouldn't dilate. Each head splitting contraction got me absolutely nowhere. It was the worse constipation I'd ever experienced; I gulped oxygen and Kay did too. I was given

Pethidine for the pain and it made me giggle. Spaced out, I started telling Kay how it was similar to taking opium in the hills of Thailand. She pinned me down and started giving me a lecture about taking drugs before she realised now wasn't quite the time – we still had a baby to get out. She turned on the ghetto blaster we had brought in with us.

'Shake those fucking hips and get it out!' my sleep-deprived sister screamed.

'Wooo-hoooo!' I yelled, throwing my arms up in the air, remembering full moon parties in Thailand as we held hands and shook our booties. 'I don't know why people are so right-on about having a natural birth, this is much more fun,' I slurred, drugged out of my head. We both looked like wobbling, exhausted idiots, pushing each other to keep moving. We flapped our arms and stuck out our bums like chickens as I tried to move whatever was in me.

'You gotta get that baby's head down,' Kay puffed as I tried the pogo. A nurse came into the room to see what the commotion was about.

'You're obviously doing fine,' she said and left.

But the chicken dance and the pogo didn't work and crippling pain shot through my back.

'Why is this pain in my back? Shouldn't it be in my vagina?' I screamed. The nurse returned. She called someone else to help, and they lay me down and injected an epidural into my spine. I kept thinking, *Every other woman has given birth, surely I can do this too*. The epidural totally spaced me out and I became numb from the waist down. The nurse had to tell me when I was having contractions because I couldn't feel anything. Exhausted, I kept passing out between the contractions and at one stage I looked down and saw Kay asleep on the hospital floor.

My cervix finally decided to open.

'We're in trouble,' the nurse said firmly and calmly as though she was an airline steward informing us our plane was about to crash. I woke up. Kay got off the floor. 'We're losing the baby's heart beat.'

Kay eyeballed me. 'You've got to do this. You have to get her out. Here's a contraction: *push!*'

I pushed, trying to work out where my vagina was as I stared at the picture in front of my spread-eagled legs. It was a picture of a little girl holding a big balloon and running through a poppy field.

The heartbeat faded. The heartbeat returned. I got another contraction. The heartbeat faded. A doctor rushed into the room.

'We're in trouble,' the doctor said. 'We lose the baby's heart beat every time you have a contraction.'

'Oh God, I'm having a contraction, I can feel it,' I screamed.

'We're losing the heart beat,' Kay screamed. '*Push!*'

I took my mind into the picture, and I took my baby into the picture, too. She was running through the poppy field with a balloon in her hand. My contraction intensified, I pushed with all my physical might. Her balloon lifted her high up into the air and she laughed.

'*Push!*' Kay screamed. I was panicking. My baby was laughing as she floated back down to ground.

'We have to do something if this situation doesn't change,' the doctor said, worry showing on her face. Now I was scared; I had to fight for my baby's life. Another contraction.

'*Fucking push!*' Kay yelled.

The balloon took my child up again into the air, large red poppies floated beneath her and surrounded her as she came back to earth.

'We got the heart rate that time! Whatever you're doing – it's working.' The colour was back in the doctor's face. Another contraction came. The intense pain was stronger than the epidural.

I wailed in excruciating agony, '*I'm never having sex again.*'

'Oh my God, she's here,' Kay cried as she looked between my legs. 'This is amazing, you look like you have elephant ears down here now.'

'The heart beat is strong,' the nurse said as she grabbed hold of my leg and pushed it past my ear. 'Wow, you're flexible,' she said, shocked.

'Don't worry about her, she's a yogi. *Keep pushing, Jane, she's coming I can see her head!*'

'Don't fucking worry? I've had an epidural and you could be dislocating my hip.'

'*Push!*'

And finally she slipped out.

Kay was the first person to hold her. 'It's a little girl.' She gave her to me. I looked at her and it felt like an old friend had come back into the world.

'Hello,' I said, in tears as I looked into her little face. Finally I knew what her name should be. As we drove to the hospital, surrounding the cottage were fields of poppies waving in the wind. There was the picture of the little girl among the poppies that had helped me give birth, and there was the song that Kay played in the car over and over again about poppies. 'You're going to be called Poppy,' I said.

I gave my daughter back to Kay and passed out.

Chapter 11
A Warrior

I lay under the mosquito net in Bali with Poppy beside me and cried at the huge task that lay ahead of me. This feeling of overwhelming hardship, of having to deal with everything alone, squeezed me and brought tears to my eyes.

All I had in life now was a ticket round the world, a beautiful baby, this house and a plan. I was trying to feel gratitude to take away the pain and focus on my plan.

My plan was to get the house ready and rent it out for a year. I had thought about selling it, but all I had in Bali was a simple contract for the land it stood on. I could make more money renting the house to tourists. Also, if I did sell the house, I couldn't guarantee that whoever bought it would still employ my Balinese family. Even though I was in trouble, I wasn't about to leave another family in the shit with no job. I now knew what it was like to have the responsibility of a family to look after, and I cared about my Bali family. My plan was to rent out the house with them included; anybody who took a house in Bali always needed staff, and I knew Elu and Kadek would look after the house well. I wanted to keep them both safe, and the house was the only thing of value I had left in the world apart from what I was holding in my arms.

I wiped my eyes. This journey was not going to be easy, but my dad was a fighter. He taught me not to lie down and take any of life's punches. He taught me to get up and fight for what you want and to not give up till you get it. He told me, 'Kid, always believe in yourself.' He wasn't the best parent, but he was the only sane one I had, and as a kid I listened carefully to his words. 'Believe in yourself, Kid. You can be whoever you want to be in this lifetime. Just bullshit your way until you get where you want to be.'

More tears fell as I stroked Poppy's head. I looked out at the moon and I vowed to always protect her and keep her safe. I promised her, 'I'll get us a great life somehow, just you wait and see.'

Thinking about making a great life for Poppy always made me feel stronger. I wasn't doing this just for me, I was doing it for the two of us, and even though I felt shattered and exhausted inside, I had to be a warrior on the outside – for her.

I closed my eyes. I had to sleep. I had a lot to do in the morning.

Chapter 12

The Magic of an Open Heart

The sunrise woke us both up early, but we were tired and fell back to sleep again. Elu woke me again with sounds of the house being cleaned and when she heard us stirring, she popped her head up from the spiral staircase.

'Jane, I take Poppy? You want tea?'

No wonder Bali is known as heaven on earth, I thought, as Poppy was whisked away, happy and gurgling, and I was left alone in bed with a cup of tea to sip on. I pulled up the net, propped myself up on the pillows and looked out across the paddy fields. *Wow, rare time alone, this is heaven*. Finally, I descended the stairs because I felt way too guilty and self-indulgent. On the ground floor, I found Poppy already bathed and dressed. She was hanging out with Kadek in the garden, and a tropical fruit salad was waiting for me on the dining table covered in cling wrap.

I showered and dressed and sat at the table feeling very odd: I needed my baby back in my arms. I'd had enough of my staff whisking her away from me and felt jealous that they were holding her and not me.

There was a knock and the garden door flew open. A screaming, long-legged woman leapt into my garden and took off, jumping over the white stepping-stones towards me. Her blonde hair was flying, her skinny legs strode like an ostrich's, bony knees protruding, and her arms were outstretched. She was dressed in colourful batiks and jewellery jingled from every limb.

'My darling, my darling, I'm so glad you're home,' the vision cried out in a New York accent. I stood up and rushed to the front stairs and as she got close she flung herself at me and squeezed me so tight I had to cough. She sniffed all over my face, 'I love you so much!'

'I love you too, Kira,' I said, with a deflated heart and a crooked smile. She'd been my best friend in Bali for years – until recently.

We had been such close friends we could have easily been taken for lovers years ago, except muff diving was not my thing. When I lived in Bali we would meet every day, do yoga together, share dinners and sunsets, talk like there was never going to be a tomorrow and laugh at the absurdity of life all the time. We would go on holidays, sleep most nights at each other's houses and when one of us had a boyfriend, the three of us hung out together. Boys often got jealous of the other girl, but we didn't care, we weren't going to give up our friendship for anything. Now, though, I wasn't so sure.

Kira was ten years older than me and she had never wanted children. 'I don't think I have a maternal bone in my body,' she'd say, but I always told her I thought my soulmate was out there somewhere and I knew one day I would have a family and children. 'I'll be your baby's special auntie then,' she'd say. 'And I'll fly anywhere in the world, wherever you are, to help you give birth.'

But she hadn't. When I left Bali and got stranded in England, the only contact I'd had with her was a solitary phone call. There were no mobile phones or phones in people's homes in Bali. The only way you could contact somebody was to send a fax, which had to be picked up from a business office in Seminyak called Krakatoa. If you wanted to speak to somebody by phone, you had to send a fax and then organise a time and place for them to be near a phone. Or the person in Bali could go to a phone office and call you. That's how I had stayed in touch with Kadek. He had been used to going to Krakatoa looking for faxes for me and I had faxed him and told him in very simple English what had happened to me. He had looked after the house while I had been away and managed to rent it out to cover costs. I had faxed Kira too. I had told her I had got into trouble and had to stay in England. I also faxed her when I moved into the cottage in Glastonbury, and gave her my telephone number and fax number there. But I had only received the one call from her.

Now she was back in my house hugging me and we sat down on my bamboo day bed together. I beckoned Kadek to bring me Poppy, and as I lay her down Kira inspected her, squeezing her limbs and telling me how adorable she was.

'It's so good to see you again,' she said. 'Kadek came to my house and told me you were arriving, but I thought I'd let you get settled and then turn up this morning. I love you so much, and your baby Poppy is adorable. I'm so happy you're home. I love you.' Her last two sentences didn't make sense. Bali didn't feel like a home any more and what did 'I love you' actually mean? Somebody else had said those words and then abandoned me, and now my shattered heart did not feel safe hearing them again.

'What happened to you, Kira?'

'What do you mean, my darling?'

'I never heard from you in England apart from that one call. You knew what had happened to me and you knew I was in trouble over there.'

'Jane, you know how much I love and adore you, and it's so wonderful to have you back in Bali with me now.'

'But what about when I was in England, Kira?'

'Darling, I'm going to be honest with you. When people are with me I love and adore them, like being with you right now, but when they are not with me, I seem to forget about them. Maybe it's being in the moment?' She smiled and I was in awe of her beauty and honesty, but the 'in the moment' shit didn't impress me. My heart screeched; bits of it wanted to fall off and drop at my feet. I wanted to lock my heart up, like caging a timid bird to protect it. It didn't want to be hurt by the hands now holding mine and the long skinny arms trying to hug me. I wanted to hear a different song.

'But it's so great to be with you now,' Kira said, 'And I'm so sorry if I ever hurt you. I'd never wanted to do that.'

I sat. Maybe I had jet lag but my brain couldn't work out if Kira was carefree or careless. Deep down, I knew she really loved me, and being with her now in this moment I remembered how my mum told me people were never perfect. Maybe I'd changed? Maybe my idea of love now I'd had a child was different to Kira's? I admitted to myself that I wasn't perfect either. I used to be so happy-go-lucky with my love, and Bali was happy-go-lucky too. It was an unreal bubble of existence. Only the rich and beautiful people stayed on the island. As soon as someone got sick or ran out of money they had to leave because there was no support for them. I felt the bubble of love I used to have for this island popping, but I still felt love for Kira.

I felt lost in the past – trying to work out who I was turning into, and still struggling with Kira's words: 'I'm sorry'. How can someone simply forget what has happened and pass everything off with 'I'm sorry'?

I listened to Kira as she talked about Bali. She kept throwing her head back and bursting into an out-of-tune song every time a word reminded her of one. I tried to stay cross with her, but I couldn't. She made me laugh too much and there hadn't been enough of that medicine in my life lately. Kira truly was as free as a songbird. She had never been trapped by anybody or anything and she wasn't going to be trapped by me, either.

It was her free spirit that made me want to hang out with her all those years ago and now I was slowly appreciating her again. I watched and listened as this beautiful apparition talked, sang and threw her jingling arms up into the air like an enthusiastic child telling me an exciting story.

I loved the way children could be so free. I remembered when I thought the whole world was a fairy tale, and Kira still lived in that world. It was part of her appeal, that she had kept her child's spirit. She was carefree, naughty and wild. She took no responsibility for anyone in her path and she truthfully had no idea how much her absence had deeply hurt me. Where had my child's spirit gone? I didn't feel like a child any more; maybe because I was holding one in my arms.

As she talked on, I felt an intense love for Kira return, and forgiveness, and it helped to heal my pain. I felt maybe I was only now really learning to love somebody unconditionally. My heart reached out to her and, as I held her hands again, I felt a piece of my heart get firmly put back into place.

Chapter 13

A Bunny Life

My dad was a lover and his love kept moving all his women around. Dad decided he wanted the big house he had bought for my mum back, so he gave her some money to buy a smaller one and we all got moved out. My older brother George now worked at the Playboy Club as a croupier and he helped rent out all the rooms in the big house to Bunnies and Penthouse Pets. That's when the Bunny Mother of the Playboy Bunnies came into my life.

Dad started picking me up regularly from Mum's house to visit her every weekend and I liked her. She wore fur coats and nice-smelling perfume and she'd give me a Bunny outfit with fluffy ears and a tail to play with. The blow-dry specialist didn't like her, though. She discovered Dad was sleeping with her and the next thing we knew, the blow-dry specialist had moved to Las Vegas to get away from her adulterous husband, Dad had moved all the girly tenants out of his house, and he had moved in there with Bunny.

Bunny was beautiful and glamorous. She had Marilyn Monroe blonde hair and huge tits. She had lips always covered in lip-gloss that would stick to your face when she kissed you, and she carefully rimmed them with a red pencil. Every day with a brown pencil she would paint a beauty spot on her cheek. Dad would look at her with silly goo-goo eyes and she always took the time to speak to me with her pretty soft voice. When I got tired I would lie down and she would lay one of her furs over me and I'd go to sleep, the bunny ears I'd been playing with poking out of the top of the coat. I'd nuzzle deep into the fur. I adored the way it felt and the way it smelt of her Marlboro cigarettes and perfume.

My new Bunny Mummy was called that because her job at the Playboy Club was to look after all the Bunnies and keep their standards high. She used to make sure their shoes weren't shabby. Was a Bunny's lipstick too pale? It had to be brighter! Did a Bunny have an unkempt tail? Were her ears bent incorrectly? All of these things were an offence in the Playboy Club. Bunnies were also not allowed to date customers. But Bunnies were naughty, and they liked to practise breeding.

Bunny told me how I could aspire to become a Bunny too, if I did the right things in life. 'When girls come for interviews with me, Jane, they have to walk around in a bikini or undies so I can see if they have the body to be one of our special girls. So don't ever let yourself get fat, Jane. Girls should always be sweet and beautiful on the outside, but also have a good personality on the inside as well. Some girls I'll hire to be a Bunny not because they are strikingly pretty, but because they have a personality and confidence that shines through everything else you see, and this makes a woman stunning!' I would smile at her and Bunny would hold my face with her hands smelling of Marlboro cigarettes and she would say, 'Always be confident, Jane. Let your beauty shine out from your inside as well as your outside, and you're lucky. You're already pretty.'

I learned all about Bunnies, their moves and their outfits. Bunnies worked for a man called Hugh Hefner. His mum lent him $1000 to start up a magazine called *Playboy* and it became so successful he then opened up Playboy Clubs so people could give him more of their money by gambling. I learned that:

A Playboy Bunny is someone who works for Hugh in one of his clubs and wears a Bunny uniform.

A Playboy Model is someone who poses naughty and nudie in his magazine.

A Playboy Playmate is the girl who is really good at being nudie and you'll find her in the middle of the magazine where the fold is.

When I went to visit Dad and Bunny, I used to wonder if other lovers were as regal as they were. Dad had a set of gold-leaf furniture, including a dressing table for Bunny. She would sit at it naked, getting ready for the day, and I used to think she was like the Queen of England. She always had dogs lying by her feet and was always surrounded by so much gold. Beside her was a golden bed, on her dressing table was lots of gold jewellery old Arab boyfriends from the Playboy Club had given her. On the bed were satin sheets and she said they were good for the complexion. 'As a woman you should never wake up with a crumply face,' she told me, and satin sheets prevent that from happening.

I used to love slipping around on her bed, playing, as I admired her. There was a painting that hung in her bedroom that

I would think was me. It was of a young girl with long hair like mine and she sat naked, bent over one knee. Her hair covered her face, and I'd sit naked underneath the picture. Bunny's thick carpet would prickle my bottom as I'd imitate the girl's pose and wish I never had to leave Bunny's sweet side. I used to ask Dad if I could stay at their house more, but Dad always said I couldn't because Bunny was busy with work and didn't always have the time to look after children.

Chapter 14
Visualisation

Years ago when I was in Bali I read a book about dreams and positive visualisation. It said, '*You have the ability to create all you desire in your life. All you have to do is be able to visualise it.*' A Spanish girlfriend was living with me at the time and we started testing the validity of the book by simply visualising things we wanted to happen. We would then write a note with our heart's request on it and stick it on the fridge door with sticky tape. And – magic happened.

Our notes started to come true. Yolanda wanted photographic work and it was offered to her. I asked to find a new kind of factory and magically stumbled upon it when I was out driving one day and got lost. Then I thought, maybe those things would have happened anyway, so I decided to get more cryptic.

I visualised a storyteller coming into my life (because I loved how my mum used to tell me stories as a kid) and posted my desire on the fridge with more sticky tape. I posted another note underneath it for a laugh, too. A couple of weeks later I hosted a dinner party and one of my friends brought an extra guest. He'd just arrived in Bali and was a storyteller. We became lovers, and I discovered the secret note I'd hidden underneath the one that asked for the storyteller had also manifested! I learned then to be very careful what I wished for. I'd written secretly: *a lover with a really large penis.*

The Storyteller and I played with visualisation together and we dreamt up a perfect weekend retreat for the two of us. We wanted a cottage in the mountains of Bali. We wanted it small, with one bedroom, cheap to rent, surrounded by paddy fields and with a lotus pond sitting outside the door. We wrote the note together, drew a little picture and stuck it on the fridge door. Later on, during a trip to the north of the island, we stumbled across our dream cottage. In laughter and disbelief we found the owner and discovered it was for rent. It was cheap, it had a lotus pond outside the door. We signed a contract.

My love affair with the Storyteller ended because we wanted different things in our lives then. He wanted to settle down and have a family and I wasn't ready. So we let each other go to follow our own dreams. I left him with the lease on the cottage and he left me with a head full of stories and an African kalimba instrument. I would play the kalimba and tell Poppy this story when she was falling to sleep:

> Once upon a time, there was a village of Clingons. They were called Clingons because they clung on to the rocks and twigs at the bottom of the river; because above them rushed a very strong and powerful current of water.

One day a little Clingon in the village said, 'I hate my life. I know we're all afraid of that current up there and we cling on everyday so we don't hurt ourselves, but I want to let go and see where the current takes me.'

'You're crazy,' said the other Clingons, holding on tight at the bottom of the river. 'If you let go of your rock, that current up there will bash and crash you and you'll die.'

The little Clingon let go one hand to scratch his head and think about what they'd said, but was moved around so strongly he grabbed his rock again.

For the next few days he talked to his friends and told them how he trusted the current and he thought if he let go it would take him to a better place. They kept laughing at him and telling him he was crazy. But one day he called out bravely, 'I don't care what you all think – I have to let go!' And he did.

'Nooooooo,' they screamed as they saw him being bashed and crashed along the bottom of the river. And the little Clingon did get hurt a bit as the current tumbled him along, but then all of a sudden it lifted him up high and he started to float effortlessly along in the water.

'Look, look, there's a Clingon like us, yet he flies!' the little Clingon heard far below him. He looked down and saw another village of Clingons, just like his own. They all cried, 'Clingon, Clingon, come and save us! You must be the messiah!'

The flying Clingon laughed as he passed them by and shouted back, 'I'm no god and I can't save you – all you have to do is let go!'

I listened to the little voice inside me and it kept telling me it was time to let go of Bali.

Chapter 15
The Plan

On the couch in Bali I filled Kira in on everything she had missed in the past few months.

I told her how I freaked out about my life in Glastonbury. How my real mum had ended up alone, a single mother living in the English countryside, and I'd had a horrible life with her and I didn't want a similar experience for my child. I wanted a different life for us both and I told her about my list of questions and the plan I had come up with. I told her how I'd kept writing and writing for days until I finally had answers that felt good. My worst-case scenario was that if things didn't work out, I'd only end up back in England in the same situation. So I had nothing to lose.

These were the questions I wrote down:

What do I want in life for Poppy and me?

How can I get it?

What can I do to make money to get what I want in life?

How can I do that with a baby?

What am I good at?

Is this a good idea?

Where do I want us to live?

What country?

The plan was a three-part recipe for a new life:

PART 1: ENGLAND

1. Travel around England and collect everything you own and ever left at friends' houses over the years.
2. Pack it all into your car *[Dad had given me the money to buy an old car]* and drive back to Glastonbury with it.
3. Empty out your wicker trunks with all your precious designer clothes. That means: the Katherine Hamnett, the English Eccentrics, the Vivienne Westwood pieces. *[I'd always kept two wicker trunks of clothes at my friends' house in London. They had been stored there for years and contained precious clothes I never took to Bali because I didn't want them to be ruined by the humidity. The trunks also stored childhood memories, such as pictures I didn't want to be thrown away.]*

4. Iron, prepare and sort everything. 'Everything' means: everything in the cottage that has been given to you to survive here by friends: bedding, crockery, baskets ...

What to do next: sell it!

Note to self: In Glastonbury there are heaps of second-hand shops and you know places to sell to in London, too. You're good at sales. Don't stop selling till you've sold absolutely everything, including your car, knives and forks. You have more clothes in Bali, you don't need to take much there, so only keep a few things to travel in.

Result: You will have enough money to buy a round-the-world ticket.

Note to self: You don't need to buy a ticket for Poppy until she is two years old. You have to do this plan now while she's still cheap enough to travel with: you don't have to buy her food, she just needs your boobs at this stage. The longer you leave this plan, the harder it will be to travel with Poppy and to be able to change your life.

PART 2: BALI

1. Make Bali the first stop on your ticket.
2. You have to sort out the house, make it look really nice and rent it for a year. Get the money upfront. Put money in a bank account for the year for your Bali family's wages. Invest the rest of the money to make more.

3. Empty out your jewellery boxes in Bali.
4. Take your old jewellery apart and combine it with the beads you've collected on your travels over the years.
5. Use the rental money you get from your house to make components of a necklace range you've been inspired to design in Glastonbury.
6. Place all jewellery components into fishing-tackle boxes. When you travel through customs in the different countries you'll hopefully look like a hippy mama with a beading hobby – and not someone doing business.

Result: You will most likely have no money leaving Bali – but you'll have a bag full of components that you can make into jewellery.

Note to self: This is a good idea!

Remember this when you have self doubt!!!

You have other friends in Bali involved in the jewellery business and you've always admired how they can travel simply with a small bag and within it have the potential to make hundreds of dollars. In the garment and gift businesses you have to ship huge boxes and containers to make your money. You can't do that now. You have to be light and able to move around with little luggage and take Poppy with you at the same time. With this idea, you have the potential to be like Jack and the Beanstalk. From some small beans he grew a huge beanstalk that took him to a pot of gold.

Don't be frightened of the giants in your mind who might try and stop you doing this!

PART 3: GLOBAL GYPSY

1. In the different countries you visit, at night-time when Poppy is asleep, you put the jewellery components together and make necklaces to sell.
2. Travel to the places on your world ticket: Bali, Australia, Hawaii, America, Europe, and search for your new home and life.

Note to self: You don't want to live in Asian countries any more, or travel across them with a baby. You want to be in countries with fewer diseases and good medical facilities. You want to keep your child alive. P.S. You also don't have enough money to buy medical and travel insurance.

HOW TO MAKE MONEY

1. Sell your jewellery to expensive art galleries and gift shops. You need to make each piece expensive (so make the components expensive) as you will not be able to do Asia-style mass production with a baby attached to your tit. You will also not be able to carry that many beads. You should sell your necklaces to shops and art galleries for about $100-$200 wholesale. They will then sell the necklaces for approx. $200-$400 apiece.

Note to self: You need to make each piece special and unique, the same way women are. This will then appeal

to customers. You can also use the necklaces to give as gifts and to barter when you stay in people's homes and they help you along the way.

'I know my plan might sound crazy, Kira, but fuck – don't you think life is?'

'Sure is, honey,' Kira replied, and I knew she'd understand me and wouldn't think I was crazy either. I hadn't told many people in England what I was up to, but I knew I could confide in Kira because we were similar in so many ways. She had also had an odd life. She started out her journey as a global gypsy living naked on the beaches of Goa. The people she hung out with were called freaks, but they all thought the people living conformist lives in the West were freaks too. She sold bracelets she made from string and shells and one day someone told her she should use precious stones instead. So she went to Nepal to get some, and her business took off from there, and somehow she ended up living in Bali.

I told Kira how I enjoyed selling everything I owned and she asked me, 'Why didn't you contact me, Jane? I would have lent you the money for the ticket.'

I dropped my head in shame. I was too proud to ask people for help and I remembered how my mum used to be proud like that too.

Chapter 16
A Beautiful Garden

Maybe it was time to allow people to get closer to me and allow them to help me? Maybe I didn't need to struggle against the world alone any more?

'Well, maybe you could help me, Kira,' I said, and asked her if she could lend me some money so I could get the house ready to rent and start my jewellery business. 'I'll be able to pay you back as soon as I get the rent money for the house.'

'Of course I'll help you,' Kira said happily, and it was good to feel her by my side again. She gave me the added power I needed to make me feel the Bali part of my plan could work.

I had to get to work. I had to do up the house as quickly as possible. I only had a two-month tourist visa for Bali, and Kira made me laugh about my new predicament. She gave me lots of tips for my new business and her light-hearted approach to life helped to lift the elephant-load of pressure I'd been feeling on my shoulders. She helped me to brush the elephant bottoms off with more laughter. I often thought it was no wonder the Blond flitted around the world not taking responsibility for his actions. This path of responsibility was not an easy one to walk.

After Kira left, I looked around at my Bali house. I noticed how it had fallen apart.

Bali houses were built on shallow foundations on reclaimed paddy fields. The houses always moved and shifted. Cracks would appear in floors and walls, and sometimes whole walls would fall down. Floors could sink and lumps of roofs would often fall off. The constant humidity made everything else go rotten and mouldy and bugs hung out in hoards and ate whatever came loose or seemed tasty. To live in Bali was a constant battle against the elements and I now wanted something more solid in my life. I thought of the three little pigs and told the story to Poppy. I didn't want a house of straw or a house made of bamboo and coconut sticks any more. I wanted solid foundations and I craved friends who could love me and be with me in all seasons, including during typhoons or El Niño effects.

I went upstairs and looked out over the paddy fields.

I wanted to be normal, but I felt so abnormal; it made me sad. I remembered wanting to be normal as a child. I used to want to grow up and be a factory worker. I wanted to be someone who knew what was going to happen to them every day, without any surprises. I wanted to work in a factory putting cherries on top of iced cupcakes.

I thought of Kira and the straight train-driver boyfriend she used to have. I thought that relationship was odd then, but now it made sense to me. Kira had found her new boyfriend on the internet and had a long-distance relationship with him.

He came from New Jersey and drove trains for a living. When all us Bali freaks asked her why she was going out with this guy, she said it was because she thought he was exotic.

'I'm over all these male travelling freaks you meet,' she said. 'They all think like they have Borneo up their arses and Africa in their pants and I don't want anything to do with them any more.' She said, 'I'm in love with my sweet train driver. He's so normal – he's absolutely adorable.'

I shook the thought of her out of my head. I had so much to do and I had to concentrate on that, but I remembered something else she had said to me when I was in Bali and becoming increasingly frustrated with the Blond. I'd rushed over to Kira's house to get away from him for a while and calm down.

'Jane, relationships can be like a garden,' Kira said. 'Sometimes one of you is a gardener and one of you is a flower. It's a gardener's job to look after flowers. They water them, care for them, they make sure they get enough sun and shade to survive. Flowers are very beautiful, but they are delicate and always need help. With a relationship, it's difficult to have two flowers together because the result is they can't look after each other and they die. The best relationship is to have two gardeners. That way, they can enjoy the fruits of their work – and have a bountiful garden. What's wrong in your relationship, Jane, is that you're a gardener screaming at your flower to do something to improve your garden and Jane – you have to smell the roses and realise – *he's no fucking gardener*!'

Kira was right. I couldn't dwell on the fact he wasn't here to help me. I had to get busy. I made another list. With Kadek's help, I had to fix the cracks in the walls, repaint and patch. With Elu, I'd throw out rotten clothing and bed sheets and replace mouldy bug-eaten cushion covers. I'd buy fresh flowers and put signs around the island to rent out the house.

I worked each day fixing up the house and starting my new business. At sunset I'd meet up with Kira again and we'd go down to the beach together on her scooter. There we would join other friends and watch the day come to an end. The sky would turn into sheets of Indian saris and we'd all sit under it admiring the colours and munch on toasted corn.

One night on the beach, I met up with an old friend called Jonas. I hadn't seen him for a long time and it was good to see him again. He was a trust-fund baby who told everyone he was an actor, but had never had a part in a movie. He was always highly entertaining, though. He told me about the new movie he was auditioning for; he lived between Los Angeles and Bali. I thought it would be nice to have some male company for a change, so I invited him to come and have dinner in my garden. Kira didn't want to come; she said Jonas drove her mad.

Before he arrived, Elu helped me cook and Kadek moved my lounge furniture into the garden. Jonas was dramatic, so I thought he'd appreciate eating dinner under the stars surrounded by the bobbing fireflies that danced in the garden. He arrived when Poppy was already asleep, and Kadek and Elu had left. Together we had fun as usual. We shared stories. I listened to excerpts from the movie and told him about my new plan and he said it sounded like a good adventure. I scooped up the empty dinner plates and left him reclining on my couch, staring at the moon. A sarong covered his legs protecting him from the mosquitoes.

I went into the house and found the fruit-and-nut dessert Elu had made and placed in the fridge for us. When I skipped back into the garden with it, I discovered Jonas had already made himself the dessert.

My skipping turned into very slow steps and I loudly placed the dessert plates on the coffee table, hoping to stir him into some kind of movement. I didn't know quite what to do. So I sat down and looked at him instead.

Instead of lying horizontally, as I'd left him, he was now sitting up in the lotus position at the foot of the bamboo couch. And he was naked. It was hard for a naked person to shock me because I'd grown up in nudist colonies as a child, but now I was finding it difficult not to laugh. I thought he must have heard me giggle, but he still didn't move. His eyes were closed. He clenched a red hibiscus flower in his teeth and I was sure the grass he was sitting on must be poking him up the arse. I giggled at him. He sat as though in deep meditation with one of his hands on his knee, his thumb and middle finger touching. His other hand was holding onto his massive hard-on. I looked up at the stars and then down at the view again. He was putting on quite a show – even for Bali standards – and I'd never seen his penis before and I couldn't help looking at it.

I looked back at his face and coughed, hoping to get his attention. He still didn't move, but I knew he was harmless because he'd kept his socks on.

'Excuse me, Jonas, what are you doing?' I asked and he opened his eyes, but there was not a flicker of humour on his face. With his meditating thumb and finger he took the flower out of his mouth and started to speak. Now the flower was waving around in the air and I looked around for hidden cameras. Is this a welcome-back-to-Bali moment?

'I have wanted you for a long time now,' Jonas said, breaking silence, 'but you've always ignored my advances. So now I want to offer myself to you like this.' He gestured towards his body with the flower, in case I didn't know what he was offering me, and his other hand kept tight hold of his dick.

'You know you're quite mad,' I told him.

'I'm mad for you,' he replied, and I was blown away by his courting ritual. 'You love beauty. This is obvious by your home and all that surrounds you.' He flapped the flower around again. 'So here I am in my naked beauty offering myself to you.' He brought the flower down to his penis and I sat in silence, smiling. Sometimes a fucked-up childhood can really make any situation seem tame. Jonas continued to talk; I think he was beginning to feel nervous.

'You teach yoga, there are stone Buddhas in your garden and a large Buddha head painting in your house, so you are obviously very spiritual. So here I am in the spiritual lotus position offering myself to you.' He flapped the flower at his rock hard penis and my face fought hard against laughter.

I did admire him, though. He had courage. I could never have opened my legs like that in front of a stranger and masturbated and then told them how much I liked their home decor.

He continued, 'My desire for you, Jane, is shown here with my hardness,' and with that he reached out both his hands.

Oh yuck – was I meant to take hold of them? Or maybe I was meant to give him a hug or drop my head and give him a blowjob? I covered my eyes; his performance had become too much to watch, but he thought he had lost my attention.

'And if all that I have offered you doesn't woo you, then I have this red flower to give you,' and he sweetly offered me back the red flower he'd picked from my garden. I reached over and gave Jonas the sarong so he could cover himself up.

That night after he left, I thought to myself how nice it would be to meet a different kind of man, maybe one who wore a suit to work. One who had a proper job with a regular wage and lived in a house made of bricks. One who was good at gardening. I turned all the lights off and went upstairs. I climbed under the mosquito net to lie down next to Poppy. It was hard to sleep. The vision of Jonas naked in the lotus position kept returning, and I thought back to when I was a teenager and my dad first took me to a nudist colony.

Chapter 17
The Nudist Colony

When I was a teenager I lived in a pub my dad owned in the countryside. He picked me up after school one summer's day and said it was perfect weather to visit a club he had just got a family membership for that had a swimming pool. He had towels on the front seat of the car and I was excited. It was rare to go to a swimming pool in England.

Dad drove along leafy country lanes about 20 minutes away from the pub, and when we got to a secret marking on the road, he said this was the marking for the club and we turned left. We drove along a gravel road and got to a locked gate. He told me to get out and unlock it and then close and lock the gate behind us again. After driving through another couple of fields, there was a car park and we drove into it. I looked left into a clearing and suddenly my breath shot forcefully down my throat.

'We're here,' Dad said as he parked the car.

In front of me were high trees and bushes that surrounded a field. The field had been made into a perfectly mown lawn, and on it stood naked people with their own bushes in clear view. They were playing games, walking around, or simply standing and laughing with no clothes on, drinking mugs of tea together.

'Oh my God,' I exhaled as I turned to look at Dad. 'How did you find this?'

'Harry and Mary who come to the pub introduced me.' Dad smiled and got out of the car, but I couldn't believe what I was seeing. Up until now, I hadn't fully computed what going to a nudist colony actually meant. Dad had said the club was a nudist colony, but so many people in his pub said so much drunken rubbish I often didn't completely listen to what people said and all I could think now was: *This is so wrong. I've just grown pubes and breasts, I'm a teenager, insecure about my life, I've just learned how to take drugs, and this is not going to help me.*

Dad strode towards the clearing and I jumped out of the car, keen to stay beside him for protection. As we walked, he started to take off his clothes and people smiled and waved at him, and he waved back. He was the famous British wrestler who had joined the nudist colony and everyone knew him.

To the right of the clearing was a badminton net strung high up over the grass and people were jumping up to hit shuttlecocks and their penises and titties were flying too. They were wearing hats to protect their heads from the sun, but their genitalia had no protection at all and to my mind they all looked like roaring, flying prehistoric animals. I moved closer to my dad's side. At the back of the field were tents with more naked people loitering around and to the left of us was a Flintstones-looking swimming pool with a large plastic rock formation in it. Naked children that were younger than me were screaming and dive-bombing off into the deep water and I wondered if any of them felt like me: drowning. Dad really knew how to jump in the deep end of life, and he always told me, 'You have two choices in life, Kid – sink or swim.' Dad waved to tea-drinking parents, who waved and blew kisses in return. Dad waved to the badminton players; more waves and shouts of 'How ya doing, Joe?' came back. Someone shouted to us from the only building on the lawn, 'Come and have tea, Joe?'

'Lovely,' he said. 'This is the club house that everyone uses,' Dad informed me as we walked onto the patio where English tea was being served. We politely sat down and accepted china cups of it.

I drank my first cup with my head lowered, trying to avoid the obvious sights. My dad was now completely naked, sitting with his naked friends. Men were sitting with their legs slightly apart, as they do, and women were sitting with all their various breast and nipple sizes exposed. I never knew nipples could be so huge, lumpy, dark and elongated, and I was grateful the women sat with their legs crossed so I couldn't inspect their noonies too. All the friends were enjoying their conversation, their tea and biscuits. I still had my clothes on but no one was saying anything to me about taking them off. I looked up to try and relieve the pressure valve inside of me that wanted just to be the same as everybody else, and found a hairy ring looking down.

It belonged to a little old man balancing on the clubhouse roof. He was wearing a gas mask and army boots and his thick grey chest hair looked like it had been stuck on, because he had so much of it. He was balancing on his hands and knees, and because he didn't have any pants on all the people below could look right up his arsehole. His ball bags swung low.

I nudged Dad and whispered to him, 'What's going on up there?' and rolled my eyes upward to indicate my concern. Dad stopped talking to his friends and followed my gaze.

'Up there,' said Dad loudly and I cringed. 'Woooow nice view, Tom!' He shouted and Dad lifted up his teacup at the old man in approval.

The old man waved down to him and said, 'Hello, Joe.'

'The roof's being tarred,' Dad said nonchalantly and then grabbed another McVities Digestive biscuit to dunk into in his teacup.

Strangely, I now felt I had permission to look up a man's bottom, and I'd never done that before. Black, steaming tar was wafting up from the roof towards fluffy white English clouds and I could see the clouds were looking down in fascination too. How come these people thought nothing strange was going on? I looked around, hoping someone would save me from this experience. I was worried; I was sitting with my only sane parent. I looked down at myself. Maybe I was overdressed?

Everyone was naked: the brave man on the roof, the jolly badminton posse, the swimmers and campers and the children. Only I had clothes on. No one was pressuring me to take them off, but I wanted to fit in to society. I wanted to be the same as everybody else and I knew I had to get undressed so as not to stand out. I also needed a pee because of all the tea I was drinking. I begrudgingly stood up and grabbed at a towel and asked where the changing rooms were.

'Good on you, girl!' Dad shouted and I hunched my head into my shoulders and slinked into the inner sanctum of the clubhouse. With all the fields and gates we had to go through to get here, I knew I couldn't get out alone. I felt trapped; I was in Tolkien's *Lord of the Rings* story and I couldn't escape until I found the golden ring.

I sat on the changing room bench for ages. I took off my clothes. Wrapped my towel around me. Sat back down again. It was the wooden slats under my bottom making painful grooves that told me to get in the shower and kill more time. I dropped my towel and got into the communal shower and soon after another naked woman got in too. This was all getting too much to handle. I put my head on the bathroom tiles and let hot water cascade down my back, trying to calm myself down. Bunny and Dad walked around naked, but I hadn't seen other people do this. I closed my eyes trying to block out more information, but then I couldn't help myself and I peeked through the showering raindrops. *Oh my God, women style down there!* I'd seen Bunny's pubes, but I thought they were naturally contained and my mum's were a mess, but these women were obviously getting the scissors out and having a trim around down there. I looked down at my own noonie. My hairs had been growing and getting quite long, and I wasn't sure what I was meant to do with them. Maybe I could learn a few things here, I thought.

The hot water helped to calm me down and wash away my insecurities and as my fingertips became water-sodden and wrinkled, I became a sweet bubble of freshness, thinking, *I now know what to do with the hairs on my noonie.* That knowledge made me courageous and I started to pull my shoulders back like my dad had taught me to and I finally stepped out of the sanctuary of that shower ready to face the world.

I felt like a brave African warrior. Some children in rural Africa had to perform scary initiation rites to become grown-up. In middle-class England, I simply had to face a nudist colony.

Chapter 18

Chopping Down the Trees

In Bali, I met up with other friends, too. One of my girlfriends had two kids and she asked if I would like to go for a car ride with her, as she was taking them bike riding. She said we could hang out together in the car and chat while they played.

'They won't ride around for very long.'

'Sure,' I said.

Sarah picked me and Poppy up and we all drove out of Seminyak into the back of Kuta. Bali had been getting busy. When I first arrived on the island, we all used to get around on bicycles, then we bought motorbikes, and as people got more wealthy and the tourist trade boomed, everyone started buying cars. They were building new roads everywhere. I had only been away from Bali for eight months, but already I felt lost. Skinny old roads were closing, new ones were opening, and majestic banyan trees and rice paddies were being slaughtered to make room for the new development.

We drove up a main road and then turned left onto a sealed road cordoned off by red plastic police cones. Up ahead we could see construction workers in masks pouring hot tar onto the road beyond the red cones. In the hot, humid weather, the tar created warped apparitions in the air. Sarah drove closer to the workers, away from the busy road, and parked her jeep. Her kids clambered out, and she dragged the bikes out of the back. The kids rode off towards the workmen.

'Stay close,' she cried out as she got back into the car and turned up the air-conditioning. We sat in the front seats, with Poppy on my lap, and watched her kids warp in front of us in the heat haze.

'Don't you find this odd, Sarah?' I asked her.

'What?'

'That your kids are riding up and down on this road, in this heat, with the lunacy of the traffic behind us and those workmen tarring roads in front of us.'

'There is nowhere else to ride a bike in Bali,' she said. 'They can't bike down the pebbly alleyways. The wild dogs run after them and they keep falling over.'

'Why did you buy them bikes then?' I asked.

'Because they're kids! They have to learn to ride a bike and I have to do something with them. When they were little it was fine to hang out on the beach or in the garden playing with flowers or sand, but now they're older I need to occupy their time somehow.' We laughed together at how Bali life could be quite mad and I even wondered if it was safe for us to be breathing the tar in the air.

I thought about the traffic jams I kept finding myself in; the increasing pollution, the green paddy fields disappearing under the weight of new villas and hotels. The beaches had become filthy. Where once you could bodysurf and dive in clean water, now you had to avoid plastic bags that initially you mistook for jellyfish and often you had to swim away from floating turds. Effluent sat proudly on the beach looking at you on your morning beach walk and sewage pipes were pumping straight into the ocean. A few syringes had started turning up on the beaches, too. Schools were limited, and friends who had been admitted to hospital were lucky if they got out alive. There was also nothing for children to do when they became teenagers.

In Bali we had all created these beautiful homes, but I felt we'd now become prisoners in them. Before Bali used to be safe, and we never locked our doors, but now we had to build our walls higher with barbed wire and glass on top of them and hire security men with guns so we could sleep at night. Friends had even started building closed-in rooms in their homes so they could control their environment and cool it down. Bali was fun, and it was nice to pass through as a tourist. To have a holiday home here would be fabulous, too, but it was not where I wanted to plant my family tree. I didn't want mine to get cut down with all the others.

I made a new friend. He was a tourist who accidently blew into my life on the beach, and his name was Bro. He had come to Bali to buy a house and we instantly became friends. He was in love with life, happy all the time. He cruised around in colourful batik shirts and I basked in his enthusiasm for life because I was struggling with the changes in mine. I was still the wild child who had arrived in Bali years ago, but now I didn't want to be wild and carefree any more. I wanted to grow up and be responsible, have sensible surroundings, but the changes in me kept spinning out into dark confusion and when that happened, Bro would show me the light again. At the same time, he annoyed my friends.

'I'm brother of the ocean, brother of the sky. I'm brother of this beautiful planet earth and I love it, like I love you,' he'd say, his arms making exaggerated movements, with a grin like a beauty pageant winner.

'He's a fucking nutter,' friends would say when I'd take him to their houses for dinner parties because I didn't want him to be lonely. We would sit and eat and he'd tell them how beautiful their dinner plates were and their lighting fixtures ... and their cutlery.

'Jane, there's something about him I don't trust,' they'd say, but I couldn't see it. For me, he always brightened up my day and he made Poppy laugh. My friends would tolerate him because I told them to be kinder, but I should have admitted there and then: I was no good at judging people.

My childhood was full of eccentric characters and as a sweet and innocent child I learned to love them all unconditionally. I had to: they included my parents. But now as an adult, eccentrics were drawn to me like zombies in a Michael Jackson video and something in them knew, 'Yes – Jane will be my friend.'

I knew Bro drank a little too much and he was overly happy, but apart from that I couldn't see what his problem was. 'You're so positive and optimistic all the time, Jane,' friends would say. 'Use your brain if you're going to make new friends.' But for some reason my brain and heart weren't connected. I think the link had been severed as a kid so I could accept everything I saw back then.

Bro also helped me deal with the Blond, who had arrived back on the island.

Chapter 19
A Brother

With the Blond in Bali, I needed Bro by my side more than ever. I needed him to glow happiness and light all around me.

The Blond had met a new girlfriend in Australia; that's why he liked it so much. Now he was using all the contacts I'd shown him in Bali to run his own clothing business. He was here to oversee production of some new lines he had designed.

I'd see him driving around on his motorbike. I'd hear him laughing at the neighbour's house. He'd say he was going to come to my house and spend time with his daughter, but he often wouldn't turn up, or would arrive hours late. He'd say he had money to help me out, but then he'd have a reason why he didn't again. He'd hurt me but I kept wanting to stay open and be nice to him because, whatever I felt about him, he was still the father of my child and I didn't want her to be without one.

It was Bro who lightened my load. He would arrive in my house, bouncing over the white stepping-stones. *'Aloha, beautiful Jane, aloha,'* he would call out and I'd smile back at him and wave.

'Jane, take me to the best place on this island for lunch and in exchange for two beautiful women's company, I'll pay. Where's Poppy?' He would hug me and then go to find her and scoop her up and make funny faces until she laughed too. She adored Bro, the love and attention he gave to her, and so did I.

'Go grab your bag, Janey, let's get outta here,' he'd shout. 'Life's too short not to have fun.'

I'd stop work, quickly pack up a bag and happily rush out of the house with him. He'd take me to the swimming pool and restaurant of a five-star hotel and I'd get to sip on virgin cocktails and nibble on delectable treats by the pool. He'd tell me how he'd like to have an affair with me one day, and I'd tell him I wasn't interested: now or ever. I'd tell him he was lovely, but honestly he was too old for me and I didn't want a relationship until I sorted myself out and worked out where I went so wrong with the last one. Bro said he'd be happy if I just had casual sex with him and I'd laugh and tell him there was no way I was ever going to bonk him either! We'd clink our cocktail glasses in a toast to our platonic friendship and he made me promise to visit him in Hawaii on my continuing journey.

'I want to see that little girl of yours again and how she's growing up,' he said. On my plane ticket, Australia was my next stop, then Hawaii, and Bro promised to pick me up from the airport if I made it to his island of Maui.

The Blond finished his business on the island and then flew off, and I felt the pressure lift. I'd seen him more at a distance on his bike than close up in real life, and the pain I'd felt seeing him was excruciating.

I had to get ready to leave Bali too. My visa was running out and I had my own journey to deal with.

I found someone to rent the house for a year and paid Kira back her money. I designed components for my necklaces, such as beads and trinkets, and had the clever craftsmen in Bali make them for me in silver and gold plate. I paid all my bills and carefully filled up my fishing tackle boxes with jewellery and lots of prayers. I said goodbye to Bro, and thanked him for all his love and kindness. Then I packed up my house and handed the keys to the new tenant. I placed money into a bank account for Kadek and his family for a year. It left me with only enough cash to get to the airport and get to Australia. But I was used to being broke and I tried not to think about it too much; it only made me feel sick again.

I got on a plane. It was time to leave Bali.

Chapter 20

Penises and Buddhas

Melbourne, Australia, was our next destination and I struggled down the narrow aisle of the plane with my five-month-old daughter in my arms. It was a night flight. One hand was stabilising Poppy, tied onto me in a sling, and my other hand was holding my boarding pass. My hand luggage had got considerably heavier since I'd left London and it was cutting a painful groove in my forearm. I gazed at the first class passengers as I slowly passed them by. They were already seated and drinking champagne and the sight of them made me feel like a little girl at an ice-cream van with no money in her pockets.

Money really can buy you happiness, I thought, at least when it comes to buying aeroplane tickets. I staggered on by.

The passengers in economy class stared at my baby threateningly, worried I was going to sit next to them, and their looks made me angry. I wanted to jump on their heads and attack them. Since the pregnancy, a lot of anger had been bubbling up. Whenever I felt someone was not being kind or loving to another human being, I now wanted to beat them up. I avoided the passengers' eyes and focused on counting the seat numbers. *Babies fly too, you motherfuckers. You were one once!* I was very tired, and this plane was boarding very late.

I found my seat and the unsuspecting woman in the next seat didn't notice us at first. She was staring out of the window and looking content, not realising her fate. She mesmerised me and her appearance made me smile.

She had wild, flaming red hair and her clothes, all various shades of green, had not been acquired from any chain store. What looked like thick blue rivers wound over her hands. She had large knuckles and wore oversized stone rings; the stones intrigued me because I didn't recognise them. She looked like a painting that had escaped from a museum and I was still admiring her when she turned to face me. Not wanting to be rude, I looked away. I tried to haul my bag into the overhead locker without knocking Poppy's head off and through my up-stretched arms I looked down at the woman again. She was smiling.

'Let me help you,' she said.

I sat down, and I could tell the two of us were kindred spirits. If she had the openness to present herself to the world like this, I knew we could be friends. She was happy to be sitting next to Poppy. She helped me entertain her, and as she did we talked about our lives. She also dealt in jewellery. She lived in Africa and was on her way to discover Australia, where she wanted to meet Aborigines. She dearly loved indigenous cultures and within her bag in the overhead locker, she also had beads and trinkets to sell to pay for her journey. As we continued to talk, the plane took off.

I fed Poppy under a sarong so the changing air pressure would not hurt her ears and I found her to be a good little travel companion. I couldn't understand why people thought travelling with a child was difficult. Poppy would simply sleep for the whole trip and only wake up for booby snacks. On both flights now I'd even been given a bulkhead priority seat with a baby cot attached to it. We would fly and Poppy would have her own cot for free and I thought it was a bargain. The only downside I could see about travelling with a baby was moving through so many time zones. It meant it was difficult to keep Poppy in any routine. Some mothers in Bali suggested I travel with cold and flu medicine so I could drug her when I wanted her to sleep. But I didn't think that was necessary.

The red-haired woman told me tales from Africa and Australia and I too felt like a travelling tribal person. I had read somewhere that the constant rocking motion of a mother's walking calms the child and that new experiences stimulate it and help with its development. To stimulate Poppy so far, all I'd given her were plants and twigs and she'd been particularly fond of the mango tree in my Bali garden. She also liked frangipani flowers and red hibiscuses. I always put new things in her hands to smell and taste, and Kadek and Elu did the same. There was no room for plastic toys in our bag and her only toy was a rag doll I'd bought her as a treat in England to say thank you for coming into my life.

Poppy was asleep by the time the fasten seatbelt sign was turned off and I wrapped her up in my spare top so she could still smell me and placed her into her cot. I rocked her gently until her breathing became heavy and then eagerly turned back to Belle, my new friend, because I wanted to know more about her.

We told each other about the kinds of jewellery we were going to sell and it didn't take long before we rushed to get our bags down from the overhead lockers to discover each other's treasures. As Belle rummaged through her bag, I giggled because we both had similar packing techniques. I watched Belle reveal trinkets hidden up sleeves and in the lining of her bag and I revealed mine hidden in nappies and clothing. As other passengers entertained themselves with movies and glasses of wine, we entertained ourselves by looking at trinkets and telling stories. We told each other the origins of our pieces and how they came into existence. We told each other how we thought the jewellery should be worn, and our personal vision for it. The pieces we held in our hands were so precious to us both. We laughed at how we didn't want to part with any of them because they were like children, but we had to, for financial reasons.

Belle really liked some of my blue turquoise. I'd bought it in Bali, and it had been carved into baby Buddha-head beads. I loved her tiny and ancient battered penises. They were made of old silver and I imagined a silversmith in Africa, dressed in a loincloth, passionately hammering them out on a rock. Belle told me that was probably how they were made and I stared at them carefully, rolling them between my thumb and index finger, looking at all the little dents. The idea of any penis anywhere near me grossed me out, but I liked the look of these little harmless battered ones and I was sure other women would find them appealing too. I thought I could secretly place one at the back of a necklace, so nobody knew it was there unless they wanted to show it to somebody. Excited, we both traded: Buddha heads for penises. I thought the little dicks would make wonderful conversation-starters when I was trying to sell my jewellery. That's what I liked about selling, wherever you were in the world if you had something to sell you always had an excuse to talk to people and hopefully make friends.

I looked through more of her jewellery and she looked through mine. She admired the goddess pendants I'd made to put on my necklaces and I told her how I'd been inspired to make them while living in Glastonbury, where I had given birth to Poppy. I told her how Glastonbury is meant to be famous for its feminine goddess energy and how all over town you will find healers and workshops available so you can get in touch with your feminine power. Even the landscape is shaped like a woman, with small hills that rise from a plain, like a giant woman lying on her back. One of the famous hills, the Glastonbury Tor, is said to be the home of the fairies who live with their queen. They were forced into exile when humans decided not to accept that fairies were real, and legend says if a person walks the hill they will often come back a changed and happier person. I told Belle how I used to be able to see the Tor from my cottage and often walked to the top of it for exercise. The view at the top was stunning. Belle asked if I thought living in Glastonbury had changed me.

I felt I had changed a lot there, from a girl into a young woman, and even though my heart was shattered, I felt being in Glastonbury delicately held everything together for me, like a mother carefully holding her child so she doesn't fall. I also felt being around so many goddess statues and folklore helped to give me the strength as a woman and mother to take on this journey alone. That's why I'd wanted to make goddess jewellery. I wanted to give other women something to hang around their necks to remind them of the great abilities and strength inside themselves. I smiled at Belle; she wasn't a girl any more; she was a woman and the two of us acknowledged the wisdom that can only come with age.

As she looked carefully at the goddess pendants, Belle said she would go and visit Glastonbury one day.

Belle was as precious as her trinkets. She was one of life's characters and had been travelling the planet for years. She told me, 'I like to live simply and I like to see the world,' and she reminded me of Kira. By the time I was Belle's age with blue rivers on my hands, I hoped to feel as happy and content with my life choices as she was.

Belle, Poppy and I flew deep into the night and we all drifted off to sleep. Before my eyes closed, I felt happy I hadn't stayed in Glastonbury because I now felt alive. I wanted to grow old and beautiful and have colourful life stories like Belle's, but I didn't want to grow old alone. Belle didn't talk about a partner, but on that plane I wished for my heart to one day find its soulmate. I wanted a real man by my side now. A man whose words I could trust, and trust with our lives, too. I didn't always want to have only tiny bashed up penises.

The plane bumped down onto the Melbourne tarmac. We had arrived in Australia.

Belle and I said goodbye to each other on the plane. With the jewellery in our bags it was not a good idea for us to go through Customs together. I watched the other passengers competing to see who could get off the plane first, but I was in no rush. It was easier to move down the aisle with Poppy when everyone had gone. Belle got up to leave and we hugged and said goodbye again and I watched her red hair slowly bob away. She had brightened up the flight and I was sure she'd brighten up Australia, leaving trinkets that told her story in her path. She didn't look back or wave again and I felt sad at how being on the road bought people into your life – but then took them away again.

I got my bags out of the overhead locker and strapped Poppy to my chest. Walking down the aisle, I felt nervous about going through Customs and I made another life decision: I don't want to be smuggling and doing this kind of travel when I have blue rivers.

I stepped off the plane, moved through passport control, picked up my bags and put them on a trolley. I went to walk through Customs and – got stopped.

They asked me to open my bags. They looked at my bead boxes. They looked at me. I was struggling with Poppy in my arms. She was whingeing and wriggling as I tried to hold her. I saw the sympathy in their eyes and – they passed me through. I sighed with relief.

Jet lagged, with a dry, nervous mouth, I pushed my trolley towards the arrival gates. I was in desperate need of a cup of tea to get rid of the shock.

Chapter 21

A Family Home

My sister met me at the airport and we hugged liked we hadn't seen each other in years, though it was only five months since Poppy was born. Now we were together again and Kay took Poppy in her arms and kissed her all over her head. She was so happy to see how much she had grown and I was secretly hoping Australia would be my home.

Kay drove slowly and cautiously back to her house, so we had lots of time to catch up on news. She kept looking at the speedometer to make sure she was within the limit and I kept thinking how different we were. We had come from the same parents, but she was happily married with three kids, had a nice house and played by the rules of life. I was a homeless single mother. As we drove I looked out at the big empty roads and the endless sea-blue sky. Poppy was strapped into a car seat, asleep again. Kay was strangely quiet and I found myself doing most of the talking. Kay kept saying she had something important to say, but it would wait until we got to the house, and I felt something odd in the air.

When we arrived at Kay's home, her husband Jim and their three young kids grabbed us and made a huge fuss. They dragged us down the hallway to their kitchen, excited we'd arrived, as they'd prepared us a breakfast of berries, yogurt and gluten-free waffles. It was heart-warming to be around such a lovely family. I never got this response at Dad's house, and most of the families I knew in Bali were already broken and in a mess too.

Now in a real loving home in Australia, I ate breakfast with Poppy on my lap while Kay's children played with her fingers and toes. We shared laughter and the washing-up together and I admired Kay and Jim's new house renovations.

When I used to live in Bali, I would visit them each year, and when they first arrived in Australia they didn't even have the money to rent a house. They would house-sit other people's homes for free when they went on holiday, but it meant they had to keep moving every few months. They had no money for clothes; they lived in tracksuits from Target. Kay pronounced it 'Tar-jay' to pretend she was shopping somewhere stylish and French.

Kay and Jim had met at university in England and when they graduated they started a recruitment business together, which was a big success. They franchised offices around the world, but in the early 1980s there was a financial crash and they lost everything they owned: the business, house, cars. There was one franchise office in Australia that was still making a little money, so they decided to take a huge risk and move the whole family there. In Australia, Jim started out selling manuals to make enough money to put food on the table; his office wasn't making much and he'd drive along Beach Road in Melbourne, look up at the city skyline, and dream: one day he would make a big deal in one of those offices. He never gave up on his dream and one day he did make that deal ... and now as a family they were financially set up again.

I always found Kay and Jim inspirational. They were loving; they worked hard together; they didn't have any family money that could soften life's blows. I felt proud of them as I sat in their newly renovated home. I remembered when it was a tumbledown weatherboard shack with a garden you couldn't see because the weeds had grown into a forest.

After breakfast Jim took Poppy in his arms and Kay led me down the hallway saying she had to talk to me. I remembered how this hallway used to give me splinters, but now there were beautiful varnished floorboards that shone instead of tortured. The walls were painted white instead of being covered in old wallpaper. I passed the guest bathroom, which used to have a makeshift shower with a plastic-stained bottom that leaked. Now a white porcelain bath sat proudly on iron claw feet. Their bedroom used to always be a sea of cardboard boxes, but now the bed was covered in crisp linens and there was a fireplace and glass doors led to a stone tiled courtyard with orange trees. On the hall table were pictures of the family. Kay said to me, 'We need to talk in private.'

I was so happy for her; she'd been the sensible one in the family all along – and now her house looked very sensible, too. I walked into her formal living room with sofas you could easily disappear in and we sat in front of another fireplace with more family pictures on the mantelpiece. I remembered when Kay and Jim were first thinking about buying this house.

I'd asked to borrow some money for a business idea in Bali and they gave me their house deposit. I promised I'd pay them back in two months and I worked like a dog until I had paid back every penny. With the money I earned, I built my Bali home and with their deposit back, they had bought this one.

When I was in Glastonbury, I didn't want to ask them for financial help. I was embarrassed by what had happened to me. I also had no way to pay any money back and I didn't want them to pay for my life's fuck-ups. When I had faxed Kay and told her I was pregnant, she sent me a fax and asked me if I thought I was doing the right thing having a baby with the Blond. I'd faxed her back: *Fuck off*.

In the living room I sat down and wriggled my toes in the thick plush carpet. Kay had gone quiet again and now I was worried.

My sister often used to lecture me as a child that I should grow up and be responsible, and the lecture always started with her silence. I felt I was about to be lectured. Kay stood up and closed the door. Oh shit, I thought, this is going to be hardcore. I remembered her closing the door on my mum once.

Chapter 22
Sorry

Mum called up the stairs, asking me to bring her hairbrush down. I was about five years old. As Mum's calls turned into shouts, I kept shouting down the stairs, 'No, I won't!' Kay and I both hated Mum brushing our hair. It always hurt, and when we cried out she'd smack the brush over our heads. Neither of us ever understood how our mum could be a hairdresser or how people would pay to go and see her.

'No!' I replied again as I sat on the steps, giggling to myself about how naughty I was.

'*I'm warning you,*' she shouted back.

'*No!*'

'*I'M FUCKING WARNING YOU.*'

I giggled because Mum always used to say, 'Don't fucking swear,' and, 'Always act like a lady.' The next thing Mum was raging up the stairs towards me. Her bony hands flew at my face and I leaned backwards to avoid them. She grabbed my hair and I took off, bumping down the stairs, screaming. I held onto my hair, not wanting it to be ripped from my scalp. I screamed out for God and landed at the bottom of the stairs in a crying heap. At the top of the stairs I saw my saviour.

My sister Kay yelled, '*STOP IT, MUM*,' but Mum grabbed my hair again and dragged me into the lounge like a cave woman. I was in tears and Kay charged down the stairs to save me. Mum threw me onto the sofa and started kicking me. Kay jumped onto Mum's back and grabbed her arms, taking her off balance. She spun her around and threw her out of the lounge, slammed the door shut and barred it with her body. Kay used to practise wrestling with Dad when she was very little and she was good at it. The lounge door kept bouncing. Mum wanted to get back in, and I knew she would kill us both. Kay and I screamed together on the other side of the door for someone to come and save us.

Kay and I both learned as kids: no one ever comes to save you. You have to save yourself.

Now Kay closed her newly painted door and sat down on her sofa. Butterflies were flying around in my stomach. I heard Poppy squawking in the kitchen and I wondered if I could make an excuse to leave so I could see how Poppy was doing.

'Mum died,' Kay said.

Butterflies then massacred themselves inside me. I grabbed the couch as years of suppressed internal pain came roaring back. They roared back for Kay too and we took hold of each other and sobbed. Nobody had gone through what we had together. Nobody had ever understood our pain.

'Why does this hurt so much, Kay?' I asked. 'I thought we got over Mum leaving us a long time ago.'

'I don't know,' came her muffled reply as we kept holding each other and crying.

I stopped seeing my mum when I was 15. Kay had stopped seeing Mum a few years earlier. I left because I felt my life with Mum had become a wrestling ring. A wrestling ring has ropes around it to contain the fighters: you fall against the ropes and the ropes bounce you back into the fight. You always get bounced back in for another round, but when I was 15 I felt I'd been in the ring for too long and my family was seriously hurting me. My dad told me he gave up professional wrestling when he was still at the top.

'Don't keep fighting, Kid, when you know you can't win. Get out while the going is still good.' I felt back then that I was on the edge of huge internal damage, but it was deep and no one could see it on the outside. I felt no one would ever be able to find my injuries in time to save me. My opponents were good, very good. Every time my sister or me got hit, the hits never left any physical marks, just fine cracks in delicate organs. One day my heart screamed at me to stop the fight and fight for my life instead. It told me I had to get away from my parents, especially my mother. It told me it was time to turn my back on the ring. I prayed that someone, somewhere, would help me, and my dad's words kept ringing in my head: 'Everything will be all right, Kid. Your life will always be all right.'

Kay stopped seeing Mum just before her final exams at university. Mum had been locked up in a mental institution again and Kay made the four-hour journey from her university in her old Morris Minor car with a broken side mirror. She'd been to the hospital many times before; she was always alone dealing with Mum's situation. She'd asked Dad for help again, but he'd said the same thing he always did:

'She's your mother. She's got nothing to do with me. I married her and now we're divorced. You're my flesh and blood and she's not.'

So Kay kept driving alone to the hospital alone and there she was asked to sit in on a meeting with a psychiatrist and our mum. The psychiatrist said it would help her mum get better, but Kay was already under a lot of pressure at university. She should have been studying for exams and not sitting in a London mental hospital. In the meeting, Mum and Kay screamed at each other and the psychiatrist told Kay, 'This situation is very clear. It's you, Kay, who's unstable and needs help, not your mother.'

Kay sat back in her seat as though somebody had struck her. She had grown up for years living around Mum's turmoil and had become a sensible adult way before her time and now she was being told by a man in authority with a white coat, a man who had the ability to lock someone up: 'You're the one who is in need of treatment. It isn't your mother that's insane, it's you.'

Kay was scared. If she stepped out of the firing line she knew I would be the next to be hit – and she had been protecting me from our mum for years. Mum was ill, but she was a smart lady and over the years her intelligence combined with her poor mental health had turned her into a manipulator. Mum had been throwing manipulating punches at Kay for years and Kay had caught every one and deflected them away from me. At university, Kay had met Jim and he showed her what her mum was doing to her and helped her to get away from her. But now Kay was back and Mum had fired a direct hit. Kay could hardly breathe. She didn't know what to do.

Kay had always been my protector. She had been the one in touch with Dad, telling him I had to be taken away from

Mum. She'd always stayed around to protect me, but now she was being attacked herself and there was nobody protecting her.

She fell back on the only thing she knew: you only have yourself ...

Kay held on tightly to her chair. She was happy with her life at university. She'd worked so hard to get there. She wasn't going to lose everything she'd worked for now and her soul stirred. She stood up shakily with that soul strong and she turned her back on Mum. She walked out of the psychiatrist's office and never looked back, never to see Mum again.

Together now, holding each other on the couch, we cried. We cried for the parent we wished our mum had been and we said sorry to each other. It was the word our mum should have said to us, but was never able to. 'Sorry,' we kept saying. Hoping the other sister could hear.

Chapter 23
Let There Be Love

During the next few days in Australia, grieving brought up many unresolved pains for the two of us, and the newly painted walls of Kay's home protected us both. This was what a real home should feel like, somewhere safe. This was the kind of home a child should be bought up in. 'Poppy, by the time you know what is going on in the world, I hope I can give you this too.'

The home kept the world outside, while we dealt with our grief safely inside. My head would fall against the walls as memories of Mum resurfaced and they'd cripple me in the simplest situations. I'd be washing the dishes, getting a dress out of a wardrobe and thoughts of her would flood me. My sister would hear me crying, come and find me and wipe the snot off my face, like she did as a child. She was by my side again, strong as always, and it felt so good.

Mum had died when I was in Bali, just before I left for Australia. Kay didn't want to tell me when I was there, though. She didn't want me to be alone to deal with this. She knew every blow can be easier when loving family are around you. Mum's funeral service was to be in a couple of weeks; it had been delayed because Mum had died in strange circumstances. They said a fire might have killed her, but they had to do an autopsy to make sure. Mum's social worker had phoned Kay to tell her the news and asked whether we would come back for the funeral. Kay replied that she didn't know, as she had to speak to me first, and together as a family we all made the decision. This family Kay had created was what she had always dreamed of having: a family that didn't ignore problems, but simply dealt with them before they got out of control.

We finally got the results of Mum's autopsy. She had been drinking and smoking in bed and had fallen asleep. She had dropped the cigarette on her bed. It made her go up in flames.

Her apartment caught on fire. Thick smoke blew out the window. The fire brigade was called. They protected the rest of the residents living in the flats and saved their homes but they weren't able to save our mum. The autopsy said they didn't think Mum suffered any pain when she died. They said, 'It was the smoke that killed her.'

Kay and I told the social worker we would not return to England for our mum's funeral. I had no money, and Kay couldn't leave her family again. We both also felt we'd said our goodbyes to our mum many years before and we wanted to have a ceremony for her in Australia instead. The social worker was sympathetic; she'd worked with Mum for years and knew us both well. She asked us what music and flowers to get for

Mum's funeral and we told her we'd call her back in a couple of days.

In the night, I heard Mum singing to me in a dream and I woke up freaked out. The bedroom was in shadow. Poppy was asleep by my side. The wardrobe stood tall and scary and I heard people turning over in their sleep. I closed my eyes again after my heart calmed down.

I never like hearing voices; Mum used to hear voices all the time. I remembered a story my older brother George told me before he committed her to an institution.

He'd come back from America and was living with us as Kay had gone away for a year to live with a friend of Dad's in Germany before she went to university. Before Kay left she kept telling Dad, 'Jane can't live with Mum without me. She needs to stay somewhere else full time.'

'Where?' Dad would ask.

'With you.'

'She can't,' he'd say. 'Bunny and I are too busy working.' So George came to live at our house again and it made Mum happy. She smiled a lot and sang songs from the movie *Funny Girl* all the time, thinking she was the star, Fanny Brice. She would sing all night and day and she'd sit next to her record player carefully writing down the words to songs so she could memorise them. I'd sing along to them too.

I wasn't home one afternoon when George returned to hear Mum singing loudly upstairs. He went up and found her spinning and dancing around in the hallway. Her arms were flying and she screamed, '*You're the devil, you're the devil and Jesus is going to save me.*' George tried to calm her down, but they both frightened each other and he ran out of the house looking for help. He thought there was no use going to the police; his mum hadn't done anything wrong, but she kept talking about Jesus and it was as though she was talking to him directly, so he went to a church to find a priest. He thought maybe his mum needed an exorcism.

He found a priest and begged him to come back to our house. As the two of them went upstairs, Mum looked calmly at the priest but then she started screaming again. '*You're the devil in disguise, you're the devil in disguise.*' The priest tried to calm her but it made her madder, and he looked at my brother and said, 'I'm no good at this.' And he grabbed George's hand and they rushed downstairs together.

The priest comforted my distraught brother. He rubbed his back and held his hand and told George he should go to church more often for tea and support. My brother was a very good-looking man. Women dropped at his feet and men's fashion at the time was to wear tight jeans, leaving nothing to the imagination. George looked at the priest and was dumbfounded.

'What the fuck are you doing? I don't need fucking help, it's my mother who needs it!' And George brushed the priest's hands away as he heard Mum now wailing outside the lounge room door, having another monologue with Jesus.

'You need to call a doctor,' said the priest. 'This isn't a job for the church,' and he opened the door and Mum started singing loudly again, '*Doooon't rain on my parade.*'

George rushed to the kitchen to call a doctor; the priest was praying; Precious, our poodle, was shaking in her basket; there were lots of pretty cupcakes that Mum had baked sitting on the sideboard, ready for our tea.

A doctor arrived and it took three people to pin Mum down and drug her with a needle so she wasn't funny any more. It took three signatures to commit her to a mental institution: a son, a priest and a doctor.

The next morning in Australia, sitting at the breakfast bar in the midst of a kid-feeding frenzy, I nervously sang the song Mum had been singing to me in my dream. I wanted to know if Kay recognised it, because I didn't.

'Why are you singing that, Jane?' Kay asked. 'Mum used to like it.' The hairs on my arms stood up. Kay being older than me remembered lots of things about Mum I didn't.

'You know the song I'm singing?'

'We have it,' Jim said and he went off looking through his CD collection. He found what he was looking for and put it on and the blood drained out of my face.

'Are you all right, Jane?' Kay asked.

'I think this is the song Mum wants to be played at her funeral.'

Kay's eyes opened wider and Jim made us more tea as I told them about my dream. In it, I saw Mum no longer with a screwed-up body and fucked-up mind, and she seemed finally at peace with her life and happy. The song of hers kept playing in the background as I told them the story. It was 'Let There Be Love' by Nat King Cole.

Mum had wanted to feel love all her life but sadly she never had. She'd been born into an abusive family. Her husband was unfaithful to her and left her. All her children left her too for their own self-preservation, and in the end she had no friends either because her behaviour had become so difficult. When I was young, I remember my mum asking me, 'Jane, why is there never anyone around to love me and care for me, like I love and care for you?' And I'd tell her in my youthful innocence, 'I love you and I'm here for you,' but that was before I left her as well. The music kept playing on in the kitchen.

It was the song we asked to be played at Mum's funeral. Mum's social worker was the only person who attended.

In Australia, Kay and I held a beach ceremony for our mum instead. Just the two of us sat on the sand in bare feet. Next to us was a ghetto blaster with a CD ready to play her song. Under the twilight sky, we each recounted all the good memories we still had of our mum. They were from when we were both very young, when she was still normal and happy. We let go silver helium balloons and they floated high up in the sky and we prayed that Mum would completely let go of this life and trust that there was love waiting for her on the other side. That's all our mum ever wanted: to be loved and free of her illness. Hopefully now she would find what she had always been looking for.

My sister and I held onto each other tightly as we watched the sun go down. We said our final goodbyes and we didn't want to have regrets. As the sun dipped below the water's edge we threw our mum's favourite lilac-coloured roses into the water, but then a huge Alsatian dog ran at us, splashing and barking. We got up and screamed. His owner screamed at him too. But the dog didn't listen and he bounded over to our mum's flowers and ate them.

Our Mum had an unlucky life – right to the very end.

Chapter 24
Paper Bricks

I had to move on from my emotional baggage. I had to keep the wheels rolling forward on my life. When Poppy went to sleep at night, I started making my jewellery. It would have been better if I could have worked during the daytime, but I realised that was now impossible.

When I was busy working in Glastonbury getting ready to leave, Poppy was younger and always asleep. In Bali, I had Elu, so I could easily work there too, but in Australia, with Poppy now a fully awake six-month-old baby, she constantly needed to be entertained, and sadly was only entertained by me. Maybe she felt insecure; her surroundings had changed constantly since she was born. I was the only stable thing in her life she could relate to, and she wanted me all the time. Kay was busy with her three kids, and was also helping her husband with the new business and she didn't have the time to babysit. This was my baby and I had to deal with it. Working at night-time after Poppy went to bed was now my only option. The most work I managed during the day was to tidy up my jewellery boxes or unpick bad necklaces I'd made in the night in my sleep-deprived state.

I should have really been going to bed early. I'd already be drained from looking after a young baby all day and breastfeeding, but I had no choice. It was summertime in Australia and trying to put Poppy to sleep each evening was a nightmare. The sun was against me. It would keep shining through the windows, excited that Christmas was coming and the days were getting longer.

I fought with Poppy, trying to get her into a night-time routine and even thought of drugging her with cold medicine – but I didn't. As the light streamed in through the cracks in the curtains, I'd give Poppy her bedtime feed with my hand covering her eyes to try to get her to sleep. She'd rebel and scream and throw my hand away and I'd look at the big strong wardrobe wishing it would come to life and help me.

In Bali the locals and expats all drove around on motorbikes with their kids strapped to them. It was the quickest way to get around and the vibrations on the back of the bike always put Poppy to sleep, so in desperation I tried to replicate the sensation.

I'd scoop Poppy out of bed, strap her to my back in Kay's old backpack and get on Kay's bicycle. I'd then peddle off around the block. Around and around I'd go, with Poppy pulling at my hair and screaming in rebellion. I'd keep going, sweating and bumping over as many lumps in the road as I could find and charging across grassy fields trying to get some Bali-style road friction happening. Her high-pitched squeals would eventually quiet down and people would stop looking at me. I'd feel the lump on my back get heavy and limp and there would be no more kicks to my ribs. Drenched, exhausted and panting, I'd return to Kay's to put Poppy back into bed, now asleep.

I'd look at my sleeping angel and it always blew me away the love I felt for her. However much she screamed and rebelled and made it impossible to do the things I used to be able to do, the more I loved her. I stroked her golden hair and kissed her head. I wished I could curl up and go to sleep next to her, but I couldn't.

I'd then start work. I'd choose a goddess pendant, place it at the bottom of a black velvet board, the type used for jewellery displays in shops, and lay out beads in a necklace arrangement above it. I'd keep changing the beads around until I felt they formed a harmonious necklace instead of a rainbow, haphazard mess. I would then carefully string everything together. Each necklace was so individual, using different beads. It was incredibly time-consuming and I would think of how people often thought designers simply threw things together. It takes time and skill to make something proportioned, balanced and well-designed. That's why it takes years to study the art of it. Often tired at night, I'd make a necklace only to discover in the morning in my refreshed state that it was crap. The bead combination was rubbish, the colour scheme out of whack and the next day I'd have to unravel it and put the beads back in the box ready to start from scratch again the following night. I'd be lucky if I could complete two good necklaces in an evening and I always went to sleep after everybody else in the house.

Working in the silent home, hearing adults and children stirring in their sleep, I'd feel draughts creeping under my bedroom door and I'd wish I was in dreamland too. But this was the only opportunity I had to pull my life back together again and I'd keep working. I'd rummage through my fishing tackle boxes hoping to make something somebody would love. Often I would wake up cold and find my head on the desk with beads stuck into my face and dribble running down my chin. I'd get up from the desk and get into bed next to Poppy to try and keep warm and then I would start work again. Often I would wake to find beads running all over the bed.

It was gruelling. I used to think a heavy labourer, after being on site all day and then drinking 15 scotches, might feel the same. My new job description was milkmaid, clown, chef, cleaner, night-time jeweller, financial advisor, constant worrier.

During those silent nights, I often questioned my whole decision to be on the road. Staying in Glastonbury on the dole would have been an easier, stress-free option. I didn't even know if my necklaces would sell.

When I'd made enough necklaces, Kay organised a jewellery sale for me. She called all her friends and tempted them by saying, 'My bohemian sister from Bali is in town. We're having a sale of her jewellery designs as she is travelling around the world with her new baby looking for a home and paying her way by selling her work.' I'm sure people turned up just to see what was going on, and Jim helped by buying lots of bottles of wine so we could loosen the women up and into the spirit of Christmas shopping.

I hated being reliant on others. I hadn't been since I was 15. It sucked and it hurt my pride. I was 28, and I felt too old to live off people and I should have had my shit together by now. That feeling kept me working through the nights. It told me to stay awake and not flake out, and I made a big collection for my first sale.

On the day, women arrived in clucking groups. They came on time and as we opened the door, it felt like the opening of the Harrods Sale in London. We told the women I was selling at wholesale prices to get my business started and as soon as the women entered the house they rushed to the display table. Kay helped sell and pass necklaces around, and Jim poured the happy-juice. Women started bickering. Mirrors moved up and down the table. 'Ooos,' were heard.

'Ooo I love that one.'

'If you're not having it, can I?'

'Can you make a special one for me to go with a dress I have?'

'I love the silver penises.'

The more the women drank the more they got hysterical about buying genitalia and I wondered if Australian men would have been so keen to have silver whelks strapped around the back of their necks.

Money changed hands. More orders were placed. More wine corks were popped and women slipped jewellery into their bags and slipped money out of their purses and gave it to me. I'm sure some women who knew my sister well bought necklaces purely to help me out. Surely no one in their right mind needs six necklaces to give as gifts at $200 each, but I didn't complain. I was beside myself with happiness and intensely thanked every woman who swapped her money for my talent.

I wished they really knew the extent of my gratitude though. The money they gave me meant I now didn't have to live off donations and that felt so good. It didn't feel good to live off my sister. Those notes the women handed over to me felt like precious bricks. If I kept working hard and getting more of them, I could re-build my future.

And word spread. Women we didn't know started calling and asking if they could come and see the range. They would arrive. They would always buy. They would give me cash and I started putting money under my bed again, tying the notes together with Christmas ribbon, making little bricks and placing them in my bed vault. The women kept coming ... I kept working ... Life felt like a blurry Christmas snowstorm, but in Australia it was boiling hot and the turkey planned for Christmas dinner was going to be cooked on a barbecue. Beading. Cleaning. Playing. Nappies and lots of baby shit. Feeding – so much feeding. Laughing and simply hanging out with my baby. Sleepless nights. Poppy awake. Beads found in her poo. Selling. Stashing more bricks in the bed vault. Very sore fingertips. Sore nipples too. Making special orders. Selling all the penises. Australian women loved them! Cooking for the family. Helping Kay with the kids and trying to act normal instead of like a sleep-deprived Christmas elf. I had to keep going. Christmas elves have to keep working too. Get everything finished before Christmas. Can't stop. Christmas is coming.

'Christmas is coming,' Kay's children kept telling me as they became my helpers, finding beads in the carpet with their little fingers and putting them back into my fishing-tackle boxes. I made it a game for them: who could find the most?

People kept dropping in to buy presents; I had to stay awake to make them. *I'll stop at Christmas – that's what insanely busy elves do, right?*

I fell asleep, exhausted, on the toilet once. Other nights because of exhausted tears, I would find it difficult to keep my eyes open, but those silver strings never stopped moving and my beads kept dropping and it was a fine line I was working on. Money was now my motivator; it could change my life. Money was my whip. I'd stand up, swing my arms over my head and throw my legs around trying to wake myself up. A rhythm would be in my head and I'd quietly sing the Flying Lizards' song 'Money' while I worked. But unlike the song's implied meaning, money wasn't all I wanted – but earning it had become very, very important.

Chapter 25
Christmas at the White House

Christmas Eve finally arrived with a 40-degree wind blowing in off the Australian desert, but I was told not to worry, as a cool breeze was on its way for Christmas Day. Husbands were still blowing in; they'd arrive at our house in a dishevelled state, hoping to find a last-minute gift for their wives. And as the cool Australian breeze finally arrived, the husbands cleaned me out of stock; it was a welcome Christmas gift.

My inner temperature dropped too and I went to bed early on Christmas Eve. I was now sleeping on a mattress full of colourful wrapped bricks. It felt like Santa had come early and given me my Christmas bonus. Now I just had to work out what to do with it.

At an unearthly early hour on Christmas morning, Kay's kids screamed in my ears '*Santa's been!*' And I could have throttled them, but seeing three little people bouncing up and down made me soften.

'Santa ate the mince pie. Rudolph ate the carrots. They've made a terrible mess.' Bounce, bounce, bounce. I met Kay and Jim in the hallway and they looked as sleepy and bedraggled as me. Jim put his hand up, a sign of morning acknowledgment; Kay hugged me and wished me a merry Christmas. The kids bounced around us grabbing at our hands, grabbing at Poppy's feet, and dragging us into the lounge.

'*Look, look, look.*' Santa had left footprints. He must have fallen into the pantry, got his boots stuck in the self-raising flour and then walked circles all over the carpet, I thought. He was obviously confused about where to put the presents. '*Look, look, look.*' Santa had found the plate the kids had left out for him and surprisingly he had taken a big bite out of the gluten-free mince pie and Rudolph had munched on all the carrots and spat bits everywhere. The kids dashed around picking up bits of Santa's beard and putting it into our hands and closing our fingers over their precious finds. Santa had dropped at least a bag's worth of cotton wool, and then they brought us Santa's empty whisky glass.

'Santa's been very naughty,' they told us and I looked at Jim and he rolled his eyes.

The kids dragged us to sit down and then the three of them started to try and read the Christmas labels and distribute the presents. Squeals of delight were heard as the kids got lost under a colourful mound of boxes and wrapping-paper and the unwrapping began. Jim played Christmas music and Poppy kept showing us her gums. This was her first Christmas and she knew something very special was happening!

Santa gave me two huge presents and I looked at them in disbelief. How the fuck was I meant to travel with them? Each was bigger than my backpack, and when I opened them, I discovered a stroller and a plastic car seat. Did Santa not know I was travelling around the world light? I nodded appreciatively, trying to fake my feelings, and smiled and hugged everyone, thanking them for their kind thoughts.

We ate a breakfast of croissants, eggs and ham and I sat back down on the couch to breastfeed again. Kay and Jim played board games with their kids. How nice would it be to have a home of my own with boxes of fun, instead of having to search for it all the time, I thought. Then we went into the garden to play rounders.

I sat on the grass with Poppy and we watched everyone play and I looked back at Kay and Jim's house. It looked like the White House in America, so big and white and with a lawn that went on forever. Passionfruit flowers bloomed on fences; I'd only ever seen them in magazines before. I shuddered at the amount of upkeep this house must need and then looked over at the pool. Jim mowed the lawns and cleaned the pool; Kay constantly moaned about keeping the house clean, too, because of its size, and I wondered if the home I was actually searching for was something like this. Looking at this house made me shudder, and the grass beneath me tickled my legs. Poppy picked at it intently, watching the kids playing. They kept running over to her, holding her hand, looking into her eyes and telling her she was still in the game even though she was too young to play. They'd kiss her head and dash off again and Poppy would look up at me, thrilled: *Did you see that?*

What other kinds of home are there? I felt confused. This was Kay's home and this was Kay's family and that felt right, but it didn't feel like my home. I looked down and started picking at the grass too and putting some into Poppy's hands.

Kay came running over and plonked herself down next to me to have a rest and asked me to stay in Melbourne again. She'd already asked me a few times and I guess was eagerly waiting for my reply. She said we could work out Australian immigration together and it would be good for both of us to be one big family again. I told her I was seriously thinking about it, but I still couldn't give her a definite answer yet and she ran off to play with the kids again.

I thought about staying and living in Melbourne – but something about it didn't feel right.

I really liked Australian people. They were open and friendly. The weather was nice (not like England) and what I considered to be my close family was actually here in front of me, running around on the lawn. I kept pondering ... I picked at the grass. Maybe if Melbourne doesn't feel quite right, maybe I should look somewhere else in Australia? Maybe I am close, but it's just not here I should settle down? I had the money to travel again and I thought it would be better to keep moving now, while I had surplus cash, instead of waiting until my money ran out again. Maybe I should visit the north coast of Australia, I'd been there before and liked it. But then I remembered Poppy's father was living there now and I didn't want to be anywhere near him. I thought about a girl I'd met in Glastonbury. She came from Perth and kept speaking about a magical spot south of there called Margaret River. When I'd been selling my jewellery, Melbourne ladies kept saying I should go to Margaret River too. They told me it was full of galleries and gift shops and I could easily sell my work there. Sitting on the grass, thinking about all my options, Margaret River felt like a good place to check out.

The kids wanted to go swimming and we all trundled off to the pool. The kids put on their Australian swimsuits, which looked like neon condoms, and squeezed on their floaties. They jumped in the pool and I took off all of Poppy's clothes and mine, leaving only our knickers on. The two of us looked like European tourists instead of Australians and we went swimming in the shade. I'd noticed on Australian beaches that women kept their tops on. Maybe I should, too?

Christmas was one game after another, food, snoozes, booze breaks, lots of cartoons. Boxing Day was the same and as the New Year came closer, my mind became clearer. After the holiday break, I was going to Margaret River.

Kay was disappointed. I said, 'This is your home, Kay. Melbourne feels right for you and this is why you stayed here, but I'm not so sure it's right for me. I don't know why. Maybe I just need to go and look at Margaret River to know what is really good – and then perhaps I'll come back here to stay.' She grunted in disapproval.

Chapter 26
A Unit

I got my sister to laugh again as she drove me to the airport. 'How am I going to manage now with all this extra luggage you've bought me? In Perth I have no one to meet me.' We continued to laugh about my situation, but inwardly I was angry with the Blond again. Jim would be there for Kay when they travelled. The Blond was such an arsehole. This had become my pattern lately – to blame him for everything that went wrong and, weirdly, it felt good.

Kay helped me get all my luggage checked in at the airport and we waved goodbye to each other at the departure gate. We always cried when we said goodbye to each other.

Poppy was awake when we got on the plane. Some mothers go to baby clinics to check on the progress of their child; I simply got on planes to keep track of her development. On our first plane trip, Poppy only woke for feeds; on the second one she was awake for longer periods, but would lie quietly and I just had to play with her hands. Now I became a children's entertainer lost for acts. I didn't travel with toys so I found myself reading aeroplane magazines to her and ripping bits out and making balls to play with. Do I need to travel with a bag full of toys, too? The reality of travelling with a baby bit me on the bum again.

We arrived in Perth and waited at the baggage carousel for our luggage. I saw it, chased after it and dragged it off as Poppy kicked me in delight in her sling. I kept picking off luggage and it grew into a tumbling snowman pile at my feet. How am I meant to carry all this? I stood for a while staring at it as other people easily dealt with their bags and simply walked away. People were nice and asked me if I wanted any help but I told them 'I can manage, thank you.' I needed to see if I could deal with all this alone.

I unstrapped Poppy from her sling and strapped her into our new Christmas-present stroller. I put Poppy's cabin bag on the handles of the stroller. I put my backpack on my back and my hand luggage containing jewellery on my forearm. It instantly carved a groove. Quickly, hoping Poppy wouldn't notice, I balanced our new Christmas present car seat on top of her in the stroller and pushed. Poppy screamed. The car seat went flying. She now had very strong arms.

Round two. I strapped Poppy back onto me. I put the backpack in the stroller and balanced the car seat on top of that. I put my hand luggage on the other forearm, so it could cut a groove in that one too, and as I put Poppy's hand luggage back on the stroller handles the stroller collapsed. It was the smallest and lightest one Kay could buy. 'Mother fucking shit,' I cursed as I walked off leaving everything in a heap on the floor.

Round three. I returned with a trolley and felt sad that nobody had stolen my luggage. On the trolley I balanced my backpack, car seat, stroller and hand luggage, and staggered off with Poppy smiling on my sweaty chest.

I arrived at the car hire desk and Poppy was bouncing in her sling. She was loving this trip, having so much fun, everything was so exciting – all these new things to see and she couldn't stop laughing and trying to talk to the rental lady and me. With car keys in hand I puffed and pushed my trolley towards the car park. As we stepped outside, the heat hit me.

It was Perth's summertime and it felt like the Gobi Desert. I sped up and raced around the car park trying to find my car. There were heat hazes in the distance and when I found the car I quickly opened all the windows. I put Poppy in the back seat with a bottle of water and fought with the baby-seat next to her. So many straps, so many buckles. In Australia they wanted to keep their citizens safe. I thought back to Bali and driving around on a motorbike with Poppy strapped to me with a sarong – *that was so wrong*! She kept opening her mouth in a cheesy grin and I'd keep stealing her bottle to have a drink. I continued to fight with the buckles to keep her safe. It was hard to get my head around the instructions, and Poppy was very amused by my wet t-shirt.

Finally, with us both strapped safely in, and air-con blasting, we drove off.

'Be good, Poppy. Please. Chill out.' I rasped as she screamed in the back seat. 'Let's drive around for a bit, cool the car down and then I'll feed you.' Her screams grew high pitched. She didn't like being strapped into the seat; she hadn't been very good at it in Melbourne either. 'I don't have a bicycle, Poppy,'

I screamed at her in the rear-view mirror as the air-con blew a freezing storm and tried to cool me down. We drove out of Perth's pounding heat and things did cool down.

On the road we stopped for lots of fluid breaks and to get Poppy out of her seat. I kept hoping she'd sleep, but she had no intention of doing that any more and kept throwing her water bottle at me.

'Yes, you're getting very big and awake now, aren't you,' I'd say into the rear-view mirror as she glared at me. Open roads lay ahead and we kept driving south to Margaret River. We passed cafés with signs promoting emu, kanga and croc burgers, and there were loads of art galleries. Wow, it looked like this area was full of artists eating strange animals and getting inspired. Would that be my destiny if I called this place home? I cringed at the idea of ending up wearing a long hippy skirt and chewing on a crocodile's leg as I sat by a river and painted.

I used to be a vegetarian until I met the Blond and got pregnant. We were in New Zealand, getting him re-qualified, when I started to act oddly. In the towns we visited he'd always go and have a look at surfboard shops. He would then find me with my hands squashed up against a butcher's window. I didn't want to buy the meat, though, and hurt a living being, so I found a hill with a bunch of sheep grazing on it and went to sit with them to regain some sense. The sheep would come up, cock their heads and stare at me with their weird marble-glass eyes. More of their friends soon followed. I found myself surrounded by a halo of cute woolly things as I tried to find the angelic loving part of myself. I tried to communicate with them, tell them my plight and how something inside of me now desired to eat them. I'd pat them and stare at them too, the same way they were staring at me. I was hoping to feel a deep connection. The problem was: I didn't. I felt they were stupid, bleated a lot and their sole purpose in life was actually to be eaten. I struggled on that hill until I couldn't take it any more. Pregnancy had changed me. I stood up, stomped off the hill and informed the Blond that I needed to go to a restaurant to eat lamb chops.

Poppy had started to eat solids, too. Little organic jars of it and a small hand blender were in my bag. Bottles were also in my bag as the summer was hot and she needed more fluids than just my milk. We stopped for picnics, and we stopped and looked at paintings in galleries and stared at llamas in fields. She was loving this journey; she was my little best friend who liked to chew on everything and dribble a lot.

At the art galleries, I happily discovered they liked my work. I didn't have very much, as I had only been able to make a few necklaces before I left Melbourne, but they bought everything, and I made sure the galleries were far enough away from each other so each didn't infringe on the other's business. That was easy. There was so much land in Australia and so few people – everything was so spread out.

It was supposed to take us three and half hours to drive to Margaret River, but with all our stops and adventures we didn't arrive till sunset.

I found the tourist information bureau, where I was told about the accommodation available in the area, and found a newly built unit attached to somebody's family home for rent. It wasn't cheap, but I needed that kind of accommodation with a baby. Before, alone, I could have got a bus from the airport and rented a simple room near the beach, but now I had so much luggage and a baby, I needed a car and a place where I could cook and that had a clean space to crawl around in. I paid the deposit and watched my hard-earned cash slip out of my hands.

I drove off with Poppy angry about sitting in her Christmas present again, but finding the unit made us smile. It was right on the beach and only a road separated us from the dunes and a glorious stretch of white sand. This was Prevelly Beach and the studio was divine. It had new terracotta floors, a comfortable bed, new linen, a tiny shower and a compact kitchen. The windows opened on the beach side and you could feel a cool breeze coming in on the early evening air. The studio was clean and we both loved it. I put Poppy on the cool tiles and she scooted off around them, dragging her bottom along. I took off my shoes and felt the coolness under my feet too, but it was getting late and I wanted to see the beach. I whisked Poppy up, grabbed a couple of things and we skipped out of the studio, over the road and over the sand dunes.

We sat on the sand together. The ocean was sparkling and the sky was full of colours and the air was still warm. Australians have a good life, I thought, as I watched the surfers in the distance. Maybe they've just finished work? I thought about how my life had changed as I watched Poppy grabbing at the sand. Travelling with a baby was easy when she was a feeding blob but now that she was becoming more human it was getting trickier. I grabbed Poppy's hand to stop her putting sand in her mouth and she struggled away from me, now wanting to crawl into the ocean. I took off Poppy's clothes and let her play in the sand and thought about the studio I'd rented instead of a hotel room, and I liked the change. Poppy was more fun now and getting more expensive to be with, but I planned to work that night to get more necklaces made.

I looked around. Margaret River was magical; I liked the idea of being Australian. Some other people were further down on the beach. Where else in the world do you get clean, white, sandy beaches like this with hardly any people on them? Nobody was close so I took off my clothes down to my knickers and took Poppy to the water's edge. It was chilly, so we backed off and decided to keep playing in the sand instead. Poppy was beaming.

'I'll get us a wonderful life, little girl, don't you worry, even if I have to work at night for years!'

I felt so grown up that night watching the sun go down. This life was different to my old carefree wild one, but the change felt good and I was ready for it. 'You stupid Blond for giving up on us and taking the easy option. Look what you're missing out on, dickhead!' I screamed up to the crimson sky. Poppy looked up at me, her brow crinkled, and I apologised for swearing.

Chapter 27

Trust My Life in Your Hands

The family I rented the unit from were really friendly. 'G'day mate,' they said to me, and I thought their greeting was really cute. 'You a Pommy?' they asked.

'Yes, I am,' I replied.

'You're a fuckin' Pommie bastard then,' they said, and I reminded myself not to be shocked. I knew they didn't mean me any harm and I'd learned Australians love to swear. Calling me a Pommy bastard was like a term of endearment for them. The family asked me if I wanted to have a drink with them after I'd settled in, and when we came back from the beach, got showered and Poppy had been fed, I went around to the main house: it would be nice to hang out with some adults.

That evening over a stubby they invited me to stay for their barbecue dinner as well, and it didn't take them long to ask me what I was up to in Prevelly alone with a baby. I noticed when I'd told anyone what I was up to lately it never took them long to ask to see my jewellery ... The family were so friendly and compassionate towards Poppy and me, they made the unit worth gold. They told their friends my story too and my business started to roll again, with late-night beading sessions. But life was fun.

During the day Poppy and I would camp out under an umbrella on the beach. We'd splash around, play, and go back and forth from the unit for food and nap breaks. We'd pop into town to buy more food supplies and go for little drives. By night-time, Poppy would be worn out and it was easy to get her into bed so I could then work by her side and watch her sleep. I'd stroke her shiny blonde hair and admire her golden skin, bronzed by the sun even though we were hardly in it. Friends of the family I rented from would knock on my door. They would want to see my new necklaces and often asked me to join them for a drink or barbie.

'Hi, I heard from the missus next door you're alone. Wanna come for a barbie?'

'Hello, do you want to come for a glass of champagne on the beach? We're all going.'

I fell in love with Margaret River. It really was the magical place everyone had told me about. I even got invited to a bush shindig. A friend of the family picked us up in a big truck with metal bars on the front.

'What are those bars for?' I asked him.

'They're for the fuckin' roos. Don't want one of those

bastards smashin' your car, better knock 'em dead first,' he replied and I giggled as I got into his truck. I thought he was having a joke with me. Surely people don't prepare their car for smashing into kangaroos? We drove out of town along a main road and then deep into the bush, rattling over cattle grids.

The Australian bush was not like the soft green English countryside. The Australian bush was shades of chocolate and brown with stumpy grey-green bushes and sporadic, naked-looking trees. The earth was red, rusty brown and if you kicked it, dust rose up; if you spat on it, it could make cheap face paint.

We kept driving with our new friend and I saw a few of the roos he had talked about, but they didn't look like they were about to commit suicide. Australia had a raw, harsh beauty its animals shared: crocodiles, emus and the kangaroos that I watched jumping away from our headlights. Kangaroos were odd creatures, with such little front legs and massive hind legs and tails; they fitted perfectly into a kid's storybook.

We came closer to a glowing light in the bush and as we drove up to it, you could see the light was a wooden shack with a tin roof. Loud music was crackling out of the shack and we parked on the dusty earth in front of it with other trucks and I felt proud of myself: I'm now in a *National Geographic* shoot instead of looking at one in Glastonbury.

Our friend helped us out of the truck and we walked up onto the creaky wooden porch. A few men offered us drinks from the plastic coolers they were sitting on; Australian trees and bushes might lack refreshment, but these Aussies sure didn't. I was offered a cooler too so I could sit down with Poppy, and everyone was laughing and having a good time. There was an open fire outside and a whole dead animal was turning, dripping and spitting fat into the flames. Gosh, this is quite rough, I thought as I suddenly slipped back to my British roots and sipped on my aluminium can to try and find some Dutch courage. Local Aussie bands were playing from a dusty old tape machine and when I went inside to go to the toilet a kid offered me a pet snake to stroke.

The house was simple. It had two bedrooms, an open kitchen-lounge and a bathroom. I think the people who lived in it were farmers because it looked like the people lived more outdoors than indoors. All the people at the party were outside, too.

Back on the porch, sitting on my cooler, Poppy bouncing on my lap, I wondered if this would be how I would live if I chose to call Margaret River my home. In England I had to move out to the country because I didn't have the money to stay in town. If I stayed in Margaret River, would I have to live out here to begin with? There were no fences around this house like there were in England, and I started to think how I liked fences, how they kept you safe and how your neighbours were close if you needed any help. Out here I couldn't see any other houses nearby.

I felt out of my depth. I didn't even like beer. It gave me a bellyache and made me fart, and I shouldn't be drinking and breastfeeding. I took another little sip for more courage and the flies realised I was at the party and started to walk all over me.

They tried to get into my mouth and up my nose. I kept flicking them away from Poppy as I spoke to the other guests, but the other people didn't seem to be bothered by them. Everything was so Wild West here and the Australians spoke differently from the city. They spoke from a little hole they made with their mouth out to the side of their cheek and they sounded like they blocked off their nasal passages too. Maybe it stopped the flies?

I was given a round, processed white bread roll and inside it was some meat from the fire. 'Don't mind the flies, love,' said the kind man who gave me the roll. 'It's the sheep they're bastards to.'

'What do you mean?' I asked.

'The flies lay their eggs on the sheep and if you don't dip 'em in time, those fuckin' eggs hatch and the maggots eat the sheep alive.' I looked down and wondered what was in my meat bap. The flies upped their game at the smell of it and were dive-bombing Poppy.

I think I preferred the beach area of Margaret River. On the beach we'd watch dolphins play in the water and feel cool breezes drift over us in the night, and Poppy needed that coolness. One night she went into a full-blown fever. I paced in front of our open window, rocking her in my arms, not knowing what to do; she had never been sick before. I covered her in cool flannels and gave her homeopathic remedies my sister had given me and the night was very long ... The next morning both of us had black bags under our eyes and Poppy was not her usual happy self. She was now Mr Grouchy, a heavy wriggling, whining dwarf that wanted to be carried all the time. Her fever had gone, though, and I was grateful for that. I knocked on the connecting door to the family's house to ask the mum there, Paula, for some mummy advice.

Paula looked at Poppy and stuck her finger in her mouth. I wasn't into sterilising much, but a stranger's finger in my kid's mouth was a little hard to handle.

'She's teething,' Paula said. 'Don't worry. Do you want a cuppa tea?' I was relieved to hear the news and Paula told me Poppy might get sick again with the teeth, and I shouldn't worry, but that was easy for her to say – she had three kids and I didn't have health insurance. I also wasn't used to going to doctors for help. Living in Bali for so long I'd got used to using natural medicines instead of dubious Western ones. Friends who went to doctors there often ended up getting sicker and friends who ended up in hospitals often never came out again.

The next night I awoke to screaming again and Poppy's nappy filled with green diarrhoea. I paced the cold tiled floor with Poppy burning up in my arms and cursed the Blond. I remembered what an African woman had once told me, 'If your child has snot all over his face and shit pouring from his arse, but he's happy and playing normally: don't worry. It's when your child is limp, like a rag doll with no energy, then you worry.' Poppy was moving in my arms like a hot angry cougar, so I gave her more natural medicine and tried not to worry and kept repeating the words of Paula and the African woman in my head. Poppy then decided to scream the house down, and she was inconsolable. I kept trying to shove my breast in her mouth, not wanting to wake the family next door, but she didn't even want that any more.

Paula knocked on the door. It was now the middle of the night and I apologised profusely for waking her up.

'I don't know what's wrong, Paula,' I whimpered, rocking Poppy manically in my arms. She stuck her finger in Poppy's mouth again and told me it was definitely teeth. She gave me a box of some baby Panadol syrup and I wanted to cry. I wanted to be with my sister. I didn't want to be in Margaret River any more – this wasn't fun. Paula massaged Poppy's gums with some gel she'd brought with her and Poppy stopped crying. Paula felt her head. Poppy was still burning up even though I had been putting lots of cold flannels on her and I was burning up with worry.

'Follow me,' Paula said, and I would have followed her into the bush to eat flies if I had to.

In my T-shirt and knickers I followed her into her downstairs bathroom and watched as Paula opened her large walk-in shower and turned it on. 'Yours is too small,' she said as she tested the water.

'Get in here and cool your baby down.' I walked straight in and sat on the floor with my legs crossed holding Poppy close to my chest. 'I didn't mean quite like that, love,' she laughed. 'You could have taken your clothes off.'

My head was down and tears were now dripping, but she couldn't see my face through the water gushing over our heads. I felt so hopeless, such a useless mother. The water kept running. Poppy didn't rebel, she simply latched onto my breast for comfort. I shielded her face from the water with my hand and she finally started sucking. I felt so alone and frightened on the floor of that shower. Our clothes were glued to us and Poppy's nappy had swelled with water. Paula was still looking down at us and I looked up and thanked her for all her help and kindness.

'This is what motherhood is like, love,' she said. 'It's a tough road. You get the good times but you also get the bad.'

'I know,' I replied. 'But I don't like this bit.'

'None of us mothers do, but hang in there, love, that's what makes you a better mum. My babies are older now and I've already gone through this. This is now your job. Keep the connecting doors open to your unit and if you need the shower again – just use it.'

'Thank you for your help, Paula,' I said weakly.

'The cool water will bring Poppy's fever down,' and with that, Paula said she was going back to bed.

But I didn't want her to leave. What could I say? Please stay! Don't go. I'm frightened. I don't want to hang out at the bottom of this shower by myself. I couldn't say those things – I wasn't a little girl any more. Before Paula walked out of the door she looked back at the two drowned rats.

'Help yourself to towels, love,' she said and she shut the door. My chest rose and tears fell; it was time to sob out the pain.

The night was long and arduous and I fought hard not to fall apart myself. I'd get out of the shower, Poppy would snooze and then I'd have to get back in again as she was awake again with a soaring temperature.

As the morning light finally filtered in through our thin curtains, I found myself splayed across the bed like a drunkard, not remembering how I got there. Poppy was lying in front of me with my arm across her belly to keep her safe, and she was wrapped in a towel. All the linens around me were damp and my hair was soaking and I felt shivery. I was worried about Paula's bed as I felt Poppy's head: she was still warm. I leaned over her and pried her eyes open and they looked glazed. She wasn't moving. I picked her up and she was a limp ragdoll. I tapped her cheek to stir life into her and she still didn't move. I tried to feed her. She wouldn't suck and now my worst nightmare had come true.

I dashed to Paula and asked if I could use the phone. I booked the first ticket back to Melbourne. I didn't shower and the thought never even came into my head to call a doctor. Paula said it was still teeth, but in my mind I just had to get Poppy to someone who could help me: Kay. I'd done this before when I'd got sick, or a friend had, and I'd manically cross an island or a country to get help. I watched Poppy lying limp on the bed as I threw all our stuff into bags and tidied up the room. I strapped Poppy to me. I paid my bill, and apologised for the damp bed. Paula kept saying I didn't have to worry, it was just a passing fever. *That's so easy for her to say!* I told Paula I was going back to Melbourne to be with my sister and she gave Poppy more of her medicine. Then I got in the car and drove like a maniac to Perth to catch our plane.

There was not a peep from the back seat this time and I wished there was. I kept looking in the rear-view mirror. Poppy was still breathing, her body covered in a sarong. She looked like a wilted rose.

'It's OK. She's sleeping. She didn't sleep last night. She's sleeping. That's all,' I kept saying to myself loudly. The air-con was blowing full blast to keep her cool and I was hunched over and shivering. 'She's taken some of my milk,' I whimpered to myself. 'I want my sister.' I'd stop the car. I'd run round to her seat. I'd wake her up to make sure she was still with me. Try and feed her. She was warm. Hardly sucking. I'd get back in the driver's seat and drive madly again. I realised: I knew absolutely nothing about babies. *I've got to buy a book.*

At the airport I called Kay. I hadn't been able to contact her earlier. 'I need you, I'm coming back.' I told her about Poppy and she took my flight details and told me she'd be at the airport waiting.

On the plane all I wanted was to feel my sister's arms around Poppy and me and to know that we were safe. I wanted to be around people who really cared for us and who my baby could depend on. I wish I'd asked that question before I'd made a baby with the wrong man: can I trust my life in your hands?

Chapter 28
The Dragon

During the whole flight back to Melbourne, Poppy lay limp in my arms. I kept tapping her cheek, wanting to know she was still with me, and trying to re-hydrate her. I'd look into her sick little face and hold her closer to me. She meant so much to me – ever since the moment I knew about her – and I never wanted her to leave my side. I had never felt this strong a love before. I looked around numbly, but there is not a lot to look at when you're stuck in an aeroplane seat. My head and eyes felt heavy, but I didn't want to close them. I wanted to be the strong, awake, on-duty, life-saving guard for my little girl.

Kay was at the airport and I fell into her arms and noticed how, with her by my side, life's woes lifted quickly. I now felt safe and I knew Poppy would be okay too. Kay had three kids and she hadn't killed any of them. Up until now I had managed to kill all my family pets and any pot plant I had ever owned. Kay held us both close and the feeling of her arms around us was the best medicine ever.

Once back at her home, Kay gave Poppy medicine that instantly perked her up. 'She's simply teething, Jane,' she said and I cried and the tears washed away the tension that had built up inside me. Poppy kept waking for the next few nights, but during the days Kay or Jim helped me so I could catch up on sleep.

I'd wake in the darkness to Poppy screaming and quickly grab her so she wouldn't wake anyone else. I'd rock her blindly, walking backwards and forwards in the dark, feeling the carpet under my toes. I found it hard to believe that this drama was due to such little teeth. I'd rub her gums deliriously with my gel-covered finger and feel the ridge of teeth starting to break through. The only thing I was grateful for was the sounds of people sleeping in other rooms. I'd stand breastfeeding and rocking and minutes turned into hours. The naps I got during the day were the only things that kept me sane. My brain had ceased to function; there was no way I could bead; pacing the night floors was my job now. No one should ever be left alone to parent. It should be made illegal. No job in the world makes someone do 24-hour shifts, day after day, night after night. But I knew this was the most important job I'd ever do.

I remembered when my mum wanted my dad to come back home because she felt life was too difficult without him. It was my birthday, we were still living in the big house and Mum threw a birthday party for me. She thought if she tied a large yellow ribbon around the tree at the front of our house, Dad might come back to us. The song 'Tie a Yellow Ribbon Round the Old Oak Tree' was on the radio a lot and we'd sing along to it. She thought Dad would know the song too. But instead of Dad coming back to us, he didn't even notice the ribbon and soon after he got married again and made me a baby brother with the blow-dry specialist.

My mum always tried to be a good mum. She tried to the best of her abilities; she always threw me a birthday party. At one party, she stole the magician's white rabbit. He asked for it back and she told him, 'You're the clever magician, you should be able to magic it back,' but instead he searched and searched for his bunny. All my little friends, Mum and I followed the magician around the house for ages as he looked in cupboards and even went upstairs, but whenever he opened a door he never found a bunny. He would turn, look at Mum and growl. All my friends thought it was hysterical, excited that the hunt would continue. They thought we were on an organised treasure hunt and Mum kept her arms firmly crossed over her chest, refusing to tell the magician where his rabbit was. 'You're full of magic. You can make rabbits magically appear out of your hat, now let's see how clever you are.' I knew then Mum wasn't doing the right thing, but I couldn't say anything. The magician finally found his rabbit stuffed in a taped-up shoebox Mum had hidden behind our sofa. As he stomped out of our house with the box under his arm, we all waved goodbye. My friends thought it was a fantastic show.

Kay and Jim stood by my side now, helping me as I slowly pulled my shattered self back together and everything settled back into a normal routine – just as Poppy started smiling and proudly showed us her new front tooth.

As our world became calm and peaceful again, something inside me raised its ugly head and I felt it roar like a fire-breathing dragon. It wanted me to leave Melbourne. To go out into the world and find what I was looking for. It didn't want me to stay at Kay's house. But part of me didn't want to leave. I felt I was safe here.

Kay asked me once more to stay in Melbourne and I kept asking myself: why not? I obviously loved and needed her; I loved and needed Jim, too, and their kids ... But this was their family and I felt it was time to grow up and find my own family home. I needed a life of my own and for some stupid fire-breathing-dragon of a reason, I felt my life was not meant to be in Melbourne.

I looked at my ticket as I sat on my bed. I was more used to being on the road than staying in one place. Apart from the eight months I had been in Glastonbury for Poppy's birth, for ten years I had not stayed in one country for longer than two months at a time. Even when I lived in Bali, every two months I'd get itchy feet and get on a plane and go somewhere else. When I left home, I'd grown wings and they'd worked well. Now I wondered if those wings were helping or hindering me. I'd always had a problem with relationships ... Before the Blond, my longest relationship had only been a year. I'd always fly off; I didn't trust people and kept moving so they couldn't get too close to me. I thought I'd changed when I met the Blond.

My biggest fear was of being abandoned, and now the dragon that used to protect me wanted to fly. It kept telling me it wasn't right to stay in Melbourne, and I was listening to it.

Kay couldn't understand me and, to be truthful, I didn't understand myself. I wanted to tell her: 'Kay, as much as I'd like to stay, it brings up enormous pain for me and I can't deal with it. I'm sorry but it's easier for me to fly away and leave.' But all that would sound stupid and I wasn't a kid any more.

Instead, I told her, 'I want be grown up like you, Kay. I want a family and I want a home, but I don't feel it's here. Let me use up my ticket. I need to find what I am looking for. I can always come back if I don't find anything.'

She said, 'You always have a home here, Jane,' and we cried together.

Kay slowly helped me leave the family again. She gave me crash-courses on parenting and shared all her best mothering tips with me. She packed my bags with medicine and books on babies and first aid and I looked at my ever-swelling luggage. I wondered whether I should have bought a caravan instead of a plane ticket.

Kay drove me to the airport, where we said our goodbyes again. The next stop on my ticket was Hawaii and as I said goodbye yet again I didn't even like the word any more. Poppy was smiling on my chest. Kay kept kissing her head and Poppy kept trying to fight off all the embraces. I pushed Poppy through the Customs gate, following our bags. I got to the point of no return again and didn't want to look back. The strings that were so finely holding my heart together felt like they were going to break and I would fall apart in a crumpled heap on the floor. But I did look back – for my sister's sake. I waved to her and I blew her more kisses and my eyes filled with water. What the fuck am I up to? When am I going to be grown up and sensible like her?

Chapter 29

Business in Honolulu

On the night flight to Hawaii, Poppy went to her first rave. She stood on my thighs, bouncing her body up and down to techno music only she could hear. Her arms flailed, grabbing at everything, including an orange juice that coloured us both. People stared at her and smiled and I smiled back, exhausted, nodding: yes, I'm her mad party friend. The man sitting next to us didn't smile, though. I kept trying to get her to sit down, lie down, to be calm and have some booby. She would lie in my lap for a second before jumping back up again, smiling. She had discovered her strong legs and wanted to dance on them. I'd try to pin her back down and offer her booby, and she'd look up at me with a naughty glint – then chomp down on my nipple with her new tooth. She had discovered what fun her teeth could be and my eyes would roll into the back of my head and she'd bounce up again for another boogie. She had Duracell batteries in her knees.

The flight was long and I kept walking the aisles to give the poor man next to us some rest. As others slept, we played water games in the toilets. Tissues were pulled out of holes in the wall; taps were turned on; smiley faces made into the mirror. It was a relief when the loud speaker announced we were getting ready to land in Honolulu.

As the plane touched down in Hawaii, Poppy finally wanted to breast-feed and fell asleep.

Through passport control, with Poppy in a slumped heap on my chest like a sleeping koala bear, I found a trolley and waited at the baggage carousel for my bags. They arrived, oh, so many of them. I filled up the trolley and put Poppy in her new stroller and dragged her behind me as I pushed the trolley in front. I staggered up to the Customs desk and the Customs officer looked at me sympathetically. I looked back with eyes that said *I know what you're thinking and I'm so grateful for that.* He waved me through and nodded. The fact that I had now successfully smuggled into two countries gave me a bit more energy and I found a taxi, piled everything into it and grinned all the way into Honolulu.

I'd been to Honolulu before when I was 18. My first impressions were a shock to me then, and were again now. Magazine adverts for Honolulu always depicted girls in grass skirts, long white sandy beaches, rolling waves, handsome surfers and lots of coconut trees waving their fronds in the breeze, but Honolulu was simply not like that. It was a sprawling, concrete monster that towered along a stretch of sand and the sand was hard to see because people lay thickly all over it like fat mackerel packed in a can.

The only reason I chose Honolulu as a destination was because when I was here before I'd been successful selling to the tourist trade, and I only planned to stay for a few days before I flew on to Maui to see Bro again.

When I was 18, sitting on the beach in Honolulu, I met a guy called Rasta. He tried to sell me leis (the flower garlands that get placed around your neck when you arrive at Hawaiian airports or stay in expensive hotels). I told Rasta he could give me a lei if he wanted to, but I wasn't going to buy one. Instead he sat down next to me. We chatted and he asked if I wanted to learn how to make leis and, bored, I said, 'Yes.'

Rasta then took me to a hotel and told me to go in there and pick the flowers off their trees and he'd wait outside for me. He had dreadlocks down to his bottom and didn't look good enough to be a rock star staying in a hotel, and rock stars don't pick flowers unless they're tripping. I would simply look like a flower-picking tourist. So with a plastic bag he gave me, I entered the hotel grounds and soon returned with a bag brimming with flowers. I gave it to him and he was impressed. He asked me, 'Do you want to go into business with me?' and I said, 'Yeah, why not?' For a month I lived in Honolulu with a flower-picking habit and worked next to Rasta with his weed-smoking habit. We'd sit on pavements or beaches together making leis and selling them to the tourists.

Now, after a few days back in Honolulu, I was squeezed onto the beach, eating cake and looking out at the water. Poppy liked the cake too and it was softening the blow of another unsuccessful selling expedition. Apart from lamenting how badly I was doing at business this time, I pondered how Honolulu hadn't changed much in my ten years' absence. More concrete-rot had spread and grown tall and more tourists had arrived, but I couldn't find a single shop interested in buying my jewellery. All the ones I'd found were part of larger chain stores. They had fixed buying times and budgets and offices I would have to travel to. I couldn't find any independently owned galleries willing to part with their money. Then Parrot Man walked over to us.

He'd found us on our first day on the beach and kept finding us every day since. He'd cruise over with his parrot on his shoulder and Poppy would get so excited every time (I wish I did) but seeing her happy made me smile, too. I guess my smile made him feel it was okay to slump down on the sand next to us again, place his parrot on our sarong to entertain Poppy, and start chatting me up. I used to think the scene was desperate: Parrot Man and single mother fall in love on a beach. Being polite, though, I told him how I'd had another unsuccessful business day and he suggested I go into business with him, taking pictures of strangers on the beach. But the idea didn't make my wings flutter and Poppy tried to feed his parrot cake crumbs instead. He kept saying what a good idea it was and I politely made the excuse that it was Poppy's afternoon naptime and I had to leave. I scooped everything up, strapped Poppy to my chest and lifted up my heavy bag of jewels, said goodbye and traipsed along the wet sand to try and get away from him.

My feet kept sinking. Poppy was heavy and so was my bag of unsold jewellery. Life used to be so free and easy before kids, I thought. Back then I might have taken up Parrot Man's offer, but now I was trying to have a different kind of life and I shook the old one out of my head. I looked at Poppy as I struggled through the sand and she grinned at me and brightened up my world. I stopped, looked out at the water and looked at her again. Her smile was magic. It gave me strength and I started walking again, faster now, to get as far away from Parrot Man as I could. Water lapped around my legs and a breeze blew through my hair and made Poppy's blonde wisps stick up. The Hawaiian air was silky and I could smell Hawaiian Tropic sun lotion in it. I turned to see if Parrot Man was following and he was nowhere in sight. I spotted an older, responsible-looking lady sitting on the sand and I dumped our bags next to her on the beach. I took off our clothes, revealed our swimwear and asked the lady if she could look after our things while we went into the water for a swim. 'Of course,' she said, and I grabbed Poppy and we went running into the Pacific Ocean together.

In Honolulu, I walked the pavements and beaches and ate cake for quite a few unsuccessful business days and made no money. I paid for expensive tourist food and hotel bills, and Poppy's innocent smiling face and cake were the only things that gave me joy. Eating cake on the beach, looking out at the ocean, being simply happy with Poppy, I thought a lot about the innocence and beauty of youth. My mum used to bake lots of cakes, and we used to eat them together. Mum's wedding cakes were legendary. After she separated from my dad, a string of mad Polish au pairs came to live with us. They were meant to look after me so Mum could go back to work and she always found them a good man to marry so they could stay in the country. The wedding cake she'd make for them was anything but ordinary.

The cake-making would begin in the early evening, as soon as Mum had put me to bed, but I'd secretly slip out again so I could watch. It was always better than a TV show. Mum and our au pair would hand-whip a hundred eggs together. Into the night they would whip, whip, whip, carefully folding in ingredients, and by Mum's side would be her other friend, Gordon. Gordon was the gin she had grown to like since giving up Lady Valium, and she would share Gordon with our au pair. I would watch the night sky turn black through our kitchen window and I'd balance on my belly on the stairs, holding onto the banisters for support and sticking my head through them so I could see better. Mum had dragged the record player into the kitchen and Bing Crosby would be playing. Two women were whipping egg whites like lunatics, and mountains of white would be growing in Pyrex bowls.

When the au pair complained that she was tired of whipping, Mum would drag her up from her seat and show her how a good British girl danced. 'You have to stick out your arms like this. That's it, like you are being crucified with joy. Now with your arms bent you have to whip your wrists around like this to the music, that's it, like you're still whipping those bloody eggs. Your fingers, you have to get them to play the piano up in the air. That's it – just like this.'

'You so fun, Kathy,' my au pair would slur.

'Kick your legs. Yes – you're getting the hang of it. Now throw your head back – YES – YES – feel Bing Crosby in your very soul.' Mum would now be off in a spinning, dancing trance and I'd wish I was downstairs dancing with her too.

'Like dis, Kathy?' The au pair would say, kicking her legs and spinning her head around with her arms flying out and I'd giggle because the au pair looked more like an insane person than a good dancer. Precious, our toy poodle, would be cowering in her basket. 'Wooo,' would go the au pair.

'Swing your hips more,' Mum would cry in pure happiness.

In my secret hidey spot, I adored everything I saw then. Mum was so fun, and I'd know that in the morning there was going to be another party when Mum handed over our au pair to her new husband. But I often fell asleep on the stairs and would be woken by females screeching. I'd quickly stick my head through the banisters and see Mum fighting with the au pair – Mum by the sink, the au pair on her back, both of them screaming as Mum tried to shove the beloved wedding cake down the waste-disposal unit. Since Gordon came into her life, it was quite normal for Mum to have disagreements with people, and her moods had become very strange. I looked down at her in the kitchen. She was having a collywobble. That's what Kay and I called her strange moods now: the collywobbles.

Bing Crosby was jumping on the record player. Mum and the au pair were trying to choke each other. Screams were bouncing off the walls and the wedding cake was flying. Precious the dog was cringing and the swear words would be getting very nasty. That's when I'd go back to bed. I never liked the scary scenes in any TV show; I only ever liked the fun bits.

I'd get into bed and pray for the wedding cake's safety. I knew if it somehow stayed in one piece until the morning, it would be delicious because it was made with so much laughter and dancing. I'd close my eyes and think about the wedding too, and women downstairs would still be screaming . . .

In the morning, bright and early, with the two women in dark sunglasses, we would all pile into Herbie, my Mum's Volkswagen Beetle. We'd arrive at the registry office and there find a flamboyantly dressed man. He'd be wildly waving at us, crying out, 'Kathy, Kathy. Over here!' Mum loved happy gay people too. She thought they made much better husbands than straight ones.

Chapter 30

Playing Mum

I stayed in Honolulu for a few more days before I finally decided to leave; business was bad and I was getting fat. I decided it was time to travel on to Maui to see Bro.

'*Aloha, Jane and Poppy!*' Bro's voice bellowed out of nowhere. He was wearing a smile the same size as the truck he was driving and I sighed with relief to be in his company again.

We drove up towards the mountains under a rainbow, and I took it as a sign. Didn't Dorothy find the place she was looking for at the end of a rainbow? Our windows were open and a Maui breeze blew all over us. Fluoro-emerald forests passed us by and mountains dropped dramatically into the Pacific Ocean. That's why there were always so many rainbows in Maui: the high mountains and the dramatic drops into the water …

The last time I was in Maui was after I'd been working with Rasta. I made new friends in Maui, and we would pile into cars together and chase rainbows all over the island, hoping to find pots of gold.

Bro's house was as magical as the ride there. I opened the car door, unstrapped Poppy from her seat and, holding her close, jumped down and looked in wonder. A miniature fairy tale castle stood in front of us. It was made of bulbous white stones with a conical roof. Open windows ran along the second floor, which had an ornate iron balcony, the type you'd find a princess looking down from. Next to the house was a grand old pine tree; its branches reached high into the sky and made shade for the grandma and grandpa wooden loungers sitting at its base. I eyed those chairs – the perfect spot for an afternoon breastfeed and snooze. I smiled at Bro.

'I love your house,' I said.

He took Poppy in his arms. 'Go inside and have a look.'

He unlocked the wooden door, pulled down an iron handle and pushed it open. It revealed a large lounge area with a sofa bed. Mexican tiles covered the floor. At the back was a small kitchen and bathroom. A staircase on the right of the pretty room invited me to come up and have a look. I crept up the stairs slowly, excited at what I would find. A large bed lay in front of me, the open windows revealing the pine tree's branches. The room had the visual effect, even the smell, of a Walt Disney pine forest. I took a deep breath and walked over to the balcony. Standing next to it was an enormous telescope to look out into the starry night skies. This was a perfect home! The kind of home I'd like to live in! The house wasn't big, but it had everything you needed in an easy-to-look-after, adorable little package. Bro looked up at me standing on the balcony.

'It's not mine, Janey, but I thought you'd like it!'

'You're so right!' I called down.

Bro was such a considerate sweetie and the three of us settled down into a comfortable little routine together. We spent our days like happy tourists, with Bro driving us around in his big truck. He didn't seem to work, but often his mobile phone rang and he'd always excuse himself, saying he had an important call to take.

It was wonderful to see Maui again. We drove through rainbows; we sat on mountaintops and beaches. We watched whales prancing high in the air, and Bro reminded me that around 3500 humpback whales migrate to Maui every year. They have sex in Maui and give birth and I could understand why . . . Maui could make anyone fall in love and want to breed. It was a similar feeling to Bali. But I had no intention of falling in love with Bro and there was no way I wanted to slam panky him either.

Slam panky was something expats did with tourists in Bali, and Kira even considered making t-shirts saying I'M A MULE for all the people we knew who were doing it. Mules are made from breeding a donkey with a horse and they are infertile. When two mules bonk it results in nothing and it's called slam-panky. Being a mule in Bali did have its benefits, though. It was fun, you never got your heart broken and if you ever had problems with a tourist you were shagging, you always knew their plane would be leaving soon. Some expats, though, were like mosquitoes. They would land on a tourist, have a bite and then spit them out. They always had new tourists to choose from because new planes arrived daily full of them.

In Maui, Bro tried once more to see if I wanted to have a relationship with him, but I again explained clearly that there was no way it was going to happen. So instead, like a family, we'd walk through forests together and discover waterfalls with natural stone baths. When we were hungry, Bro would take us to delicious restaurants and treat us to lunches and I would insist on buying food and cooking us dinner.

My mum taught me how to be passionate about food. She always said, 'Jane, use only the best ingredients.' When I was little, she would take me all over London collecting them in Herbie, our Volkswagen. I loved those trips in Herbie. She would tell me Herbie was real and each morning we'd kiss his steering wheel hello as though we were greeting a good friend.

We'd drive across London to where the Indians lived so we could buy rice smelling of jasmine flowers. We'd drive to Belgravia to buy meat, as Mum said the best meat always hangs out where the best money is. We'd travel across London to famous fish markets to get fresh prawns and the catch of the day. Mum taught me to look into a fish's eye to see if it was fresh. 'A fresh fish has clear, beautiful eyes,' she'd tell me and, 'A fish's eyes that are not fresh look like a liar's, cloudy and full of doubt.' We would go to fruit markets and pick up figs and berries in season and we'd go to Italian shops to buy sugared almonds. 'Children's treats should always be made of real food,' Mum would say. We'd travel to the East End where the Jewish people lived and find salt-beef, crunchy dill pickles and chewy bagels, and always before we'd drive home we'd buy some fresh bread and flowers for the table. The flowers we bought were nearly always lilac roses. Mum liked the way they made the house smell of violets and they'd fill Herbie with the same heady scent. We would dance in our seats driving home. Frank Sinatra would be playing on her music system and we'd wave our arms out of the windows pretending we were making Herbie fly.

All the men at the markets, butcher shops and florists liked my mum. They would save her the best cuts of meat, the tastiest fish and the freshest fruits in season. They would also give her special smiles and I'd watch my mum's face carefully to see what she did in return. But Mum was never interested in any of those men. I think she stayed secretly in love with my dad forever.

I was secretly still in love with the Blond. Even though I knew how wrong he was for me, deep inside I still wanted him to come to his senses. I secretly wanted him to come and find us, tell us he'd made a terrible mistake and that he wanted to love us again. I secretly wanted him to be the one at the steering wheel of Bro's car, not Bro, and I wanted him to make Poppy laugh so much she dribbled.

Late in the afternoon in Maui, after our daytime adventures, we'd drive home and in our castle I would play mum and clean the house and cook.

I only remember one holiday with my mum. Mum's collywobbles had been getting worse and she had given up her job hairdressing because she couldn't stand on her feet all day long. She took up cooking for rich London families instead. Her belly had swelled up, making her look like she was pregnant, and she was always tired. One night we all drove off in Herbie to the hospital. Sitting in the hospital corridor holding Kay's hand, Kay told me how Mum had gone to the toilet and had pooed blood and that's why we were there. She said I shouldn't worry though as the doctors would fix our mum's bum. The doctors gave Mum more pills and Mum said, 'Bloody doctors, they never know what's wrong with me,' and I felt sad for her. Mum was sick all the time lately and didn't have the energy any more to be happy. She'd tell me, 'Be happy, Jane, always be happy.' Other people wanted her to feel better, too. Our Scottish neighbour came round to speak to my sister about our mum's situation.

'Kay, your mother's fucking mad and you need to do something about it,' she said. But it was our Italian neighbour who offered to help us. She said we could go on holiday with them to her brother's farm in Italy and in exchange for board, Mum could cook for everyone. Mum said yes to the idea and we all got excited: this was going to be our first family holiday.

We went to Italy on a train. We had packed dinner, breakfast and lunch and we had bunks to sleep in. I fell out of the top bunk and cracked my head, but arriving in Italy and seeing fluffy yellow chickens made me forget all about my pain and smile again. But Mum didn't. In charge of the farm was a fat, grumpy farmer who Mum hated.

I would keep her company while she cooked for the family. I'd sit at an old wooden table in the kitchen and rest my elbows on it. There I would listen, smell, watch and get little tastes of what she was cooking. She taught me to use my senses: to observe, smell, feel, taste and to listen to what was going on in the kitchen. She would let me touch food, sniff it, and look for signs, but rarely did I get to actually try and cook anything: that was her job. She would put tastes in my mouth and say, 'What flavour is missing, Lady Jane?' She would put things under my nose, 'What herb does this need, Lady Jane?' She would get me to look in the oven, 'Do you think it looks ready?' I would sit cross-legged on the floor, looking at the oven, listening to the cooking sounds it made. I liked doing that and when dishes came out I was always allowed to touch them. 'Do you think it feels cooked?' Mum would ask, and it made my senses bloom. I watched her cook in that Italian kitchen with my legs too short to touch the floor and I knew she wasn't happy.

She didn't like the fat farmer. She called him a fat pig. A fucking fat chauvinistic pig, a bastard, and that fucking farmer. She took to always being upset. Chickens would run into her kitchen and scamper around and then scamper out with Mum chasing behind them with a tea towel. 'You're fucking dinner next time!' she'd scream at them.

One night when Mum was carving up a roast chicken for dinner, a chicken scampered in and shat on her floor. Mum had already been cursing the fat farmer, but now her eyes grew wide and her cursing became operatic. Her arms rose up to the ceiling and I knew there was going to be trouble. There always was when her arms rose up like that. The Italian family was already keeping their distance and Kay spent all her time away from us doing homework. Everyone was in the dining room waiting for their dinners and they must have wondered what Mum's screaming was about, but no one came in to see her.

Mum stared at a kitchen floor covered in shit, then spun around and threw open the oven door. She got a warm plate from the oven and slammed it onto the kitchen bench and she got two spoons out of the wooden drawer and faced the chicken shit again. She bent down and scooped up the poo. She turned and plonked it onto the warm plate. She then got the gravy jug and poured some on top of it. She laid stuffing on top and mixed it all up. She washed her hands. She taught me: always wash your hands. Then she delicately laid on some carved roast chicken and neatly arranged green vegetables, potatoes and carrots on the sides. She poured over some more gravy and wiped her hands on her apron. She picked up the plate with her apron and whizzed past me into the dining room. I jumped off my chair and ran after her, and watched as she served the plate to the farmer. She smiled at him; he smiled back at her. She sailed back into the kitchen with me chasing behind her. I clambered back onto my seat. This was a good TV show! She came over to me and whispered into my face, 'He's a fucking bastard, Jane. He fucking deserves it.' Then she continued to serve up the rest of the food with no poo and used her apron again to take all the hot plates to the dining table. We all sat down. The farmer had his face hovering over his plate. He was gobbling up all his food. He hadn't waited for anybody else; my mum taught me: you should always have manners. 'Delicious, Kathy, delicious!' My heart was beating and I hardly dared to eat as the farmer picked up his plate and licked it bare. Mum looked my way and winked.

We left the farm soon after. Mum couldn't bear it any more and we moved to an Italian village where a rich American fell in love with her. He became besotted, actually. She was still beautiful, groomed with style and grace, and he didn't know she was special. That's what I started calling people who were different from other people. 'They're special,' I'd say, just like my mum. The American was very rich and wanted Mum so badly he offered to send both Kay and me to the finest schools in Switzerland. He wore white linen trousers and a blazer with a badge on the breast pocket and his hair was slicked back. He would take us out for dinners and buy us presents. Kay begged Mum to love him.

'Switzerland, Mum! He wants to send me to Switzerland, to a great school!' My sister kept pleading with her and hoping she could get a different life, but Mum still loved Dad and wasn't interested in the rich American, and it devastated Kay.

Mum was a delicious cook whatever she made, and she inspired me to cook too. I found when travelling, it was a good way to say thank you to friends or strangers who let you stay in their house for free. It made your stay with them more enjoyable, and everyone likes a good meal.

Chapter 31

Where the Special People Reside

Bro's favourite subject of conversation in Maui was aliens, and he constantly made me laugh because he was so passionate about them. He believed they regularly flew down to Maui and he'd use his big telescope in his princess bedroom to look out for them at night. Most of the time, I had no idea what he was rambling on about, but he loved to talk and I never met any of his friends, so I didn't mind listening, because I thought he was lonely. He was so animated about everything. I'd make him a cup of tea and he'd go into an orgasm about the joy of drinking tea with milk. 'Janey, it's so good to be around the

English again!' he'd say, and I'd let him know it was good to be around him too.

Bro also tried to help me sell my jewellery. He'd look after Poppy and take her for a walk in her stroller while I went into shops to speak to buyers, but each time I came out my head would be low; I'd been unsuccessful again. Bro would say, 'You don't have to worry, Janey. I have enough money to look after us all,' and I'd smile again, but deep down inside I felt sad because I didn't want to live off him or anyone. I loved Maui and would have loved it to be my home with Bro nearby as a good friend, but I knew I couldn't stay if I couldn't make any money here.

One afternoon, Bro decided to tell me how he got to be so financially independent. In his youth he was a farmer and a whiz at cross-pollination and he invented a very profitable weed. People now worked for him growing, pollinating, harvesting and selling his crop. He told me he was the inventor of the plant called Maui Wowie. I sat back, impressed. When I had had my business with leis, that's what Rasta smoked all the time and that's what tourists asked him for, too. It was a cannabis bud picked young and sticky and when you smoked it, it blew your brains out. Poppy sat on my knee listening to this conversation, and Bro told me the real reason why we weren't staying in his house and he'd rented the small castle instead. He told me his house was not safe at the moment. My eyes widened and I sat up straight.

'That's why I have so much money, Janey. I'm a profitable farmer, so don't worry about making any money, I have enough for both of us.'

How do I always get into these kinds of situations? I don't want to be with a drug dealer hiding out from the police. Actually, I don't want to be hanging out with a drug dealer, period! I'm over all this shit. As I watched his mouth move and his hands gesture enthusiastically, I now understood why Bro was so happy all the time. I'd never met a person on Maui Wowie who wasn't happy! And all his strange prattling on about aliens, that made sense too now. My life flashed before me. All the people I'd ever hung out with on drugs talked some crap or other, and I was sick of it. I wanted to smack myself in the head, and I felt like smacking him in the head too. Poppy was bouncing 100 miles per hour on my nervous knees and was so thrilled with the story she screamed out in ecstasy. I stilled my legs. I thought about all the times Bro had talked about aliens and I had sat and listened to him because I thought he was lonely. Why am I so useless at judging people? I asked myself. What if the police come now? What if he has drugs in this house? What if he is using the two of us as cover? My daughter is in danger!

I was panicking. I had known that he smoked a bit of weed. He'd do it late in the afternoons when he'd retire to his princess room and I'd smell it wafting out of his windows, and I knew he was happy all the time. But I was good at justifying people's eccentric and bad behaviour.

When Mum's collywobbles got worse and she stayed in hospital a lot, I went to live with my dad and the Bunny. Bunny was very sweet and funny in our early days together. She liked to walk around naked all the time. We all did and Dad taught me how to play chess naked, too.

We'd sit in front of the telly watching children's cartoons together and Bunny would came in with her big tits swinging and a smile on her face. She would serve us Bird's Eye frozen fish fingers, peas and chips and I'd watch them as they ate their dinner on their laps watching the TV and wonder if other families did this. I'd be sitting at the coffee table eating my TV dinner and I'd watch them with oven chips hanging out of their mouths and pubes hanging behind their plates. Bunny's large breasts would be in close proximity to her fish and I was sure Dad's penis shouldn't be so close to his chips either. They would tell me, 'You should never be embarrassed about your body, Jane. You should always be proud of it.'

Bunny had a wardrobe for the clothes that she hardly wore and it was very special to both of us, because we both had secrets in it. When nobody was upstairs I'd run to her wardrobe and carefully open the doors and get inside it. I'd quietly close the doors behind me, leaving just a little crack so light could filter through. Inside the wardrobe was clothing heaven. There were shelves of soft cashmere jumpers and I would cuddle them close to my face and smell her perfume. They were better than any cuddly toy. Bunny had sparkly shoes I'd try on and she had lots of bags that I would drape on my shoulders too. Her silk clothes would hang down over my head and I'd reach up my arms and rub the soft fabric against them. My favourite part of the wardrobe was right at the bottom. There, I'd carefully dig a hole and build myself a nest to sit in. It was tricky because I had to battle with stiletto heels, bags and glistening glass. Using my bottom to push things out of the way, I'd snuggle into my nest and reach up and feel all the fabrics around me and I'd play with the musical glass instruments that twinkled in the dark. I had to be careful though, I didn't want to break them and they were often very difficult to pull out of the pile because they were buried so deep. I'd sit with my legs sticking out sideways with Bunny's shoes dangling off them, I'd have her handbags dangling off my shoulders and I'd blow into the musical instruments, making music.

I asked my Dad why wine bottles smelled of old vinegar. He told me, 'That is how you can tell if a wine is off,' and I felt confused. Why would Bunny drink so many bottles of off wine and then hide the empty ones at the bottom of her wardrobe? I didn't tell Dad about them, though, because I knew she wanted to keep them secret, and in the wardrobe I continued to play the vinegar-smelling flutes for years. I liked their home and started to prefer living there instead of with my mum. In the wardrobe, I would concentrate on the perfume in my life instead of the bad smelling stuff around me.

As I listened to Bro I got more and more angry with myself. I was angry I'd put my daughter in danger. I was angry at how I always justified people's bad behaviour and I didn't want to do that any more.

My head and my heart were now on a collision course. My heart was trying to be open, trying to love Bro and accept him unconditionally.

'Don't worry,' Bro said, 'I never keep a large stash in the house. I just keep a little bit in the tiles on the roof.'

My head was now screaming at my heart. Holy fuck, what are you doing here with this man? Get out *now*!

My heart replied, don't worry, life's cool ... Bro's a nice man.

What are you fucking talking about? said my head. He's a fucking dealer! He can't go home! He's obviously in a lot of trouble – and so are you!

Mmmmm, I think you're right, said my heart, I should start paying attention.

Wake up to yourself! Of course I'm right, said my head, He might be a nice man, but you and your baby are in danger around him and should get away fast.

Oh my God! You're right! said my heart, I probably could have hung out with him before, when I was younger, but now I'm grown up and sensible. I have to get out of here.

Hallelujah! cried my head. You've been unconditionally loving people for years, but now it's time to wake up and see reality.

I felt a shock of electricity run through my body. My mum had got zapped when she was in hospital. The men in white coats thought it would help with her strange behaviour, and when she came out of hospital she got very hungry and we would buy enough food to feed all the Polish au pairs in London, but Mum never put on any weight.

The more my mum ate, the skinnier she got and the more she wanted to fill herself up with food. We would go shopping together and she taught me how to change price tags. 'It will help with your math,' she said.

We would whizz around Marks and Spencer's together and she'd find things she wanted to buy, show me the price and then I'd run around the supermarket finding labels with cheaper prices on them. For being such a good math genius, I'd then get to sit in her trolley and she'd push me around really fast while I had my head down, quickly peeling off labels with my little fingers and putting on cheaper ones. When a package had no label on it, I'd hold it up, and Mum would grab it and put it back on a shelf.

It was during Mum's obsessive cake eating period that a new friend of hers came to live with us. I think he arrived to fill a gap left by my sister. Kay was getting older now and preferred to stay at her friends' houses instead of with us. I'd been riding my Chopper bike around the block when Mum's new friend arrived. She had told me earlier to go and play with the traffic and give her some peace.

I came in the gate and Mum was sitting on the doorstep very excited to see me. 'Jane, someone special has come to live with us,' she said. 'Come on in and I'll introduce you to him.' I dragged my bike into the hallway and she beckoned me to follow her upstairs. I climbed up after her and watched as Mum went into Kay's bedroom. I followed her and found her sitting on Kay's bed. I looked around.

'Where's your new friend, Mum?' I asked.

'He's here,' she said. I looked around again. Kay had a very small room. There was a bed, a dressing table, a large white wardrobe and nobody else in the room.

'Where is he?' I asked.

'Can't you see him?' Mum asked me.

'See who?'

'Jesus.'

'Where is Jesus?'

'There on top of Kay's wardrobe.'

I followed her gaze. There was a small amount of space between the wardrobe and the ceiling.

'I can't see anything, Mum.'

'Look harder,' she said and I squinted, but I still couldn't see anything and felt frightened to stand up to look in case someone jumped off the wardrobe.

'Mum? Is Jesus a mouse?'

'No. Jesus is Jesus from the Bible,' she said.

'I can't see him, you must be very special to see him,' I said.

From that day on I knew my mum was very special; she was different to every other mum I knew. So was my Bunny Mummy, and my dad.

Bro was still talking. I was still dumbly nodding. My head was reconnecting to my heart and I knew they hadn't been connected for years – but at least they were trying to connect now. The jolts I was experiencing were transforming me.

I have to get out of here! I want a normal life!

Chapter 32
Aliens

Bro said he was going upstairs for a rest and I nodded numbly. I hadn't spoken during his revelations. It was the same as hanging out with drunk people in my dad's pubs. They talked crap, and all you needed to do to keep them happy was to nod and pretend to listen.

Bro slipped up the stairs to his princess bedroom and I rushed outside with Poppy. I put my hand on the big old pine tree for support and took in deep breaths of fresh air. My friends in Bali had warned me about Bro. They could sense something wasn't right. Why couldn't I? I span around, paranoid, now with the tree at my back and Poppy close to my heart. I looked for undercover policemen hiding in the bushes. Life had switched on my electricity and now I was seeing big words in flashing neon:

GO GO GO. I wondered if I should go to another Hawaiian island, but the electric neons flashed again: *NO NO NO*.

I pushed myself off the tree and walked in circles on the grass, bouncing Poppy on my hip, trying to work out what to do, how to escape this mess. The earth underneath my feet grounded me and I calmed myself down, took more deep breaths, checked in on my reality. There were no police around and I knew Bro wasn't dangerous. I knew he wouldn't ever intentionally hurt either of us. Poppy was jiggling and wriggling in my arms, bored with walking in circles. How am I going to entertain her and get us out of here fast? I looked around for policemen again. It was hard to think and to be a child entertainer and a watchman at the same time. Poppy was now whining badly, she wanted to play.

Reality check.

Nothing dangerous is going to happen in the next 15 minutes.

I could do a lot to get us out of here without Poppy in my arms.

Bro has only been sweet and hospitable.

Action! I need his help to get out of here.

I shouted up to the window.

'Bro, can you do me a favour? I need you to look after Poppy for ten minutes while I sort out some stuff.'

'Sure, luv, bring her up in five,' came the answer.

I grabbed Poppy's arms and swung her down onto the grass so she could practise walking with my help and tried to calm my paranoia. *We're safe. Nothing is going to happen to us*. 'Can I come up now?' I shouted impatiently.

'Sure!'

I took Poppy upstairs and found Bro lying back on the bed propped up on his pillows. All the windows were open, but I could smell the joint he'd just smoked and there was a big smile on his face. I looked around. There was no sign of an ashtray. It must be under his bed. An alien movie was playing on his TV and his high-powered telescope was at the end of his bed. That's where he looks for his friends when he's fucked up, I thought, and I handed Poppy over to him. I knew she would be safe for 15 minutes. Whenever he smoked even a cigarette he always did it away from us. I waited impatiently until she was settled with him.

'You should watch this alien movie, Janey. You'd really like it.' I declined with a nod. Poppy was content. She was kicking her legs happily in the air and singing on the bed, and the pine tree was looking in through the window to check in on her too. It was a shame. It was nice to see her happy with a man, but I just wished I'd chosen a better one – and a better father. I watched them both – Poppy was now giggling at the TV – and I turned and dashed downstairs.

I ran around. I collected up all our things and packed them into our bags. I'd go to LA, the next stop on our ticket. I collected my jewellery and beads and packed them away too. I hadn't sold anything in Hawaii, but at least I'd made lots of new stock. I could hear Poppy gurgling upstairs and my face relaxed into a smile. I dashed to the bathroom. Piled our things in our wash bag. I tried to work out an excuse as to why we needed to leave so abruptly. Help me get out of here, God, I asked the bathroom walls.

As a child I was never given a religion. Dad said his kids should be able to grow up and choose their own beliefs, and sometimes Mum would take me to church. She said it was a nice place to sing songs and if I was well behaved through the service she always let me go up to the altar to get a rice-paper thingy to stick on my tongue as a treat. In church I always got bored by the man in the black dress and I became fascinated by the little red wardrobe instead. I used to wish I could go in there and play. It had a curtain instead of a door and Mum said it was a place where people could go and speak directly to God and apologise for bad things they'd done. I would ask if I could go in there. I wanted to say sorry for my bad thoughts, for wanting to hang out with Bunny and Dad instead of her, but Mum said I was special and didn't need to go into the wardrobe. She told me I'd been built with a direct telephone wire in my head and I could talk directly to God any time I wanted to. All I had to do was think what I wanted to say and he could hear my every word. She said the church and its little wardrobe were only for old people like herself. Old people hadn't been so well wired as me, with direct telephone connections.

In Maui, I was now talking to God very loudly in my head and asking him to get me out of here, and at the same time Poppy's gurgling upstairs had turned into laughter. Everything was in our bags. I found a phone directory. Searched for numbers of airlines. I could now hear her in full-blown belly laugher and I couldn't remember her laughing quite that hard for a long time. My whole body froze. I looked up. My ears pricked up like a bunny rabbit's. I have to go up there to check on her, I thought, I'll creep quietly upstairs because I don't want her to hear or see me because then she'll want to hang out with me again and I have to get this mess sorted. I'll check she is okay and then creep back down again.

I held onto the stone wall and my feet made slow and quiet progress up the stairs. I could hear loud music; it sounded like they were watching a tragic horror movie and I thought that was a good thing because he wouldn't hear me when I called the airlines. The stairs emerged at the back of the bedroom, and as I got to the top I slowly raised my head over the stone wall and was immobilised.

They were watching a movie. A tragic man was dressed in a green alien suit. He had a large head with antennas madly flapping around on it and he was moving around a lot. He was wearing over-sized lizard-looking gloves and they had hold of an earthling's arse. He must have captured her. She was screaming out. Poppy and Bro were sitting at the end of the bed close to the TV screen. Bro had the remote control in his hand and Poppy was hysterical with laughter. The earthling was cute. She had blonde hair and Bro was giggling and pointing at her and whispering to Poppy, 'Look at the funny alien, Poppy. Look at the funny alien.'

The earthling was bent over and the alien was fucking her up the arse.

'BRO!' I shouted.

I stormed over and grabbed Poppy and he cowered away from me like a puppy dog.

'I'm sorry, Janey. I got bored with the other alien movies and thought Poppy would like this too.'

'You're not fucking funny any more, Bro,' I shouted. Poppy gurgled to disagree and I slammed off the telly. 'We're leaving.' I spun around with Poppy and ran downstairs. At the bottom I couldn't help but laugh to myself. This was my perfect exit plan! Thank you, God!

Bro stayed upstairs and I grabbed the phone and called the airlines. I found the first available flight to LA and got a ticket from Maui to Honolulu. Bro finally slinked downstairs and moved around us apologising and I said I forgave him, but it was obviously time for us to leave. He insisted on taking us to the airport, but our flights didn't leave till the next morning and I kept praying to God to keep us safe that night. As we walked through Customs in Maui and Bro was finally a safe distance away again, he bellowed out, '*Have fun in California, love!*'

And I turned back and waved, '*Thanks for everything, Bro! Goodbye!*'

I knew I wouldn't see him again even though he'd helped me in more ways than he possibly knew. Now with my heart and head finally connected, I waved goodbye again.

Chapter 33
Angels

Poppy was nine months old when we flew into Los Angeles. I had a friend there called Ted who was going to pick us up from the airport. I knew Ted from when I first went to live in Bali and he had one of the most beautiful, non-judgemental minds I'd ever come across. I stayed in touch with him wherever I was in the world and he even came to visit me in Glastonbury.

In Hawaii, with telephone calls cheap to LA, I had been calling him often for advice. I'd waffle on about the past and how different my life had become now I was a mother. He kept telling me I should stop living in the past and be more accepting of the now, as it would bring me untold happiness. I'd laugh at him. 'Being happy in the moment might be easy for you, Ted, but you don't have a baby to look after!' I'd then continue to waffle on about the things I missed doing: hanging out in groovy nightclubs and dancing, going to restaurants, wearing nice clothes and simply doing whatever I wanted, whenever I wanted. I kept making him laugh when I told him how I spent my time now: hanging out in people's lounges, crawling all over their carpets, pushing swings in playgrounds and often I was now covered in vomit and shit. I'd tell him about the mothers I'd see in the West and how they were so different to the yummy mummies in Bali.

'Western mums wear tracksuits covered in vomit prints and they always have trainers on their feet so they can move fast chasing their toddlers. Without maids, drivers, cooks and massages, Western mums always have a look of pure exhaustion on their faces – and I look like one of them now.' He would remind me there were different kinds of joys in my new life and I'd sigh and tell him, 'The transition from wild child to Mother Nature is not a simple one.' I also told him about my inability to make any money with my jewellery in Hawaii, and he kept telling me to come to LA and stay with him. He was sure I could sell my jewellery there and that I'd like his new girlfriend.

Ted was waiting for me at the airport and his new towering beauty was draped over his shoulder like a fur stole. She had legs and arms that resembled golden linguini and blonde hair that fell and kissed her tight little bottom, which was wrapped in a clingfilm miniskirt. I looked down at my stained and practical baggy dungarees. Ted's new girlfriend was Italian. She didn't speak much English but that didn't bother him and we all piled into his truck back to his apartment.

They were fun to be around. Neither of them was stressed about life in any way, and nothing ever seemed to bother them. They'd both made a decision that life was about being free and having fun, and they chilled out in their apartment a lot because they didn't work much. Ted was a well-respected DJ who played some weekends and Linguini was a genius computer cartoon animator who sometimes worked on short animation projects. They didn't need much money because their life was simple. They had no desire for material possessions and there were no plans to have kids. Ted had had the snip; he thought the planet was populated enough.

We would spend our days with Ted and Linguini, mainly in their apartment. Ted would practise playing his music and Linguini would be draped over something, being beautiful eye-candy. She would quietly read her books or gaze up at nothing, and Ted would constantly admire his muse. She was an inspiring temple of beauty and they were perfect for each other, blissed out in every moment, even when a baby was screaming right next to them.

Their relaxed attitude to life managed to intensify my serious one. As their minds melted into a single union of peace together, my mind turned into a fucking raving lunatic and split into two personalities.

One part of my brain wanted me to change: to be more serious, stop being so carefree, to get my shit together. *It's time to change, girl.* The other half of my head would hiss back: keep being carefree, keep being free and wild. *Do whatever you want to, you don't have to change.*

I would talk to Ted and Linguini about my schizophrenia and they'd laugh at me and tell me how often the mind is crazy and the only way to be free of its lunacy is to train it and get it under control like a naughty puppy. They'd tell me I was stressing too much and instead of listening to the crap going on in my head, I should sit back and listen to the thoughts and simply watch them play out like a TV series.

'Is that what you do all day, Linguini, when you lie back on those cushions staring at the ceiling? Are you really looking at the movie going on in your head?' I asked.

'Yes.'

'The thoughts in your head, they are only thoughts, Jane. They always go away,' said Ted.

'But my mind can be like a friggin scary movie,' I told him. 'How can you not get totally engrossed and caught up in what you are thinking sometimes?'

He told me I should focus more on being in the moment. I should simply practise being here and not somewhere else in my head and focus on what I was actually doing, which at the moment was mothering Poppy.

'So this is like karma yoga? Like when you get a job in an ashram, cleaning toilets, you have to be happy with what you are doing all the time and not freaking out about what you would like to do instead?'

'Yes,' he answered, and my mind instantly wandered off, out of control, to the time I spent in an ashram and they gave me the job of cleaning the toilets. Instead of being peace-loving, all I kept thinking, with a shitty toilet brush in my hand, was how fucking dare they give me this job. I struggled badly in those toilets until I went up to the head-guru-geezer and insisted he move me into the kitchens. I told Ted about my experience and he said I should have concentrated on cleaning the toilets instead and been grateful that I was helping everyone have a nice clean bathroom.

'Fuck that,' I said, and I also told him I wasn't very good in ashrams. When the time came for the head-guru-geezer to give us all a spiritual name, I went up to him again and complained, saying I didn't want one.

'Why didn't you want one?' asked Ted.

'Because my friend went up and got one and she got called Cunti.'

So with Ted and Linguini, I practised meditation and they kept trying to bring me back into the moment and into simply happily being. But too often I'd spin out and start internally beating myself up.

I would watch them go clubbing or watch Linguini being a patio lizard, sunning herself, and my mind would boil with envy. I didn't want to play with a baby all the time. I wanted to go clubbing. I wanted to chill out and sunbathe. I wanted to have a shower alone. I wanted to lie on a couch and listen to music through earphones.

Instead of being happy in the fucking moment, I was having every negative emotion I could have.

I'd ask Linguini, 'How can you be so blissed all the time, Linguini, is there no struggle that goes on in your head?'

And she would say, 'Life is beautiful, Jane, you simply have to enjoy it,' and I'd want to throttle her.

Being with them all the time, in all that bliss, all that quiet, made my mind become tragic instead of better. Ted would say to me, 'Your mind is like a lotus pond, Jane, the only way you can come out of its mud is to keep practising, keep being present. That's how you eventually rise up and out of all that delusional crap. You have a good mind, Jane. It's strong, it just simply does not want to be under control right now and it's trying to rebel – just laugh at it.'

'It's hard to imagine my mind will become a fucking lotus,' I would say, angry at my lack of ability to meditate.

'Keep practising, eventually you'll get it under control,' he'd say and I'd nod and say I'd keep practising …

Secretly I was highly motivated to practise. I never wanted an out-of-control mind like my mum's.

I used to go and visit Mum in hospital when her mind went completely nutty. It was a special hospital for special people and it smelt of bleach. The doctors wore scary white coats, and the ward where Mum slept was filled with women stranger than her. When I visited, my mum would always have saved her red jellies to share with me and she'd say, 'Jelly is the only thing I look forward to now, apart from seeing my girls.' The people in white coats would keep looking at us as we ate the jellies together, and Mum said they had to keep a close eye on everyone in the ward to stop people running off. She tried to run away, too, but the men in white coats always brought her back. She said she had been committed.

That hospital always upset me, and Kay and I were the only people who would visit it. Mum wanted to get better no matter what it took, and that's when she agreed to the doctors giving her electric shock treatment. Mum told me it was a bit like sticking your fingers in an electric socket and 'You should never do it.'

Now as a mum myself, it was scary to look at my thoughts and not have them under control either, so I kept practising and listened to every word Ted said.

I'd watch Ted and Linguini go out for the night so he could DJ, and I'd get angry and frustrated and think *Poor me, I can't go out*. I couldn't lie on the couch reading books for hours, either. I couldn't do what I wanted, whenever I wanted. I couldn't go and buy clothes and go for a coffee by myself. Where was the fun in all this relentless mothering? I was so tired of having a baby constantly attached to my tit. I was tired of never having a full night's sleep. I wanted a boyfriend who loved and cared for me. I wanted a boyfriend who would help with my child, too.

I'd think *I'm having a nervous breakdown!* I often thought I was going to die of exhaustion. I'd watch Poppy crawling, going to grab the vase on the coffee table, and I'd find myself reacting like an angry teenager: *I don't want to run after her again!* Thoughts of the Blond abandoning me would return. Thoughts of my mother leaving me would come, too.

When Mum came out of hospital, I lived with her again and not at Dad and Bunny's. Chocolate was always melting on the stove, cakes were always being mixed in Pyrex bowls. The fridge was always full of bowls of freshly whipped cream and in our bottom kitchen cupboard there was a huge glass jar of vanilla sugar. I'd sit on the floor, unscrew the metal lid and bury my head in the opening, sniffing.

I kept trying to meditate. Be in the present moment. Watch my thoughts. Not get attached to them.

I would watch Poppy pull out all the pots and pans from the kitchen cupboards. I'd put them back, leaving a few out for her. I'd place rice in a Tupperware container and let her use it as a rattle. I would open the jars of chutney we'd bought from the farmers' market and let her sniff the contents.

My mum grew so fond of cakes after she came out of hospital, she got addicted to Cherry Bakewells. They came in boxes of six. They were crumbly cakes that smelt of almonds and had shiny white frosting on the top with a cherry. Each cake came in its own little aluminium cupcake holder. I used to want to grow up and work in the factory that made them, carefully placing cherries on the top of cupcakes. I used to play with the aluminium cupcake holders pretending they were swimming pools for my dollies.

As Mum watched me play, I often asked her, 'Why does Jesus still live on top of our wardrobe?' And she would tell me because he'd given her a special gift and he likes to live high up. 'What's that gift?' I'd ask her.

'I can heal people, Jane,' she'd say.

As a kid I started to wonder if I should die and live high up, too. Apart from when Mum was cooking, our house had become so boring. I used to pretend I actually lived in a castle that was under a dark spell. Kay would come home from school, go straight upstairs to her bedroom and close the door. I would open her door and she would tell me she was busy doing homework or I would find her already asleep. Mum, when she wasn't cooking, would be asleep too and I'd ask her why everyone slept so much in our house and never wanted to play and she'd say, 'It's because of the naughty fairy dust in the air.'

I'd find a corner. I'd sniff the magical dust and pretend I was a dormouse in the boring castle. I'd curl up and with practice I discovered I could easily fall asleep and that dreams could be really good.

In them, I'd find magical lands and go on fun adventures. Asleep, I would never feel sad or bored any more and I'd dream that Mum found the answer to her health problems and all her tummy aches and pains disappeared. I'd dream I was living with Dad and Bunny again and he was taking me to Selfridges to eat crème caramel and buy me new clothes. I'd dream I was wrapped up in Bunny's fur coat, smelling her cigarettes and perfume. I'd dream our family of three girls was wide-awake again and happy and we were all far away on another holiday... We were laughing on the holiday, we were in the sun and Mum was giving us her homemade suntan lotion of olive oil and vinegar to put on our skins. We were all wearing sunglasses and looking up at the sun – there was no more darkness in our lives any more.

I'd curl up in corners, at the top of the stairs, under the Christmas tree, and I'd fall asleep. I learned as a kid that life can often be better in your dreams.

Travelling and being busy meant I didn't have time for memories of my past to surface. Always changing locations. Different situations. I'd been running from my memories for years and I packed my bags several times in LA, ready to leave, but Ted would ask me to stay and face everything for once, and I'd unpack again. I knew I was running on a hamster wheel in life and I knew I had to get off it. I knew I had to face myself one day, and now with a child in my arms it was too hard to keep running … So I stayed in LA and the combination of time and space in that LA apartment let everything bubble to the surface and pop. That apartment became my ashram as I continued with my motherly duties and mad thoughts kept coming, but eventually, I noticed – they also left. Though sometimes they would catch me off guard. They would spin me out and I would think I was going out of my mind again, but instead I'd be patient; I was now a mother, learning to be patient. Ted and Linguini stayed lovingly by my side, patient with me and Poppy.

I asked Ted, 'One day will I no longer have this mad urge to keep moving and travelling around the world all the time?'

'I can't answer that for you, Jane,' he said. 'All I do know is you'll eventually find peace with yourself, wherever your journey takes you. Your thoughts won't have the power over you they had before, and instead of them torturing you, you'll have the ability to watch them and they will end up amusing you instead.'

Ted and Linguini were angels sent from heaven above. I never thought angels wore big white dresses or had white flapping wings that knocked over your cup of tea when they came to visit. I always thought they looked more like us. They were secretly always around looking out for us and some had good record collections and some wore big earphones and some simply looked like delicious hand-made spaghetti.

Chapter 34
On the Edge

In the apartment, days turned into weeks as we shopped at farmers' markets and I cooked organic dinners. I found galleries that bought my work, and Ted and Linguini entertained Poppy outside the shops while I sold. In every moment we all practised being present and Ted was a very good teacher.

He'd dedicated his whole life to the art of letting go and there was no clutter in the apartment either. The kitchen was bare apart from basic crockery, pots and pans, a blender and a juicer. The two bedrooms had simple curtains, a comfortable mattress on the floor and minimal bedding. Ted and Linguini's room had a music system at the end of their bed and there was another one in the lounge next to another mattress with throwovers and cushions and blankets. A small coffee table sat next to the mattress and a vase of fresh flowers was always on it. The vase was a Poppy magnet. I would place her at the other end of the room and it would encourage her to crawl forward. Outside the apartment was an open deck. There was no furniture on it, but we would go out there with a blanket and all share it together, having a picnic and getting some morning sun.

I'd take Poppy out each day to the playgrounds to entertain her and I would push swings with other mothers. I'd ask them if they found the job of mothering difficult compared to their old lives, but none of them would admit it. They'd all just smile sweetly and tell me how adorable their kids were and I'd be left pushing Poppy backwards and forwards, thinking how fuck-numbingly boring this was. I was trying to get Poppy into a routine so I could finally sleep through a whole night. She still thought I was her night-time dummy, because we shared the same bed and I couldn't say no to her and let her scream, as I didn't want to wake Ted and Linguini. I was always tired. I often needed an afternoon nap even if Poppy didn't. My breasts were exhausted too; I hardly had any juice left in me.

I'd go home to Ted and Linguini and they'd be smiling, and looking at them would remind me: this was my life now. I had to find the joy in simple things like pushing a child's swing and making mashed carrots. We'd sit around together and surrounding us on the walls were pictures of Ted's gurus. He said being in the presence of someone truly enlightened could often make your mind melt into submissiveness. One day Ted announced, 'Woo hoo, an enlightened guru has come to LA!' We all piled into his truck to see him.

The Enlightened Man was speaking at a large yoga studio in town and we all took our shoes off to enter. People were already sitting cross-legged with their eyes closed in meditation when we arrived, and Ted and Linguini went to sit at the front.

I indicated I'd sit at the back with Poppy and found a spot next to the wall so I could support my back. I carefully lay my sleeping Poppy in my crossed legs and covered her with a sarong and prayed she wouldn't wake up.

The room quickly filled with people. They entered, looked around for a spot, quietly padded over to it, then spun around and sat down cross-legged. I noticed that the people who searched for enlightenment were very nimble. Everyone was now sitting with their eyes closed, but I kept mine open. I had learned with Poppy that meditation with your eyes open is possible and I wanted to see what was going to happen. I looked around and thought the event was similar to going to a rock concert on sleeping pills. The Enlightened Man finally entered – late.

He didn't look anything special apart from being dressed in white with matching very clean white socks. He slowly walked up to the small stage. He turned around like everyone else had and sat down cross-legged. He looked around, smiled, and then he closed his eyes. I closed my eyes too in case I was missing out on something.

'Ommmmmm ommmmm ommmmmm.' The chant indicated that the meditation session was over and everyone opened their eyes, including Poppy. Oh shit, she's awake, I thought. The Enlightened Man looked around. He had a strange beam on his face like he'd been having sex in his head, and as I looked around other people had the same expression on their faces, and they were now acknowledging each other with little nods. No good shit ever happens like that in my head, I thought. He began to talk, and at that moment Poppy began to scream.

I held her close to me and quickly put my top over her head, trying to distract her with my breasts. People turned to glare at me and I gave them back one of their earlier, sexy little grins and hoped I'd be accepted as one of them. Poppy went quiet for a moment and then fought off my top, wanting to see what was happening. I knew if I didn't get her back to sleep straight away, I'd have no chance, so I threw my top back over her head and rocked her madly. I couldn't concentrate on a word the Enlightened Man was saying and obviously neither could anyone else. Poppy was now making super-loud sounds of protest and more of the sexed-up meditators were staring at me in disapproval because I was screwing up their bliss.

I need this too, I shouted at them in my head, I need inner fucking peace more than you do. 'Please stop, Poppy, please,' I whispered into her ear, but Poppy wasn't listening to me. She pushed me away. She threw off my top. She let everyone know she didn't want to be there and screamed, flapping her arms in case anyone hadn't noticed her. I quickly stood up and bowed my head, mouthing *sorry* to everyone, and clumsily stepped over people as I tried to get out of there. I grabbed hold of random shoulders and heads for support when I lost my balance, manoeuvring through their bottoms and kneecaps. I couldn't even look at the Enlightened Man for fear my embarrassment would cause me to self-combust. Maybe mothers are simply not meant to be enlightened, I thought, as I kept on nodding to everyone, acknowledging I shouldn't be there. I continued to trip up as Poppy gurgled, but she was happy now.

In reception, Poppy looked around and gave me a little smile, but I found it hard to smile back. I really wanted to hear what the Enlightened Man had to say and I wished I could go back in and listen to him, but I couldn't. I was now a mother; I had motherly duties and I didn't dare ask the receptionist if she wanted to babysit. I was angry with myself again, angry I wasn't a good mother, and my mind flipped into schizophrenia again.

Why can't life be about me?

It can't, you silly cow; you're a mother now.

I don't want to be a mother right now.

Fucking grow up!

Poppy picked up on my tension, stared at me and went ballistic. The receptionist came up to us and gently ushered us out of a side door towards a fire-exit. I looked like a homeless Indian mother with a baby in my arms, a blanket around us the two of us and no shoes. She pushed a door open and led me into a corridor. The walls were dirty grey concrete and there were stairs leading upwards. The receptionist told me I could go upstairs and sit on the roof. *What does that mean? Am I meant to fucking jump?* My expression must have relayed my thoughts and she told me it was a nice place to go and I wouldn't disturb anyone up there. Frustration was now running through my veins like a volcano about to blow. I ran back into the room, found my shoes and stomped up the grey concrete stairs.

What is it with enlightened people and me? When I lived in India I travelled long distances a few times to try and see them. Whenever I got to my destination I'd always discover they'd just died or gone on holiday.

I kept stomping upwards. I puffed. The stairs were never-ending. I wanted to see a fucking enlightened man. I'm the one who needs peace of mind, not those peace-loving fucking hippies.

At the top of the stairs, I found the roof. While beneath me people sat in blissful silence I yelled at the top of my voice: *'I WANT LIFE TO BE ABOUT ME!'*

I was definitely having a breakdown.

In response, Poppy screamed. I now wanted to throw her off the roof and that scared me even more. Motherhood was intense. I couldn't get away from it. I stood in the middle of the roof, scared to go any closer to the edge in case we both tipped over.

'Why am I travelling around the world looking for a home when I don't even know what the fucking word means any more?' I wailed, as I squeezed Poppy to me, not wanting to accidently throw her over the edge. '*WHY PUT ME IN THIS SITUATION? YOU'RE AN ARSEHOLE, GOD!*' Poppy screamed louder and we wailed together. We were lonely wolves howling in the LA night, wailing up at the moon, begging our clan to come and find us. I didn't dare take a step forward and I held Poppy more tightly, hoping she'd stop crying.

She went limp.

I held her away from me and dangled her in mid-air, thinking I'd killed her from too much squeezing. She looked at me and hung like a rag doll. The stars up above winked at us and vulnerability was everywhere. We stared at each other and blinked. We balanced. Poppy reached her hand out to me. The corners of her mouth lifted. Mine followed. We both started laughing. We had been so silly.

Later Ted found us sitting on the blanket in the middle of the roof, pointing up at the sky and giggling at the stars.

Maybe I needed to completely lose my mind to make way for a new one. Maybe that's why mothers lose the plot, because they have to lose their old selves so a new grown-up person can emerge. Poppy and I had so much fun on the roof that night. We laughed and talked to each other and I even went to the edge and looked over. Below, the cars and people looked so small, so I stepped back again to keep Poppy safe. We were happy together and I felt grateful to be sitting on the roof with my daughter, instead of in a silly yoga room smelling of old socks – and I was finally able to laugh at myself. I had given birth and was automatically supposed to know how to be a mum – but that just wasn't so. The reality was, I was still trying to work it all out. I wasn't perfect, but I was Poppy's mum and she loved me and was laughing with me.

'I'll get better at this,' I said to Poppy, 'I promise you.'

Chapter 35

Love and the Race Track

Ted and Linguini helped me to get Poppy into her own bed. I bought another piece of luggage, a travel cot, and they stayed up with me for a couple of nights while Poppy adjusted to sleeping in it. Then I knew it was time to give Ted and Linguini back their space. I had been staying with them for over a month now and even though they never once complained about us being there, I knew it was time to move on and let them be a young couple in love and alone.

I was also running out of beads.

Feeling happy and content with my life, I rented a car for my baby and luggage and planned to drive to San Francisco.

Ted gave me a parting gift – a box of his DJ mix tapes – and as I drove off, I played them loudly and waved out the window and yelled, 'I'll see you somewhere in the world again.'

On Highway 1 it took a while for Poppy to stop screaming in the back seat, but her shouts simply drifted over my head. She was fed. She had a clean nappy and I knew it was only her bad attitude that was the problem. I looked into the rear-view mirror. She was struggling to get out of her car seat and was thrashing her arms and kicking her legs. I smiled. I liked the way she had fight in her. I'd pass her some snacks and she'd throw them back at me. I passed her a whole seat full of things and they went flying, too. I looked out at the views in front of me and they helped take my mind off the rebel in the back.

We passed a cow farm with shit piled as high as blocks of flats. We passed petrol-guzzling American cars the size of boats. I sang to Ted's music and felt happy and alive. We arrived at Big Sur and there we got out of the car. Hugging each other, we saw seals singing into the sky and clapping their flippers as they hung together on the rocks. Waves crashed and Poppy was calm. Maybe she'd just been testing out her lungs in the back seat? We watched the crashing ocean and the wildlife and became mesmerised by the power of nature.

I held Poppy's hands and she toddled about and bounced up and down, thrilled. I then had to strap her back in her car seat and she started screaming again and I became mesmerised by the power of her lungs. We drove off and I turned up the music and we both sang loudly all the way into San Francisco.

I headed towards some more friends, Dave and Maria. They used to live in Bali and I hadn't seen them since they had their second child; they hadn't met Poppy. I'd called them to let them know I was coming and we were all looking forward to the reunion.

I drove up to their house, tired from our long drive, and fell in the door with all our luggage. Looking around, I noticed their lives were in as much chaos as ours. Our babies started crawling around together at a high speed and it didn't take long before Dave slipped off into a quiet side room.

Dave had his own small business, as did Maria. During the day, Maria took in two more babies to look after, and she was significantly more exhausted than I was. She was still waking through the night to feed her youngest child and now during the day she had four babies in the house. She had no help and did all the household chores herself. At night-time, Dave would come home and expect an orderly house and dinner on the table, and I'd observe Maria running around constantly, like a manic dog with rabies. She'd cook. She'd clean. She'd hold the babies and stop them crying. She'd entertain, change nappies and breastfeed. She cleaned the house, the floors and more shitty nappies. She would make meals and clean up food from babies, floors and walls. She often foamed at the mouth like a dog and her eyes would bulge in the same way too. She'd bathe babies, put them to bed, make a grown-up dinner and tidy up after dinner. Dave would come in from work, eat his dinner and then slip into his quiet side room again.

Observing all this, I wanted to give her a break and helped with the kids and the chores. When finally the clock hands said it was adult bedtime, Maria would go into the bedroom, close the door, and then I knew she had other marital duties to perform as well. I'd cringe at the thought. I was so not ready to have sex again. When I was struggling in labour for 36 hours, trying to push a watermelon out of my vagina, I had sworn I would never have sex again. Now, I was happy I was celibate. There was no way I wanted to put anything back in my vagina for a long time.

I was a voyeur in Dave and Maria's house. I moved though it, helped Maria, tried to make her laugh about her situation instead of cry. I would have liked to have left, but somehow I wanted to stay and help. I wondered if this was how Ted and Linguini had felt about me staying and that was why they never asked me to leave.

Maria would talk to me about how she felt lost in life and didn't know what to do about it. Dave would talk to me about how it was difficult for him to find Maria attractive any more.

They would both ask me for advice and I really didn't know what to say to them. I felt silly saying what Ted had said to me: 'Just accept your situation – be present with it – be in the moment!' It sounded wanky to repeat that to other people. Instead I just helped around the house.

Maria had bags under her eyes and wore a variety of baggy t-shirts and tracksuit pants. Her outfits had stains on them night and day. She frequently forgot to wear a bra so her honeydew melon breasts were clearly visible through the worn-out cotton. Often one breast would be deflated due to breast-feeding and the other would leak. Dave and the babies had new clothes, but their budget never seemed to reach Maria. Maybe she felt she had no need for new clothes because she stayed at home all day getting shat and pissed on and her only excursions were to the supermarket. Her hair was rarely brushed. She didn't wear make-up any more and she had very pale skin. I remembered how, in Bali, even with a tan, she always wore a little make-up to brighten herself up, and around the house there were pictures of them both to prove it. Pictures of them before they had children. She was pretty then, she wore nice dresses, and they were both smiling at each other.

When the extra babies arrived in the morning, I'd help Maria to look after them so she could have a break and go and shower by herself in peace. She was always so thankful and she'd dash into the bathroom – but dash out again in five minutes with a towel wrapped around her. Then she'd run around the bungalow, throwing laundry into the machine, throwing dishes into the sink, throwing toys into a multitude of baskets and throwing clothes under beds. I'd be playing with the kids and thought it was a shame she didn't give herself a little bit more time in the bathroom. Maybe then she would have noticed the hairs growing out of her chin.

I'd watch Dave, too. He was also lost in his own world, trying to make enough money so the family could survive. He'd come home from work, still in his business head, and he'd want dinner, a clean house, a better-looking wife, kids fed and asleep in bed. He never seemed to realise how exhausted poor Maria was; all he could see was how unattractive she'd become. I wished I could have taken her out for a manicure or to the hairdresser's, but I was living on the financial breadline again and all I could afford was to buy food to make dinners in exchange for their hospitality.

I thought back to Bali and family life there. Maria wouldn't have had to cook and for sure she wouldn't have had to get down on her hands and knees and scrub the floor. She would have had cheap babysitters and the two of them as a couple would have had the time and space to relax and have a little fun together. There were beaches and cheap massages, sunshine to tint your skin to a healthy glow. Clothes were cheap and colourful and it was easy to look good with maids making you delicious fruit salads and smoothies. Why did I leave there again?

Two girls who lived in Bali came to visit me when they were passing through Glastonbury. We all went into town together and I showed them the tourist sights. What they found more fascinating, though, was how trashed mothers looked in England compared to Bali and – still pregnant then – I had laughed with them and said, 'I'll never look like that.' But now in San Francisco, looking into a mirror, I raised my eyebrows at the reflection returning my stare.

Watching Dave and Maria also made me grateful I was no longer in any form of relationship with the Blond. I'd kept the communication channels open with him, so if he wanted to contact me he always could. But he never did, and now I was secretly grateful that there were oceans and countries separating us. The strings he had attached to my heart were gone. I felt free. Life was difficult as a single mum and I often blamed him for all my problems, but now watching Maria and David I was happy to be single. At least I clearly knew I didn't have any love or help from my man, and I was happy now accepting that.

As much as I wanted to stay in San Francisco to help them, I felt I didn't know how to, and it was so painful watching them struggling. They were always honest and open about their feelings when they spoke to me, but sadly not with each other. When I told them they should talk to each other the way they talked to me, they'd always say they didn't want to hurt the other person and I understood how they felt.

That's why I hadn't spoken honestly to my sister in Melbourne. I thought I would hurt her feelings and I never wanted to hurt her in any way at all.

I'd watch Maria's and Dave's emotions; they were both like race horses stamping their hooves, waiting to be let out of the starting gate. They needed to talk. They needed to be honest with each other. Then maybe Maria would realise she was not looking after herself and Dave would realise he needed to help out more with the family so she could have time to herself. But communication, love and respect are so much easier to talk about than to actually do.

As soon as the gate opens and you see a way out, people run, like I had. I used to think that was an easier option in life. I thought about other people in my life who were good at running. Dad constantly fled from one woman's arms to another, and the Blond ran too.

I thought the only way I could help Maria and Dave was to give them back their space and hopefully they'd be able to sort out their problems together. I knew they loved each other and I prayed for them that they would find their love again.

I packed our bags and we all said goodbye. We each hoped we would find what we were looking for.

Chapter 36
In the Dark

Next I drove to Santa Cruz, not far from San Francisco. I used to do African dance workshops there. I had loved the area and wanted to visit it again. Maybe this would be my home? I remembered it having groovy beaches and cafés and great art galleries. I badly needed to sell my work as I hadn't sold any while staying with Maria and Dave. I drove into town and got out my little pink book of numbers and addresses.

A friend of Kira's had given me the telephone number of a good friend who lived here, and I now looked at it and thought it wouldn't hurt to call. They could always say no. Kira's friend told me their friend was a seasoned traveller and there was generally an unspoken code among us global travellers: we all helped each other out when we could. I found a phone box and called the number. A man named Ken answered and he was excited to hear from me. He'd been told a mother and baby might turn up, and he invited us to come and stay at his house.

It was fun to hang out with other global travellers on the same circuit, because in exchange for a bed they'd get to catch up on news of other travelling friends, and often in our bags we had something interesting to sell, paying for our trip along the way.

That evening Ken and his girlfriend Jan made dinner, and into the night we shared tales about people we knew. We wove our stories together and delicately linked them up like a precious crochet project. As we talked, Poppy kept crawling off and I keep bouncing up and charging after her. This house wasn't baby-proof and it was obvious she could set off a baby bomb at any time.

Lately she had been reminding me of a soldier on a mission. She would head directly towards something she had her eye on, not letting anything get in her way. That night the two of us fell asleep exhausted. Ken had placed a mattress on the floor of his small home office and I set up Poppy's cot by the side of it. It was a joy to put Poppy in her travel cot. I knew I would get a great rest and be fresh to do business the following day.

In the morning Ken and Jan woke up early like us. They were getting ready for work and I could hear them dashing around the house. As I walked into the kitchen, Ken called out as he was leaving, 'Stay as long as you like and make yourself at home.' He waved goodbye and I thought that was a dangerous thing to say to me. They both ran out of the front door and I stood in the doorway with Poppy on my hip and we waved at them.

'Thanks for everything!' I called out, 'I'll get food for tonight and make you guys dinner.' I closed the door and was excited to start my day. I wanted to get out of the house quickly and see if Santa Cruz would be our home.

Driving around Santa Cruz that early morning was not quite how I remembered it. There was a weird morning fog that sat on the town like a bad hangover and gave me an eerie feeling. I drove down to the beach and watched waves angrily crash into the shore and the damp in the air made me feel uncomfortable and cold. I wrapped Poppy up tighter in her sling and held her closer for warmth. She snuggled her head into my chest, wanting to get her face out of the wind. Maybe when I was here before, I wasn't up this early? I went back into town and traipsed around the grey, empty chilly streets with a stroller. I looked into all the shop windows trying to work out which shops would be good to sell to. As the day heated up and the fog cleared, I decided to buy some food, return to the house, have some lunch, give Poppy her afternoon nap, pick up my jewellery and hopefully make some money by the afternoon.

Preparing lunch was not as easy as I remembered. In LA I'd get out pots and pans to amuse Poppy and she would play quietly. In San Francisco she played in the play-pen with all the kids, but now she wanted to open all the kitchen cupboards and drag everything out in search of something at the back. All the cupboards had things in them that weren't childproof and this was getting tricky. I picked Poppy up and put her on my hip and gave her a wooden spoon. She sucked on it for a while before she bashed me on the head. I fought with her to get it back and then had to dance wildly to keep her happy as I tried to steam her vegetables and make a sandwich for myself. Her hands, arms, legs and feet were so agile now. They had woken up out of their baby stupor and they grabbed, kicked and swiped at anything they could. She was now a little ten-month-old octopus. I tried to put her down, but she headed straight to the cupboards. I picked her up again and put her on my other hip. She was getting to be a really heavy octopus, and I'd lost a lot of weight lately since she had been crawling so much with me dashing after her. I felt my body had become really weak and feeble after ten months of constantly holding her, and my back was hurting badly.

Before childbirth I used to do yoga every day. I had discovered yoga when I was 18, and I couldn't believe how high you could get naturally on life by simply breathing and doing a series of exercises. But I simply didn't have the luxury of time to do that any more. If I had a moment to myself, I had to string beads or clean up a mess. I moved away from the counter top and leaned backwards to try and alleviate my pain. I didn't know how much Poppy weighed, but to me she felt like she now weighed a ton. I went back to trying to make our food and trying to keep Ken's house clean of flying debris.

It took ages to cook and to clean up. I had only managed to make a simple lunch, but I was sweating from the exertion of it all and dealing with a wild octopus in my arms. At least I knew she was strong and healthy and there was nothing wrong with her brain. She was as quick as lightning, especially when it came to making a quick grab at my tits. She thought they were her playthings and would grab at them like teddy bears. I needed Poppy to have a nap in her stroller; I needed one too, but I also needed her to be calm and comatose when I went into a shop to sell in the afternoon.

My funds were getting dangerously low. Renting a car was expensive, but I didn't have any other option. Being broke was not a nice position to be in with a baby and no other security behind me. I tried to watch the thoughts and not let them affect me.

We drove into town and Poppy looked sleepy in the back seat. I parked and put her in her stroller and pushed her around, but there was too much going on. She was too excited, and she was fighting her afternoon sleep. I kept pushing and she kept not closing her eyes. They were half shut as if in a trance when I decided to take my chance. I wheeled her into a shop and went up to the counter, hoping to speak to the owner.

Luckily the woman there did own the shop and I got her interested in looking at my range. I took my bag of jewellery off the stroller handles and carefully took out all the necklaces and made a display of them on top of her glass cabinet. I looked back at Poppy; she was still dazed: all was going well. The woman liked all the different necklaces and she picked one up and Poppy all of a sudden yelled out in protest. We both got a shock and I nervously laughed as I looked at Poppy. Her eyes weren't dazed any more, they were staring and I knew the look in them only too well. It was time to get her out of her stroller before she blew a fuse. I unstrapped her, lifted her onto my hip and a pain shot through my back. I jiggled her around and tried to smile. The woman had put down the necklaces and was now telling me how adorable my little girl was. I was agreeing with her, but Poppy was now glaring at the necklaces on the table: she thought they were hers. The woman and I went back to talking business and she picked up another necklace to have a closer look and Poppy screamed and wriggled out of my arms tying to reach it. This is a nightmare, I thought, and gave her a couple of necklaces to pacify her.

I then had to fight with Poppy as she put them in her mouth and dribbled spit all over them. My face crumpled with embarrassment; I was trying to sell these necklaces for $100 each! I made my excuses to leave. I told the lady I would return to show her my range another day as obviously today, with

Poppy on my hip, it was not a good day. I walked out of the shop and wanted to cry.

What had happened? In Australia, Poppy used to sit on my lap adorably when I was with a customer. She would smile at the buyers and coo sweetly at them, and I'm sure she helped me to sell. In LA and Maui, I hadn't noticed any difference because I guess I'd had Ted and Bro to help me, but now – this was a nightmare! I tried to think of the positive aspects of my situation. At least Poppy was showing she was a healthy and inquisitive child. I needed help. I headed to a toyshop for the first time ever. I had to buy distractions. Tupperware was just not good enough any more, no matter how much rice I put in it.

The next day I was too embarrassed to return to the same shop, so I went to a different one and planned it much better.

Poppy awoke from an afternoon nap in the house. Relaxed and content, I took her into town and she played with her new toys in her stroller as I went into a new shop. When she started grumbling, I put her on my hip with another one of her new toys and she was amused by it. I sped up my sales pitch, but then Poppy's eyes locked on the necklaces in the buyer's hand. Poppy looked down at the table where the jewellery was, dropped her toy, and swiftly swiped at my bead box. It flew. A beautiful, colourful, rainbow spray. I lurched forward to try and catch it and Poppy lurched forward and grabbed at the necklaces on the table. They flew off in another direction and the buyer watched in awe. I hit the floor. Poppy and I both scrabbled around on our hands and knees grabbing at necklaces and beads, each of us trying to get to them first. Poppy squealed with delight; this was a great game! She grabbed at necklaces and dragged them under her knees. I looked up and profusely apologised as the buyer looked down at us in shock. I grabbed Poppy. Stood up. I gave her to the buyer and didn't give a shit what the buyer thought of me, I just needed to save my jewellery. It was the lifeline keeping us afloat.

'Please hold her,' I commanded, 'or I'll never be able to clear up your floor and get out of here.'

That night tiredness hung on me like a coat of armour. I couldn't cook, I hardly had the energy to lift up my little finger. I made an excuse to go to bed early as I didn't want to hang out with anyone either, I just wanted to be with Poppy.

I wanted time alone with her, not having to worry about anyone else. I closed the door and put on our pyjamas. I wanted to watch her play before she went to sleep. I wanted to listen to her silly baby talk and simply calm everything down from the mad day. I wanted to say sorry for being such a grumpy mummy in the car earlier and I wanted to stroke her blonde hair as she fell asleep in her cot. I wanted everything to work out okay for the two of us ... Poppy didn't want to go to sleep in her cot. She stood up and put her arms out to me. Feeling guilty about being grumpy with her earlier, I got her out and tucked her in bed with me. I knew maybe I shouldn't, but I was feeling insecure too and I think we both wanted to feel someone next to us for comfort as we fell asleep.

When I was a little girl, the dark used to frighten me. I always wanted to sleep in my mum's bed and she would let me, but in the middle of the night when I needed to pee I could never wake her up. I'd shake her, but she wouldn't stop snoring. I'd shake the pill bottles next to her ear, but she never moved. I'd climb out of bed and walk to the bedroom door and I'd hear Mum's heavy breathing. I could hear my sister's too, in the next room. I'd look down the hallway towards the bathroom door and see the attic trap door above it and it would make me shudder. I'd walk past Kay's room a little bit trying to be brave but my feet always stopped moving. I thought there were boo-boo men up in that attic, and maybe Jesus was up there too, waiting to jump down on me. With my legs crossed I made a childish plan in my head, just like Poppy had when she had grabbed at my necklaces.

If I peed on the floor and not in the toilet, I knew I would get into trouble, but if I sprinkled, I thought everything would be all right. I pulled down my knickers, held onto the crotch in front of me, pulled it forward so it wouldn't get wet and I squatted and dribbled out a little pee. Then I shuffled backwards and forwards in little circles, sprinkling piddle all over our wool carpet. With knees bent, bottom out and my head forward like a duckling's, I waddled up and down in front of my mum's and sister's bedrooms, making sure I never went too close to the attic. On my face would be a smile of relief, but often I had to keep going – I always had a lot of pee in me because Mum gave me hot Ribena before I went to bed. After running out of hallway and feeling the carpet damp underneath me, I'd then waddle into my mum's bedroom and around her bed, tinkling and thinking how clever I was.

My family never discovered my nightly jaunts and they blamed Precious the poodle for our stinky carpets. I wished my mum had woken up because I knew she wasn't scared of the dark. Sometimes she would wake me up in the night.

'Come on, Jane, wake up. It's time to get up,' she'd say. Rubbing my eyes in the darkness, I'd take Mum's hand and she'd lead me into the hallway. She'd turn on the hall light and then we'd slip into Kay's bedroom. It spooked me that we'd always find Kay sitting up in bed. Mum would quietly take Kay's dressing-table chair and put it next to her bed and sit down on it. Then, she would beckon me to sit on her lap. The hall light gave an eerie glow to Kay's face and she would talk strangely into the air.

Mum would ask my sleeping sister questions and Kay would laugh at them or tell us stories about her boyfriends. Mum would listen carefully, her head cocked to one side, and when Kay's answers made no sense at all, we'd giggle quietly together at how silly she was. When Kay got animated, slapping her thighs and shouting loudly, she often woke herself up and she'd scream to find us both staring at her. '*GET OUT OF MY ROOM!*' she'd shout and I'd scramble over her bed and get out as fast as I could. Mum would be laughing and in hot pursuit. I'd jump into Mum's bed and hear her slam off the hall lights and then jump into bed too. Under the covers we would both pretend to hide. We would be breathing hard from our naughty adventure and we'd look at each other in the darkness, trying not to laugh.

I'd ask Mum, 'Why do we keep doing that to Kay?'

And she'd answer, 'Because it's good for her.'

Then we'd both fall asleep.

Chapter 37
A Village

Santa Cruz: days three and four.

It was impossible to work. Poppy had decided not to sleep in her cot ever again and started waking all through the night, screaming to be put back in my bed. Not wanting to wake Ken and Jan, I'd grab her, and Poppy would then keep me awake all night, snacking at will, thinking it was funny to chomp down on my nipple if I tried to go back to sleep. My life became a sleep-deprived haze again and it wasn't funny any more.

In the evening, I'd still try to cook for Ken and Jan so I could repay their kindness in letting us stay, but now they insisted on cooking for themselves. I think it was less stressful for them than watching Poppy demolish their house. When we met in the evenings, I was also running out of entertaining conversation.

They wanted to talk about friends, parties, travelling, but deep down inside, all I wanted to talk about was babies, poo, pureed food choices and developmental stages. Was it normal for a child to crawl across the floor at high speed with a leg dragging strangely behind her? I felt deflated and the conversations were painful.

I didn't want to be entertaining, and craved being with people who really cared about us. I was too exhausted for us to be around anyone. Obviously, it was time to leave. But my lack of funds had immobilised me.

Day five.

Another sleepless night. I felt very uncomfortable in the house now and, listening to Ken and Jan getting ready for work, I stayed in the home office, hiding. *I have to sell some jewellery and get out of here and pay for a motel.* After they left, my eyes needing matchsticks to hold them open, I made us some breakfast and tried to feel positive about the day. In the afternoon I went to look for another shop to sell to – one that I hadn't previously embarrassed myself in – and I found it. This was my last chance and I knew I had to be better prepared. I turned the stroller round and walked back out of the shop and up the road and thought through how I was going to approach them. I couldn't mess it up this time. I was desperate for money.

I walked around until I had composed myself, then I got Poppy out of her stroller and walked back into the shop with Poppy smiling sweetly on my hip. I showed them the necklace I was wearing around my neck and told them a little bit of my story and about the range I had available to buy. They were interested to see more and I made an appointment for the next day to show them my complete range.

Day six.

Conversation in the house last night had been like a dried out African river bed and I told Ken we were going to leave today.

I knew he couldn't ask me to leave because he was a sweet man and couldn't throw a mother and a baby out on the street. I told them I had planned to leave earlier but business in town was taking longer than I expected and I had an appointment to sell jewellery the next day. So I'd leave tomorrow afternoon. I said goodbye to them in the morning as they left for work. They told me where to leave their keys and my head dropped against the kitchen wall in desperation and I cried. I felt so much pressure. I was beating myself up for my embarrassing predicament and all I wanted was a hug from a supportive adult to reassure me everything would be okay. I had been on the road now for seven months. I was scraping together necklaces out of my bead box and I was still no closer to finding a home: my life sucked. At least it felt good to cry and the tears were better out than festering inside me. I started to cry louder because nobody was in the house and it was a relief to be able to let rip – but I woke up Poppy with the noise.

I made her breakfast. She emptied their cupboards. Pots and pans crashed to the floor and I was happy she hadn't found the crockery cupboard again. I now felt happy; with Ken and Jan gone, I could relax in the house, make lots of noise and not be on edge about it and not be stressed about what Poppy was getting up to. Being alone with Poppy in a home was precious and I craved a motel room so I could let her cry though the night again and get her in her own bed again – but I couldn't take that chance. It would use up the rest of my money and I wouldn't be able to eat, and what would happen the next day? I knew this desperate feeling well; it was hard to deal with. I carefully made a snack box for Poppy. I cleaned the kitchen and scraped the egg stains off my breakfast plate. I jumped into the shower with Poppy and we washed our hair. I got us dressed, packed my baby bag with supplies and got into the car to go shopping. My brain was slippery like the one fried egg I'd eaten for sustenance. I hadn't eaten any of their toast; there wasn't much bread left and I hadn't been able to bring any into the house.

I got in the car with Poppy. We drove to a toyshop and waited outside for it to open. Inside the shop, I scanned the aisles carefully, looking at all the price tags, finding it hard to believe I was investing my last few dollars on plastic toy crap. I went to the cashier with my small finds, trying to keep the toys hidden from Poppy. I then took Poppy to a playground, to wear her out. The appointment I had made with the shop was flexible. I'd said I would get my daughter to sleep first and then go there. I spent hours in that playground, pushing swings, my eyes drooping, watching the morning fog lift. I took off my cardigan that had been tightly wrapped around me to keep warm and strapped Poppy to my back with it. I then galloped around on the grass playing horsey. I dropped to my knees, my jeans got wet with the dew but I was past caring at that stage. My old Converse sneakers were soaking. I let Poppy crawl around and I chased her and we both got filthy as she yelled out in kiddy delight. I climbed up slides, slid down them. Up and over. Up and over. The sun pushed the fog away and I was grateful for the warmth. The day had woken up out of its groggy, sleepy state and my daughter was now finally falling to sleep. Her eyes looked heavy like mine felt and I took her to the car to change and feed her and strap her into her car seat. She was getting used to that seat and didn't scream as much. I looked into her face and kissed her cheek. Her eyes were still refusing to close and she looked drunk. I was so tired I didn't care what anyone thought of me any more and I changed my clothes in full view in the car park and used baby wipes to freshen myself up and wipe off the mud.

I'd known I would need spare clothes. I'd been to this playground before in the early mornings, before the sun came up, wanting to get Poppy out of the house so Ken and Jen could sleep. I knew how filthy I'd get too. Santa Cruz's damp mornings brought grey slush to the playgrounds. They became filthy cold holes that sleep deprived parents hung out in and I would occasionally see others like me. We would acknowledge each other with a tired nod.

In the car, with both of us now safely strapped in, I drove to the shop. I kept looking in the rear-view mirror and driving around the block. I kept going until I saw Poppy's eyes close and her body language indicated *Yes, I'm unconscious.* Then I zoomed to the car park and shook my head to come back to reality, away from the merry-go-round I'd just been on. I took some deep breaths before I opened the door. I needed this shop to help me get off the scary, bumpy ride.

Ever so quietly I opened the door next to Poppy and looked at a sleeping angel. Looking at her sleeping was always precious. I quietly un-strapped her and placed her into her stroller. I placed a blanket over her and tucked in the sides. I grabbed her rag doll and tucked it in the side too. On the handles of the stroller I carefully hung her bag with its investment of new toys and a snack box and I prayed she would stay asleep for me. I was losing it; my breath was heavy and I looked up to feel the sun on my face for some strength and asked God to help, then I felt guilty that I only spoke to him when things were going bad. Outside the shop I took a moment to compose myself again and then I wheeled her in, asleep. I was hoping to give the impression that I was as fresh as one of daisies I'd trampled earlier in the park.

The shop owner looked at my necklaces. I'd spread them all out on her counter, and she seemed to treasure them as much as I did. She pulled necklaces towards her that she wanted to buy and asked if she could get more when she ran out of stock. I told her I didn't think so as I wouldn't be staying in town and to be honest I didn't know how she would contact me again. She slid more necklaces towards her side of the counter and I smiled. I kept turning to check on Poppy in the stroller and the buyer kept telling me how sweet she was and how much she liked my jewellery. I told her Poppy might not be sweet if she woke up. I told her Poppy had been around the beads and necklaces all her life now and she thought they were hers and she hadn't learned how to share yet. The buyer laughed. She was an older woman and her children had grown up, but she still had compassion for a new mother. As we were sweetly talking about Poppy, her eyes opened and I took a deep breath and got out one of her new toys, placed it in her lap and stepped in front of her so she couldn't see what I was doing. I told the lady we should really speed this up now, as I have had disasters trying to sell before. I was anxious; everything had been going so well up until now ... I kept nervously turning and checking on Poppy like I was being stalked. She was sleepy. She was sniffing her toy. Feeling it. Putting it in her mouth. I was now talking like a rabbit warning other rabbits in the field we have to get out of here before we get shot.

'I'm so sorry, but I really need to wind this up before my daughter fully wakes, or this could get ugly, trust me.' As I said the words, my ears pricked up. Poppy had dropped something. I turned. I was now a smooth operator. I opened her snack box and gave her a rusk. Sweat droplets formed on my head.

I rabbit-talked, trying to get the last few necklaces over to the lady's side of the counter. Sonic animalistic hearing was going on in my head. Poppy was sucking on something. I knew my time was running out. I turned and Poppy's eyes darted behind me to the woman holding necklaces. I looked up to the ceiling and hoped Jesus was now on the shop roof and going to help me out. I turned towards the lady: my time was over. I took the necklaces she had decided to buy and put them in their individual bags. I madly wrote out an invoice and a rusk hit me in the back; I knew it would be gooey. I slid the few necklaces she didn't want back into my bag and collected my money. I wished her luck with selling my jewellery, turned and sailed out of the shop, saying, 'I'm sorry I have to leave so quick, please don't find me rude, I want to get out of here before my baby bomb blows.'

With a beating heart I wheeled Poppy fast and furiously into the car park. My sugar levels had dropped, my head was spinning. I felt sick, I felt great, I now had money in my purse. I threw the stroller and its contents into the car boot and slumped into the front seat with Poppy and her snack box.

I opened the windows to get a breeze. Shakily I unpacked our picnic. As I looked down at myself, I saw gooey rusk all over me. Fuck – I'm trying my best here! I slumped my head back and tried not to cry. I didn't know where to go or what to do next. A child needed more than one person to bring it up; I needed a village around me and Poppy.

Chapter 38
A Bay City Roller

Due to Mum being committed to mental institutions, I was sent to boarding school at the age of seven. The minimum age to enter the school was eight. My parents lied about my age to get me in and the school never asked for any proof. Mum was out of hospital on my first day of school and so both parents took me there to settle me in.

'Don't worry,' the two of them kept saying, 'one of us will always come back for you at weekends and we only want the best for you. The Queen is the patron of this school, you know!'

I was tiny sitting in the back seat of Dad's car, drowning in an itchy maroon school uniform. They had bought the smallest size but everything swam on me, including the knickers. They were rough, a disgusting maroon colour, and they looked like a nappy and itched my precious parts. I whimpered to Mum in the back seat how floppy and itchy they were and I grabbed at the crotch, pulling it forward to show her.

'Don't be silly, they're good for you,' she said. 'They are nice and big, so you will have fresh air round your noonie all day.'

The itching of my knickers never subsided, I only learned to tolerate it, and the uniform shrank to fit as I grew.

We were the first family to arrive at my dormitory. We were guided towards a bed and I was told, 'This is your bed and other children will be here soon. Please make yourself at home.' I climbed onto my new bed and looked around. I was in a huge room of little iron beds. At the side of each one was a small chest of drawers, and at the bottom of each was a wooden box. Outside the dormitory we each had a grey locker allocated to us. This was my new home. Large windows surrounded the dormitory and I could see trees waving at me from the outside. *Hello,* they'd say to me, *we are free out here with our families and yours is leaving you, they don't love you!* Mum had bought me presents because I was going to boarding school. They were all from my favourite band, the Bay City Rollers, and she started organising them around me.

She busily stuck posters on the wall behind me. She pulled out a large floppy hat from her big plastic bag and stuck it on my head. She pulled a scarf out and wrapped it around my neck. She emptied out another plastic bag of clothes and shoes and put them in the chest of drawers and the wooden box. She disappeared to find my locker; she was going to fill it up with treats from Marks and Spencer's. Mum and I had been busy the previous day changing price tags in the Marks and Spencer's food hall so we could afford them all. Mum came back and put a box of Cherry Bakewells in my hands and I stared at it – and

I stared at her. I hated her for being ill. I hated her for leaving me. I hated my dad for thinking I wasn't good enough to live with him. Dad had disappeared to do the final paperwork and I didn't want them to leave; I wasn't grown up enough for this.

Other children and parents started to arrive and they smiled at me as they passed my bed. A large poster now hung over my head stating *I'm a Bay City Roller.* The white floppy hat on my head also had a band on it saying, *I'm a Bay City Roller.* I pulled my Bay City Roller scarf up so only my nose and eyes showed and I sat there frozen. *Be brave,* I could hear my head saying, but my heart wasn't listening any more.

I was still sitting in the same position when my parents left. They blew me kisses. 'We love you,' they said as they walked away, 'Always be happy, Jane!' I looked out of the window at the trees, who were now waving at me too. They were giggling with each other and their branches were blowing fake kisses just like my parents had.

Sitting alone, watching other parents preparing their children to be left alone, I looked over the top of my scarf. I was trying not to move an inch in case anyone noticed me, but my tears fell. I missed my sister. I wanted to hear her Motown music again. I wanted to do some synchronised dancing together in our lounge. I wanted to sit on her bed and watch her draw pictures of me in my ballet outfit. I wanted to be in her bedroom and listen to her with her Indian friend gossiping about boyfriends. I wanted to share one of her Radox milky baths and watch her smell both of our knickers to see who had the smelliest. I'd always get the smelliest to wear on my head as a bath hat, but I promised myself I'd never complain about that again if she just came and got me out of here. I didn't want her to be in Germany, where she was having a year away from home before she started university. I wanted her to come back and save me.

I tried to be brave in that school, but when the nights came and I was in bed alone, thoughts of Mum in her scary hospital with all those mad women filled my head. Thoughts of people in white coats. Thoughts of Jesus on top of the wardrobe. And the thoughts in my head would make me cry. I would hear other little children crying in the dark too. I hated the dark.

As a mum now, I never wanted to leave Poppy. I wanted to work, but when she was older, I was always going to be there to take her to school and I would always, always bring her back.

Chapter 39

Learning Right from Wrong

At boarding school, my friends became so important. They were now my family and together we worked out life's problems, such as what to do with our smelly knickers.

We were meant to put our clothes into a school laundry instead of giving them to our mums, but we'd never remember to do that; we were too young. We'd wear our knickers until they got smelly and then turn them inside out and keep wearing them some more. At night-time we'd take them off and hang them off our bedposts to air. We didn't hang them at the bottom of our beds because kids would steal them. Once hung up, we'd have to climb under our bed sheets for noonie inspection.

Little white humps manoeuvring about on top of our iron beds is what others would see, but underneath serious noonie inspection was going on. Our private parts hoarded the maroon fluff from our itchy school knickers like rocks hoarding clams and under the sheets we'd be picking out all the fluff with our fingers. It was a stinky business, but we had to do it because if you got too fluffy, you got really stinky and we only had a bath once a week.

I used to get a break from school though, not like my other little friends. One of my parents would come and pick me up and I would stay with them at the weekends. Mum would come if she was not in hospital and she'd often bring my friends with her, so they could have a break from school as well. Most of my friends' families lived in exotic locations and they only got to see their parents at the end of term; often their parents didn't even pick them up. A stranger would arrive instead to put them on a plane and the stranger would bring them back again, but this time they would have mangoes or coconuts in their bags. Some parents, like mine, lived in England, but they still didn't pick up their kids. Their daughters would receive terribly polite letters from their parents and siblings would get the same typed letter, saying the same things apart from at the top of the paper, where the parent had made the effort to handwrite the different names.

I heard children were kept away from their parents because they had blue blood. It was an expression I heard a lot at school and it meant children came from royalty. I'd cut myself before and knew my blood was red, and the school put me in special classes to try and cover up that fact. The school maintained a high level of excellence and I had to attend elocution lessons to become a good British citizen. 'HOw nOw brOwn cOw,' I had to keep repeating in my scratchy, itchy knickers. 'Aaaaayyyyyyy,' I'd continue, hoping one day Britain would be proud of me.

At school, away from parents, we were being moulded into perfect British citizens with good routines. We'd wake up, sink wash with a flannel (if we could work out how to), clean our teeth, get dressed, go to the toilet, march to breakfast, march back. There was school-time, break-time, lunch-time, study-time, back-to-the-dormitory-time, change-time, play-time, dinner-time, homework-time, play-time, bed-time and end-of-day-time. I liked all the rules. We were being moulded, like cogs in the wheel of life, to be Great Britain's future and if we didn't fit in, something was done about it quickly.

An artist emerged in our dormitory. She drew large brown daisies and wrote graffiti and her identity was confidential for ages. She'd create her artworks in private, but they were always discovered with delighted shrills and shocked screams. The whole dormitory would rush to see the new exhibitions and teachers would arrive. Whispering would occur. We'd all look around, eyeball each other. Who could have been so naughty and bold?

The artist was found and sent away. Bad behaviour and poo on walls was not tolerated in Britain. In our school we got taught what was right and what was wrong.

I learned so much of my mum's behaviour was wrong. She turned up unexpectedly at school one afternoon. She made a loud entrance into the dormitory. 'Quick girls,' she shouted. 'My car has turned into Herbie and he's outside waiting for you all.' Children jumped up from their beds and rushed over to her, and I had a sick feeling in my stomach.

'Come on, Jane, move,' said my little friends. 'This will be fun.' My friends liked my mum. She always gave them lots of Marks and Spencer's treats and they now gathered around her like rats around the Pied Piper of Hamelin, and more were falling under her spell. She floated off out of our dormitory with them all.

I shook my head to see if this was for real and then ran. I ran down the stairs after my friends and saw Mum fling the doors open to the car park. Kids poured out after her and I ran and pushed my way to the front of the crowd. I looked around: there were no teachers to save us. Mum was in her high, handmade leather boots and she was towering above us all. Her audience was enthralled by all the excitement and she opened her car door and began her show.

'Now, you all know my car, children? Well, during the week, it really became alive and now it can drive all by itself!' The children started cheering and bouncing up and down and I alternated shocked looks between them and my mum and wished a large hole would appear and swallow me up. Mum started her car. It was facing away from us and she leaned into it, did something to the gear stick, and then put her foot inside to press one of the pedals. The car slowly started to move. The kids cheered. Teachers arrived from nowhere. Mum was shouting, 'See, I told you, kids! My beautiful car is alive,' and we all started to slowly jog after it as it headed towards the football pitch. '*LOOK! IT'S GETTING FASTER AND FASTER*,' Mum screamed as she jogged by its side with the door open, holding onto the steering wheel. Her mohair knitted coat was flying and everything was speeding up …

'I better stop Herbie,' Mum cried as her car gathered speed and the kids screamed and laughed. Mum tried to get back into the car, but her leg got stuck in the door and she was now madly hopping on one leg. One of her hands was still on the steering wheel and her other was trying to open the door to free her leg. Her handmade boot-heels were scraping along the gravel, and the car started to turn right. It was heading towards the school buildings. The children were in a riot. Teachers now charged forward and screamed at us to keep back. They split up and one teacher came for us and madly waved at us to retreat. Everyone was jumping up and down. No one wanted to miss my mum's show.

The teachers stopped the car and Mum's adoring fans screamed and gavc her a round of applause. She turned to face them and made a deep bow and I felt someone take hold of my shoulder. I turned. It was my dorm mistress and she had a nervous smile on her face, trying to reassure me. My mum was escorted off the school grounds and refused permission to return. The school said my mum's behaviour was wrong; she was a bad and disruptive influence on the children and couldn't be controlled. I sobbed in the toilets after her show, quietly, tears and snot falling onto the tiles.

Chapter 40
Mad Parenting

I tried to stop Poppy sucking. She had had enough and I felt she was sucking out the last of my energy. She grabbed at my top, wanting more, and tears came to my eyes. I had no energy left for myself, let alone for Poppy, and now she was crying. The noise ripped through me like shards of glass and I pushed back the front seat of the car and slumped into breast-feeding mode again. I needed to sleep, but I had to stay awake. I imagined the local newspaper report: *Sleeping mother found in car with windows open and missing baby.* I had to do the right thing: I had to protect my child.

I was ten when Dad pulled me out of boarding school because he couldn't afford the fees. I then went to live in an English country pub. It was nice to be around my family again.

Dad and Bunny worked together managing the pub. My brother George now worked for Dad, managing the restaurant. Kay was at university close by and Dad had bought a house for his mum and dad in the next village. My little half-brother Dax, who lived with his mum in Las Vegas, became big enough to fly on an aeroplane by himself and would visit us every summer. Mum sold her house in London and came to live in the next town. That time living in the pub with all my family was such a happy time ... I held Poppy closer to me thinking how good it was to be around family.

I lived four days a week in the pub and three with Mum. Kay and George never visited Mum any more and, if the truth be told, I didn't want to, either. I would beg my dad to be allowed to stay with her less often, but I was told my mum had legal rights to see me.

'Nobody else sees her,' I'd tell him.

'They're older and they have a choice,' he'd say.

'Why don't I have a choice too?' I'd ask.

'You have no choice until you're 16,' he'd reply and tell me, 'End of story, don't ask me again.'

I was 13 when Mum started sharing her new medicine with me. She said the herbs were a natural remedy to calm her nerves and they couldn't do me any harm. She taught me how to roll up her herbs into a cigarette and we'd smoke it together. I was used to puffing on her cigarettes from the age of ten, when she used to pick me up from school and she'd give me one to light for her as she drove.

Rolling herbs was like cooking together. 'You can't go by volume using these herbs, Jane, you have to go by smell. Sniff it and if it smells really good and strong, you put less into the cigarette. If it smells old and dry, then you put in more.' She would put a sticky brown block under my nose and teach me how to smell if it was good or not. Mum also used to make cookies with it, and they really made us laugh. The cigarettes we made together were called joints and I became very good at putting them together. Mum would watch me carefully, giving instructions.

'That's it, smell it again. Do you think you've mixed enough happy baccy in with the tobacco?'

'I think so,' I'd answer.

'That's it, now roll it up tight and twirl the end tight like a firecracker.' I would roll joints, concentrating like I was creating an art project. 'Rip off some cardboard from the Rizla packet and roll it up too. That's called the roach so you don't get tobacco in your mouth.' We would smoke her medicine together in front of the children's cartoons after school and we started laughing together so much …

'This is good shit,' she'd say.

'It's fun,' I'd reply.

'You're such a good girl,' she'd say to me.

At the pub, my sweet family life changed. The Bunny started going odd like my mum. She'd been hiding wine bottles at the bottom of her wardrobe all through my childhood, but now I think all that drinking was affecting her and she kept going on the turn.

I'd feel sorry for Bunny, but there was nothing I could do to help as her sweetness and happiness slipped away. She spent less time working in the pub and more time in her bedroom. I knew becoming a dormouse was not good for anyone. I'd open her bedroom door and peak through the crack and see her sitting naked at her golden dressing table. She'd have her dogs at her feet and she'd be looking into her golden mirror. On her dresser was a solitary glass of wine, but we both knew where there was more. I never wanted Bunny to end up like my mum; I remembered my mum used to be happy and normal too before she became withdrawn and strange. I wanted Bunny to acknowledge me in the doorway. I needed her to look after me. My sister had left home and now lived far away. Bunny looked in her mirror and saw me in the doorway.

'Not now, Jane,' she'd say into her mirror and I wouldn't move. 'Please, Jane. *Not now.*'

I'd close the door and feel unwanted. The pub floors were old, from the sixteenth century, and they creaked beneath me as I left, telling her I'd gone away. Bunny would go on the turn like this for days at a time. Nobody ever knew what was wrong with her, just like nobody ever knew what was wrong with my mum. All people said was: 'Leave her alone.' My mum was left alone too.

People are not meant to be left alone. Dad married Bunny to try and make her happy, but it didn't work for very long. He then bought her an apartment so she could live away from the pub. It was a two-bedroom apartment and one of the bedrooms should have been mine, but Dad bought Bunny a sunbed instead and put that in the spare room. They moved out of the pub, but they left me in it and Dad hired alcoholic managers to work in it instead of him, so he didn't have to be there all the time. He put a lock on my bedroom door to keep me safe. With the different managers, I learned how to drink.

Poppy finished feeding. This whole travelling plan of mine was crap and I was giving my child just as strange a childhood as my own, but with a different story line. I leaned my head against the car door. I felt deflated.

Chapter 41

Retail Therapy

I felt myself slipping into a dark hole and pushed my car seat further back into the full recline position.

Poppy had now fallen asleep on my chest and I was grateful for the peace. I kicked my Converse sneakers off and put my feet up on the dashboard and looked at my stained trousers. They were so scruffy, but I'd only just got them out of the wash yesterday. My gaze drifted down my legs to my bare feet, skinny toes poking upwards. They were the colour of Cadbury's chocolate. The nails desperately needed care and the feet, a scrub. I put my fingers in the hair piled up on my head and they got stuck, and I remembered I hadn't brushed it in ages. I could easily be taken for a single-mother hobo. I lurched forward and tilted the rear-view mirror so I could see my reflection. Green eyes looked back at me. I had no make-up on and tired black bags sat underneath my eyes. I had no pretty earrings on and my skin looked all dried up. I slumped back again. Poppy felt like a heavy bear. I lifted my hand up; I needed to stay awake. The skin on the back of my hand was dry too. My gaze went up my bare arm. It looked like a dried out riverbed. My gaze kept moving towards my armpit and I sniffed it. What the fuck had happened to me?

I sank my head back in disappointment at myself and looked up at the car's nylon, fuzzy ceiling. I was crap. I smelt like crap. Crappy tears fell out of my eyes as I sank deeper into a hole. I was Alice in Wonderland, lost, spinning in the dark, not able to grab onto anything to stop myself. I was going down. Thrashing. Trying to breathe. Trying to grab hold of anything to stop falling. Searching for some light – and I found a spark.

I didn't want to go down any further. I'd seen what depression looked like. I'd seen where it took people. The spark of light showed me a way out. It showed me how to be a happy again. Anything was better than being depressed. The spark of light told me to stop beating myself up, to care for myself, to go shopping! *Buy yourself a lipstick, a new dress, a pair of jeans and you'll be happy again.* I wiped the snot off my nose – and I already felt better. I knew Poppy loved hanging out in shops. This was the answer to what I had to do: *go shopping.*

With a smile on my face, but feeling very fragile inside, I put Poppy back in her car seat and we drove out of the car park as I thought about floral prints, the colour pink, a necklace and a little sparkle.

Poppy loved the new season's colours in the shops and she kept grabbing wildly at hangers. Shop assistants fought over who was going to hold her because she was so cute, and while

I was in the changing rooms I could hear her on the other side of the curtain making happy noises.

The blow-dry specialist gave Dad a son when she was with him and when he was very little and couldn't even speak she took him to live in Las Vegas. When he became old enough, Dad would fly him to England to visit us in the pub for the summertime and we would always go shopping together. He would arrive in the country skinny, with two deflated suitcases, and would return to America fat, with bulging suitcases. He was seven; I was 13. We'd run around the stores playing catch and I would pick up hangers and drape the clothes over me and Dax would say, 'You look so beautiful, Jane.' I would choose a pile of hangers and go into the changing room and Dax would wait outside the curtain for me. I would change into an outfit and dramatically throw open the curtains and strike a pose. He would cheer and applaud, telling me how fabulous I was and how proud of me he was, and we would laugh hysterically together. I'd slam the curtains closed again and change into another outfit for his next onslaught of devotion. Dax had so much love for me. My dad had taught him how to love women and make them feel good about themselves.

Dad would get Dax to practise his charm by sitting him on top of the bar at the pub and getting him to chat to the female customers. 'That's it, son, you're getting the hang of it,' Dad would say as he passed by while he continued to serve his customers.

'You look very beautiful today,' Dax would say, smiling and winking at an old pensioner who had come in on her monthly village outing.

'Ooooo, he's so lovely,' the pensioner would say, batting her wrinkled eyelids at him. 'Would you like a packet of crisps?'

'Ooo yes please,' he'd say. 'You're so beautiful and generous.'

Dax even made me feel loved when Dad and Bunny moved into their love nest and left me behind. He would still come to the pub to visit me and he would hold me tight. Dad and Bunny made Dax a bed in their apartment and when he was there they would invite me over for Sunday lunch. I always hated saying goodbye to him when he left the pub to go back to their love nest.

I started to hate saying goodbye. I always wanted to be the one to say those words first. I wanted to be the person going somewhere exciting all the time. I didn't want to be the one left behind, especially in a pub with stupid alcoholic managers to look after me.

Dad thought I was tough. He thought I was independent. He said he thought I could deal with anything. He didn't realise I was still a little girl who needed to be held. I acted tough because the outside world scared me and I created a facade of bravado to try and deal with it. I was a teenager, nothing made sense in my world and I needed love and hugs more than ever before. Only my little brother grabbed hold of me and refused to let me go. I wanted to be protected. I wanted my parents to be responsible for me, the way they looked after him. I wasn't ready to be in the world by myself – but none of the adults seemed to understand that.

Now I shopped madly. I kept taking things and trying them on. I was feeling wonderful and the shop assistants kept telling me how good I looked. Poppy was smiling. I had flashes that I should be saving my money so I could rent a motel room, but with all the excitement and feeling my life was being healed, I thought fuck it, I need to have some fun too.

I was going to see Dax in a month. His childhood hadn't been easy either. Living in Las Vegas, his mum had done a lot of naughty things so they could survive. When Dax went to the local school, kids would approach him with drugs and guns.

Instead of following the crowd, his mum sent him to the gym to learn how to fight the crowd. Dax became a wrestler like our dad and won so many tournaments that – against all the odds – he managed to get a full scholarship into the Air Force Academy. Flying away from his life had been his dream as a child. Little aeroplanes used to sit on his bedroom shelf, next to a collection of crucifixes that he accumulated all through his childhood, though his mum had never taken him to church. In England when we were together, we always felt safe against the rest of the world: the drunks, the Las Vegas strip, the fucked-up people around us. By the time he was eight he was telling me, 'Jane, I'll always protect you.'

Now Dax was graduating as a fighter pilot from the United States Air Force Academy. When I was in Glastonbury he'd called me. He asked if he could drop a bomb on the Blond and I told him it wasn't necessary. He said he was so sorry he couldn't be with me but there was no way he could get out of college. I made a promise to him back then. I promised, whatever it took, I'd be in America for his graduation.

As I ran around the clothes shop grabbing at hangers, I was thinking of him. I was going to see him soon and I wanted to be dressed nicely for the occasion. I wanted him to open his arms and be proud of me again.

I grabbed wildly at more clothes.

Chapter 42
Finding Your Rainbow

I bought a lipstick, skirts, tops, new dresses, underwear and some skinny trousers that didn't look like comfortable mummy pants. I bought clothes for Poppy and justified every penny I spent. I wished I could go to Colorado right now and be with my brother, but that was impossible: he was living in Army barracks and studying for his final exams.

I drove back to Ken and Jan's and felt guilty. I shouldn't have gone shopping. I should have spent the afternoon working out what to do next. I had told them I was leaving. They expected me to be gone. Walking back into the house, I felt stupid and rude. I knew they would be wondering what was going on as our stuff was still in the room and I'd stayed out late and even treated us both to a meal in a restaurant because I didn't want to go back there. I could hear them in the lounge laughing and as I walked in they offered me a glass of wine. I said. 'No thanks,' and I told them quickly, 'Thanks for letting me stay so long and I'm sorry I'm not out, but I had a great business opportunity today that ended really late and I promise you, I'm leaving tomorrow.'

'Do you know where you are going next?' Ken asked sweetly.

'I'm not sure, I haven't worked it out yet.' I said it without showing them a flicker of fear. 'I'll decide as I finish packing tonight.' They commented about the joys of travelling and having no plans or structures in your life and I smiled, but inside, I shook. I wished I was in their position instead. They hugged me, I think out of happiness that I was finally leaving, and they told me again where to leave the house keys the following day. I said I was going to put Poppy to bed and have an early night and they said goodbye to us.

I quickly went and got all the plastic bags out of the car and took them secretly into the room to pack them in our bags. In Ken's tiny home office, guilt felt heavier than our shopping and I plonked the bags around us on the mattress. I dragged Poppy's new toys onto the mattress too and looked around feeling lost. I had told Ken and Jan I was going, but where? I had no plan and my brain felt like the mashed potatoes I'd eaten for dinner.

Poppy crawled over and lifted up my top again. I didn't have the energy to say no. She plonked herself into my lap and I relaxed her back into my arm so she could feed. I looked at my white plastic bags. Shopping was such a stupid thing to do. I should be in a motel room now weaning Poppy, but the thought of being in a motel room alone scared me. I thought of Margaret River and the teething episode and tears started to hit the pillow. I'd become such a baby lately. But I didn't want anyone else to hear my pain; my life was my problem and somehow I had to work it out.

The exhaustion of the day, the sleepless nights, my uncomfortable situation in the house – it all accumulated as I choked back the tears. I looked at my bead boxes and dragged them onto the mattress too. I opened them up and tried to change my focus. I have to make more necklaces, rent a motel room, and get out of here. Poppy fell asleep and I sat up and looked into the box. Tears fell and made the beads wet. I tried to wipe up the water and beads got stuck to my fingers. There were no more shops I could sell to in Santa Cruz. I had to get out of here. I looked at my beads and they were hopelessly low. I couldn't work out how to string anything together and I needed precious sleep. My thoughts drifted to the following day. I have to leave. I looked again into the box through puddle eyes. Splish splash.

I stroked Poppy's head. She was beautiful and oblivious to her mother staring into a wet box. 'This life has become so hard, Poppy. I can't do it any more,' I whispered to her. 'You need friends to play with, not kitchen cupboards, and you need a bedroom of your own, not a shared mattress on the floor. I want to give you a routine and a toy box.' I cried more and dragged the guilty plastic bags towards me. I pulled things out of them, trying not to go into a deeper hole of despair. I wished I hadn't run away from all the people who were good in my life.

I always thought life was better somewhere else, but now I began to think that wasn't necessarily so. I missed my sister and her family and I wanted to be around them. I missed my Bali family too. I staggered off the bed. Turned the lights off. In the dark I shoved everything off the mattress and snuggled us both under the covers. I still had my shoes and clothes on and I didn't care. I looked at Poppy in the dark. Maybe all this isn't real? Maybe I'm lost in a bad dream and when I wake up, it will be over.

Chapter 43
A Test

My thoughts drifted back to the pub. I was trying to study for my English O-level exams. Siouxsie and the Banshees was playing on my record player and I was singing along to the lyrics, trying to convince myself I lived in a happy house too.

'*Jaaaaaane, phone call for you,*' Dad called up the stairs. He was working the evening shift because it was the manager's night off. I picked up the phone upstairs and Dad said, 'Got it?'

'Yes, thanks,' I replied and a click sounded as he put down the phone.

'Hello?' It was Mum and her voice was faint. 'How are you, Jane?'

'I'm good, Mum, I'm studying for my English O-level exam tomorrow, so I don't want to talk much. What do you want?'

Her voice wasn't clear. She talked rubbish. Things about the weather, her car, how my pets at the pub were and about my dad. 'Mum, I have to study; if nothing is important can I speak to you when I come to stay with you tomorrow?'

'Jane. I called you to say goodbye.'

'What?'

'Goodbye, Jane. Goodbye,' and the conversation drifted onto strange things and my mum said, 'Goodbye, Jane, I'm going to kill myself.' Then she hung up.

I pulled the receiver away from my ear and looked at it. I put it down and quickly picked it up again and listened, hoping she was still there. I heard an empty tone and I bolted down the stairs.

Dad was serving in the bar. 'We need to talk,' I said. 'This is urgent. Please?' He finished serving his customer and we went into the kitchen. I told him about my mum's call.

He said, 'Jane, you are my flesh and blood and you mean everything to me and I would do anything for you, but your mother is not my flesh and blood and I want nothing to do with her.' All us kids had heard Dad say this before.

'Dad, she's going to kill herself!'

'She's not going to kill herself. Stop worrying. You should go back upstairs and study.'

'I can't, Dad. She is my mum and she has just told me she is going to kill herself.'

'Then go and call the police. I'll give you their number. They deal with these kinds of things,' and he told me I wouldn't need any money to call the police, as it was a free call. He went into the bar and gave me some coins in case I wanted to call Mum again.

I called Mum from the phone box next to the front door; it was the only phone we had for outgoing calls. Mum didn't answer, so I called the police in her local town, the number Dad gave me. They were nice to me. They knew my mum very well. She was always in trouble with them: shoplifting, disturbing the peace, parking violations, being under the influence and harassing my father. They said they'd go round to her house for me and see what was going on and they'd call my dad at the pub with any news. They said if my dad was too busy to help me, I could also call the Samaritans for support. 'They're really nice people when you have nobody around to help you.' The police gave me the Samaritans' telephone number.

Shivering next to the front door from cold and nerves, I kept putting coins in the phone box trying to get someone to help me. Kay wasn't in. I called the Samaritans. I kept calling Mum. I kept calling the police to see if they had any news yet. The pub door banged as customers came in and out. Dad liked the banging door because he knew when customers arrived and left. Mum's phone was engaged: beep, beep. The phone wanted more money. Cold wind whipped under the door and I felt like I was in a Las Vegas casino playing a slot machine with someone's life, and I wasn't winning. Kay still didn't answer her phone; George was in Spain. Customers were harassing me because they wanted to use the phone too, and how could I tell them they couldn't because my mum might be dead? I dragged myself off the phone to free up the line so the police could call back and customers could ring their friends. I sat at the Space Invaders machine next to the entrance and played, trying to take my mind off things.

Dad gave me coins to put in the machine: *dit, dit, dit, dit, BANG, BANG*, it went. The Samaritans said Mum wouldn't kill herself. *Bang, bang*. The police told me she wouldn't kill herself either, *dit, dit, bang, bang*; but she told me she was going to die. *BANG BANG*. I was very good at Space Invaders, *dit,*

dit, dit. I used to practise most afternoons when the pub was closed, *dit, dit*. I'd steal the money out of the tills because I was so hooked on it, *dit, dit, bang, bang*. I didn't eat any dinner that night, packets of pork scratchings filled me up. Tiny bits of crunchy dead pig spilled from the packets all over the top of the Space Invaders machine, and underneath aliens kept stomping and battling on. At least I was winning a Space Invaders battle. Dad would come and see me every now and again as he collected the dirty glasses around the pub. He'd ruffle my hair, ask if I'd heard any news yet. The only news I heard was the laughter and stories coming from the customers in the bar. Dad would leave more coins on top of the machine.

It was impossible to go upstairs and study. My head was with my mum, my fingers were with the Space Invaders, my heart was willing my mum not to die. I was nearing my top score when I picked up the phone again to dial the police. This time they asked to speak to my dad and he took the call upstairs, asking me to wait in the bar and look after it for him. When he came back down he told me the news.

'Your mum's fine. The police went round to her house and they found her with loud music on and lots of empty gin bottles by her side. She was rude and drunk and told them to fuck off as they were disturbing her peace.' I sighed with relief. 'Jane, it's late, you better go to bed now as you've got exams tomorrow,' and with that Dad kissed me on the forehead and went back to work.

I failed my English O-level.

Chapter 44
Walking the Line

Fifteen was a very dark year. Kay finished university and went to live in London. George went to Spain to open up a bar of his own. Bunny's sweetness had all gone. Bunny had bought me lots of pets at the pub, saying they would be my friends, but terrible things happened to them.

My fluffy white hamster, Columbe, I'd let run free around the pub lounge. One day she climbed up into the Calor gas heater. I didn't know she was there and put it on to keep warm and she went up in flames.

My rabbits escaped to live in the fields around the pub, but they would always come back for food, cuddles and chats. Dad gave a man with a shotgun access to our fields and he shot them.

I had a chicken called Jemima. She would sit on the cellar

door, outside the bay window of the pub. She had one leg, a fox had eaten the other one, and due to her bad balance she'd often fall over into her own poo. Dad told me a fox completely ate her one day and my grandpa told me what Dad said was bullshit.

'Your father got the gardener to wring her neck, because she was so fucking shitty,' he said. 'She was scaring the fucking customers.'

One of our dogs used to chase the traffic on the road in front of the pub. Backwards and forwards in the car park he would run and Grandpa and I would watch his antics together. 'That's one silly fucking dog,' Grandpa would say. Then the dog started biting kids in the beer garden and Bunny had to put him to sleep. 'I'll miss watching that fucking dog,' Grandpa said.

My goldfish slipped away next, right under the kitchen chest freezer as I was trying to clean their bowl. By the time we moved the freezer and got them out, they weren't flapping any more. I walked into the bar, looking sad, and Grandpa said, 'I heard you've just killed more fucking pets.'

And a man came in the pub early one morning with my Fanny. She was my Shih Tzu dog that Bunny had given me. Bunny said a dog can be your best friend and Fanny was. When it came time to go and stay with Mum, I always took Fanny along and she made my visits with Mum bearable.

In the short English winter days, I would turn into a sleeping dormouse at my mum's, and normally Fanny would sleep by my side. One afternoon when I was in bed snoozing I was woken up by screams of '*Faaanny, Faaanny*,' and I opened my eyes and looked around. My bedroom was tiny. I slept in a single bed, next to it was a chair and a small built-in wardrobe. My walls were covered in children's cowboys and Indians wallpaper and I hated it and the matching curtains. I made a small gap in the Hiawatha and John Smith curtains and peeked out. Mum was outside in her dressing gown and slippers and she was running around in front of our house screaming, '*FAAANNY, FAAANNY.*' She was gaining momentum and her dressing gown was being picked up by the wind. The grass area in front of the house was the size of a football pitch and no children ever played on it; adults walked quickly across it with their heads down. There were lampposts and they shone a creepy glow onto my mum. '*FAAANNY, FAAANNY,*' she kept screaming as she flew around, not caring where she was going.

Fanny must have run away again, I thought, I wish I had. Mum's dressing gown was open and her nightie was showing, and I was sure the neighbours were secretly watching out of cracks in their curtains too. I got out of bed and went into Mum's bedroom and took a cigarette out of her packet. I went back into my bedroom to light it up and took a deep drag. I liked the way tobacco gave me a numb feeling about life. After a few puffs I was ready to look out of the window again – in a nice protective grey cloud.

Mum was running towards our house. She had spotted a woman on the pavement below and was charging towards her. I made the crack in the curtains smaller, so she didn't see me. The woman below was carrying shopping bags and she had now stopped walking and was staring at Mum. I thought this might be a chance for Mum to talk to someone and make a friend. She didn't have any friends on the estate and this woman obviously lived close by. Mum rushed up to her, panting, and grabbed hold of her shoulders. '*HAVE YOU SEEN MY FANNY?*' Mum shouted in her face. Ah, maybe this won't be the day she makes friends, I thought. The woman shook her shoulders free of Mum's grip. '*HAVE YOU SEEN MY FANNY?*' Mum asked more loudly and the woman sped off up the pavement, struggling with her shopping bags and taking quick glances behind her to make sure Mum wasn't following. I turned away from the window and sat back down on my single bed with my polyester duvet. I took another deep drag. I knew I had to go and deal with this and get Mum off the streets.

Fanny often ran away from Mum's. One time she even turned up back at the pub. People would find her and say they picked her up on the yellow line in the middle of the road. They'd say she was happily pottering along on it.

One morning a man turned up at our pub. Dad was stocking up the bar with new bottles and I was sitting in the bay window watching life go by. Dad looked serious as he listened to the man talking and then the two of them went outside and walked towards the man's car. I kept watching. There was tension in the air, but I'd got used to tension in my life and learned when I felt it to stay still, watch, calculate and then move fast, depending on which way life's volcano had blown. They walked around to the back of the man's car and the man opened his boot. I could feel something was wrong. Dad looked inside the boot. He leaned inside it and quickly turned his back and my heart started banging. I stood up and put my hands on the windowpane that separated us. Dad faced the man and put one hand on his shoulder and then he hugged him and I read Dad's lips, thank you, he said. My heart was now in my mouth, my face against the glass. Dad leaned into the boot and retrieved a small lump wrapped up in a blanket and he held it carefully. I knew that was the moment to charge.

The man told Dad he was driving round a corner when he saw Fanny. He tried to swerve but he was going too fast and she was walking the yellow line. He hit her. He slammed on his brakes. By the time he got out of his car she was dead. He read her collar and brought her back to us.

I should have looked after Fanny with more love and care,

but sometimes you just want to close your eyes and pretend everything in life will be all right. I thought that was what you did in life. You saw strange things happening, but just waited and hoped nothing bad would occur. That's what the adults around me did.

But I should have stopped Fanny walking the yellow lines and someone should have stopped me when I started sniffing white ones. I felt there was very little air left in the world when Fanny died and I started doing lines to try and get away from my reality too.

Chapter 45
Toast

Dad was hardly at the pub any more and I started to hitchhike home from school because he wasn't there to pick me up. When I arrived home, I'd find a pissed manager instead of my family. The manager would have cleared up after his morning shift and he'd be sitting having a drink at the bar to relax. Mum and Bunny used to say a drink relaxed them too and when the manager offered me one, I accepted. All my life I'd been around people drinking, so I thought it was normal and grown-up to have a drink. The manager was an alcoholic. He used to say how impressed he was that I could handle my booze so well for a young 'un. I'd clink my glass with him in a wobbly stupor and say 'Cheers,' but the truth was, in the beginning I couldn't handle my booze. It didn't take long to get used to it, though. It was like getting used to smoking cigarettes. In the beginning it made you feel sick, but if you kept doing it, it didn't take long before you started craving it instead. Like craving a cigarette first thing in the morning.

I learned drinking took away bad feelings and I understood why adults drank and smoked so much. I often felt my life had turned to shit, especially when my Grandpa died. Drinking and smoking was like pouring magical fairy nectar into me, making my life sweet and funny again.

Mum had taught me gin was a good drink and Gordon's was the best. People couldn't smell it when they sniffed your glass and I took to sneaking into the side bar of the pub and putting nips of it into my orange juice. In the afternoons when I came home from school, if the gin bottle looked too empty due to my consumption, I would take it down and fill it up with water.

But I didn't drink with Mum. With her I smoked.

She would pick me up from school and instead of giving me a cigarette to light for her, she'd give me her tin and I'd roll us a joint for when we got home and watched the cartoons together. Mum even started giving me pot to take back home to the pub. 'I don't want you smoking other people's,' she would say, and I didn't refuse her gift, but I didn't know anyone else who smoked drugs apart from me and Mum.

I wondered if the drugs I lit up sparked me to be creative. I started drawing naked people inspired by the nudist camp and I would turn them into flowering trees and plants. I also came up with business ideas to make money. I'd buy workmen's dungarees, tie-dye them and sell them on a stall I'd set up outside the pub at weekends. They were a big hit with the customers and they started buying whatever I made. I started dyeing thermal leggings and vests for winter, and in cold weather I'd often giggle, knowing lots of our customers had my thermal rainbow knickers on.

I was thankful for the creative entrepreneur in me. Maybe I'd been given a gift by God to make up for all the other shit around me. It was a strength I had. Something I could always fall back on. I had the ability to look at a weird or bad situation in life and see how I could turn it to my advantage, like being stranded in Glastonbury and being inspired by all the goddess energy around me and creating a range of jewellery that I would then sell to support me travelling the world.

My pub stall range kept growing. In our pub's restaurant we sold homemade pâtés in earthenware bowls. I'd collect the empty bowls, clean them and sell them. The customers, amused at my entrepreneurial skills, wanted to encourage me and the grocers gave me their extra trays of peaches to sell. The antique dealers gave me boxes of goodies they couldn't sell either and Dad let me sell Cokes, lemonades and packets of crisps to the kids in the garden. I became loaded with cash, but little did anyone know the proceeds went towards me and my mum getting fucked-up on drugs.

Kay came down sometimes for a weekend and she spoke to Bunny about me. She said she had an idea I might be taking drugs and she felt something was wrong, but she couldn't prove anything or do anything because she lived so far away in London now. She said Bunny should do something about it.

Bunny never said a word to me.

Then I made a new friend at the pub. I liked the clothes he wore. He looked different to all the other boys who used to hang out in the countryside and I wondered if he was different like me. One day I sat next to him in the bay window and whispered into his ear, 'Do you wanna smoke a spliff with me?'

He turned and gave me a big smile. 'Of course, love,' he said with a cheeky grin.

We smoked a spliff together at the back of the pub garden, and there we built a solid friendship with much laughter. Danny had one leg. He had had an accident when he was a kid and when other kids asked him what had happened to him he would tell them a shark bit it off when he was swimming in Brighton. His parents and the hospital tried to make up for his accident and they would give him lots of money and they built him a special car to get around in. He was pissed off with life too, and as we smoked pot in his car and listened to his punk music, the lyrics we heard screamed out what we felt inside: 'Fuck you, life!'

Instead of going to the village discos with school friends, I started going to nightclubs in Brighton with Danny. My dad only gave me one rule: 'Do what you want, but you have to be back in the pub before it closes at ten o'clock.' So I started staying at Mum's at the weekends because she let me come home later.

Mum liked Danny. She said, 'He's a really nice boy that one, making the effort to pick you up from home and take you out for the night in Brighton and then bring you safely back in his car.' She said she was happy that I knew him and as I'd walk out the door for the night she would slip an extra lump of hash in my hand for him. 'Go on, so you can smoke with Danny Boy,' she'd say. Danny would arrive at Mum's house and toot his horn to let me know he was there. I never let him inside. I'd brought a friend back to Mum's house in Lewes once and it had been a disaster.

Danny would beep his horn and Mum would look out of the curtains and tell me to hurry up. Once I was in his car, we'd see her looking out of the crack of the curtains and we'd wave goodbye and then drive around the corner so she couldn't see us and he'd park again. I'd roll us a joint, and he started sharing his drugs with me too.

His drugs came in little white envelopes that looked like letters to fairies and he'd carefully open them and sprinkle the powder on a flat surface. He'd chop it up with a bankcard and make a couple of thin lines. The powders would burn as they rushed up my nose but it helped us get speedy for the motorway.

The Inn Place on the Brighton Seafront was our favourite club. Malcolm McLaren's music thumped out of the speakers and his girlfriend Vivienne Westwood designed the clothes that the girls in the club wore. I'd wear heels to look older and I would darken underneath my eyes and cheekbones too. My hair would be backcombed, covering up a lot of my face, and I'd stuff cotton wool in my bra. Bunny always used to tell me, 'Large breasts can make men's minds go silly,' and I'd always hope the doorman's mind would go silly and he'd let a 15-year-old in his club again.

In the club I'd sit down with Danny. He didn't like dancing. I'd be paying close attention to what everyone was wearing. I liked the girls who wore big brown sacs of skirts with layers of petticoats. Their feet would be wrapped in rags and on their heads were bowler hats that looked four times too big. They were called Buffalo Gals and hanging out with them would be punks, skinheads and New Romantics. New Romantics wore big, floaty white shirts and the boys wore make-up. The Buffalo Gals would dance, linking arms like maypole dancers, and laugh out loud and sing along to silly lyrics by Bow Wow Wow. I used to dance and sing like that in my bedroom, but I didn't do it in the club. I didn't want to leave Danny sitting by himself. We went to clubs a lot and Danny found a new coloured powder he liked and it would make him collapse next to me on the worn-out velveteen couches. I'd shove him to wake him up as I'd be sipping my gin, lime and water and my jaw would be grinding from side to side as the powders up my nose were speedily working and Danny would keep nodding off.

We'd go into the toilets to unwrap our little white envelopes and he'd sprinkle his brown powder on tin foil and hold a lighter underneath it. He'd suck up the smoke through a rolled up banknote and it would make him retch. I'd sniff my little white line and look at him as he slumped back against the bathroom wall. He'd be trying to stop himself from vomiting and I'd watch him retching and I could smell the piss all over the floor and he'd keep swallowing, trying to keep his gorge down.

I didn't like the idea of sniffing heroin. When I'd been in boarding school, I used to have to take pink worm medicine all the time and it would make me retch and my stomach would turn just like this. His powders made him go to sleep and I didn't get why he liked them. I could sleep enough by myself. I wanted powders that made me feel excited about life, buzzing, wide awake. I'd leave Danny slumped over, sliding down the toilet wall. People would be banging on the door to get in and I couldn't bear watching him writhing in the smell of piss and shit. Powders always made you shit and everyone in the club was taking them. He would join me later on the couch and say, 'When you get used to it, you don't feel sick any more,' and then he'd nod off by my side. 'This is a fucking great buzz,' he'd say when I'd shake him awake and it reminded me of when I was in Mum's house and I would go to sleep so I could have a good time.

I'd hang out with his friends too and go mushroom hunting in the countryside with them. On those trips, I'd pretend I was Annabella Lwin, Malcolm McLaren's protégée and the lead singer in his band Bow Wow Wow. She had a song called 'Go

Wild in the Country' and I always felt those lyrics were written for me. She was 16 when Malcolm McLaren made her a singer. I was 15 when I used to sing her song, creeping over the British countryside looking for mushrooms. Danny's friends also taught me how to make a tea with the mushrooms and when I stayed at the pub I would often go to school high as a kite. I'd have hallucinogenic fantasies and think I was famous like Annabella Lwin, and wore clothes designed by Vivienne Westwood and I lived in my own beautiful home with people loving and caring for me.

When I was staying with Mum she'd tell me, 'You can come home at one in the morning, but if you're not back by then I'll call the police.' She called them a lot and they always ignored her. Danny and I would leave the club early, but we were always late and Mum would have put her alarm on for 12. She would have already called the police and we'd drive up to her house and find her peeking through the curtains again.

Hearing my key in the front door, she'd charge down the stairs. '*WHY ARE YOU LATE?*' she'd scream and I'd take her arm and lead her into the lounge.

'I'll roll you a joint. You shouldn't worry so much,' I'd say and something in me felt it was still sweet that someone cared about me. She would trundle off into the kitchen to make me a mug of hot milk and we'd sit together and have a smoke as the powders still sped around in my head. I'd tell her about the bad traffic in Brighton, the Buffalo Gals, the car running out of petrol, how we forgot the time, more about how Danny was doing with only one leg, Danny falling asleep in the club and not being able to wake him.

'Shut the fuck up and go upstairs to bed,' she'd say finally. 'You're driving me mad, you've got verbal diarrhoea.'

I'd go upstairs with an ashtray and continue to smoke more pot to try and calm myself down. I'd lie on my bed staring at the cowboys and Indians wallpaper, feeling I was lost on a fucking Indian reservation. During those nights the wallpaper often came to life. I was now a Buffalo Gal sharing a peace pipe with a cowboy and trying to slow down my beating heart. It was always sunrise before the powders wore off and my jaw would stop grinding and my eyes would finally flicker and close.

One morning I was woken by screaming. '*YOU'VE HAD SEX!*' Mum was back in my bedroom again.

'What?' I asked, my head groggy. She had my knickers in her hand and was waving them about.

'*YOU'VE HAD SEX!*' she screamed again.

'What are you talking about?' She was waving the knickers in my face and I grimaced and pushed her away from me and propped myself up on my pillows. She hovered over my bed, hopping from foot to foot, doing an Indian war dance, and then shoved my knickers in my face again.

'*YOU'VE HAD SEX!*'

I cowered back and she backed off and stood up and sniffed at my knickers. Oh fuck, I thought.

'Mum, what are you doing?' I asked.

'*YOU'VE HAD SEX!*'

I knew I needed to clear my head somehow and make sense out of her behaviour.

'Mum, you're trying to tell me, you've come in my room, you've stolen my knickers, been sniffing them, and now you're accusing me of having sex?'

'*YES!*'

My head was thumping. My knickers were waving like a white flag. Cowboys surrounded her head and I wished they would shoot and kill her. Her mouth was opening and closing and I could no longer hear any more of her stupid fucking words. She pounced forward and tried to shove the crotch of my knickers into my face again.

'*I don't want to smell my fucking knickers!*' I screamed, pushing her away and struggling to get out of bed. I pushed her out of my room.

'*LOOK AT THIS, LOOK AT THIS.*' She thumped at my chest with them.

I tried to focus. My knickers had never distressed her like this before. I grabbed at them and took a look. They had mucus stains in the crotch and I didn't know why they did. I was having periods now and in the middle of my cycle I did get mucus in my knickers. I asked a girlfriend if she got it too and she said I was juicy and it meant I was fertile. I stared at my knickers not knowing what to do. Mum was obsessing with them now. It was so sad she had nothing else in her life to obsess about, apart from my mucus.

'I don't know why its here, Mum, but I promise you I haven't had sex.' I looked into her big brown eyes. 'I promise you, Mum, I haven't had sex. Can you wash them for me and can I give you some other clothes to wash as well?'

'Give me them then,' she said, feeling needed again, and I picked up my dirty nightclub clothes off the floor and gave them to her and she disappeared down the stairs. 'I'll make you some tea and toast then,' she said.

Chapter 46
A Little Help to Fly

I opened my eyes in Santa Cruz to discover nothing had changed. I was still in Ken's home office sleeping on a mattress on the floor. The sound of Ken and Jan having breakfast in the kitchen had woken me up. Poppy was by my side, breathing heavily in her sleep. I carefully manoeuvred away from her and slipped out of bed to go and see my hosts.

'I'm sorry for last night. I'm so exhausted at the moment,' I said. We shared some breakfast and I managed to make them laugh before they closed the front door. Anyone who sees me at their front door should refuse me entry, I thought, or they might never get me out. I smiled sweetly as I waved them off and then I crept back into the tiny office and quietly picked up my bead boxes.

I was grateful for the time alone. No Poppy, as she was still asleep in bed, and no other people around either. The time alone was precious, like the precious little beads in my box, but so few beads were left. There was not a sound in the house as my index finger moved through the beads, trying to visualise them forming a pretty string. The fridge chugged in the background and I wanted this peace to last forever. I sat on the lounge carpet trying to put bead combinations together in my head and trying to work out what to do and where to go next. I really wanted to be with my brother Dax, but I knew I couldn't stay in his barracks. I crept back into the office again and slipped out with my little pink book. Only now did I feel grateful that Poppy had been awake all night and she was now happily sleeping, giving me the time to think.

I dropped onto the carpet on my knees and flicked through my book. Reality hit and I couldn't stop my eyes from welling with tears. I threw my head back. 'You're such a cry baby lately,' I said to myself. 'Pull yourself together.'

Where am I going next? What am I meant to do? I kept flicking through the pages, hoping for an answer. I had to move on to another town, and I still wanted to find our home; I knew Santa Cruz wasn't it. Home. The thought made my eyes well again. Wiping them, I looked from my address book to my beads. Beads stuck to my fingers and the writing in my book smudged. My ears pricked up; Poppy was now awake.

I went into the room and slumped on the bed in a foetal position and Poppy headed straight for my chest again like a kitten, biting into me. *Be in the present moment, Jane, think of what Ted would say to you right now. Don't lose it. You have to stay strong for her. You have to be a good mum.* I stared up at the ceiling, listened to the fridge chugging. Maybe I should just leave here and drive. See where that takes me? And I closed my eyes and prayed for help. If anyone can hear me out there, please send me a sign.

I remembered being in LA and Ted talking about enlightened people and telling me about one he used to live with in Sedona. He told me this man knew what the secret of life was all about. I opened my eyes and looked up. I had no idea what my life was about. My thoughts drifted away with my milk, and calm lay over both of us. I simply lay with my daughter. I cuddled her. I felt her warmth next to me. I came into the moment, because I had nowhere else to go, and then bounced up. I had an idea!

Poppy looked startled as I scooped her up and ran into the lounge to find my book again. 'Horsey, horsey,' I cried as I stuck her on my back and got on my hands and knees, flicking through the pages.

This whole trip had been teaching me to trust in life. All along the way I'd got into tricky situations, but life constantly showed me what to do next and moved me on. Each time it gave me little messages. Often they didn't make any sense at the time, but I trusted in them and they turned out to be the right things to do and – hey, life is crazy – I knew it was time to trust the little messages again. I had no one else to help and guide me.

I found the number I was looking for and looked at the clock. It was too early to call. Fuck it – I'll call anyway. He might have an answer for me. He might know what I am meant to do next. I've no idea, but I've got an odd feeling I should call him. The phone rang for ages and then a sleepy voice said, 'Hello.'

'Ted, I'm really sorry to bother you so early. I just want to ask you a quick question and then you can go back to sleep.'

'Jane, what's up? Are you and Poppy okay?'

'Yes, we're fine, but I want to know if your enlightened man in Sedona has a telephone number.'

'Yes. Hold on.' I heard him rummaging about and Linguini

asking if we were okay too. 'Jane, the guy's name is Robert Adams and here is his number.'

'Thank you. Go back to sleep. That's all I need, I'll call you in a few days. I love you.'

'Love you too.'

I put the phone down and stood with Poppy on my back and looked at my book with the new number written in it. I looked at the clock. It was too early to call up someone I didn't know, so I decided to get us some breakfast. In the kitchen I watched Poppy singing and hitting pots with a spoon and I made her some mashed apple and banana. I kept looking at the clock. Tick. Tock. The hands were moving so slowly. A reasonable hour came, but I missed it because we were having too much fun. I liked the way Poppy had grown up and was boisterous and fun to be with. We were now charging around the house together on our hands and knees playing hide and seek. We were making as much noise as we liked and were playing in their wardrobes. We got into the shower to wash off yesterday's woes and, sitting naked together on the shower floor, we pretended we were elephants. We poured Tupperware pots of water over our heads and I told Poppy the story of Dumbo the elephant. I liked that story; my mum used to tell it to me too.

'One day a stork delivered a baby elephant to Mrs Jumbo. Mrs Jumbo worked in the circus and she discovered her baby elephant was a miracle and could fly!' I would pick Poppy up and whoosh her into the shower jet above our heads and she'd laugh hysterically. I told her versions of the story over and over again until my arms got tired and we got out of the shower and dried ourselves, sharing a towel. I got us dressed. I looked at the clock. Now was obviously the perfect time! I got Poppy's new toys and went into the lounge room and settled her down on the carpet with them.

'Wish me luck Poppy,' I said to her, and I picked up the phone and dialled.

The phone rang for ages. *Bleep, bleep, bleep.* I thought about putting it down, but it was stuck to my ear and it wasn't going anywhere. He was supposed to be enlightened, he was supposed to have direct communication with God. Surely if I asked him, he might have some kind of answer for me? My heart thumped. My ribs hurt with the pressure. Someone picked up the phone.

'Hi, I'm sorry to bother you. My name is Jane and I got your telephone number from a friend in LA, who lives in Hollywood, who I met in Bali, who used to live with you. His name is Ted and I asked for your number because I'd really like to speak to you.' Then I remembered I was being quite rude. 'I'm really sorry, please excuse me – are you Robert Adams?'

'Uhhh uh uhhh uh.'

'Sorry? Do I have the right number? Is this Robert Adams?'

'Uhhh uhhh.'

I held the phone to my thumping chest. 'FUCK!' I now remembered the full conversation I'd had with Ted: *He can't speak to you because Robert Adams has had a stroke.* I didn't know what to do. Robert was the end of the line, literally. I was being rude, but I needed somehow to connect with this man.

'Ummm, okay. This must be Robert and I've heard you had a stroke.'

'Mmmm,' he hummed.

'Could you do me a favour? Could you grunt once for yes and twice for no?'

'Mmmm,' and I couldn't help but laugh; my life was ridiculous.

'Does that grunt mmmm mean yes?' I asked.

'Mmmm.'

I smiled; I was understanding him! 'Robert, I wanted to speak to you because to be really honest, I feel so lost about my life, and hearing about you from Ted I thought you might have an answer to what I am supposed to do with it.' A whole pile of grunts started pouring down the phone and they made me laugh again because I was actually trying to understand them, but it was like trying to understand Chinese. Robert sounded like he was laughing too. 'Robert?'

'Urrr.'

'You just said yes?'

'Urr.' He then made another continuation of urrhs and mmms and sounded like he was laughing again …

'Wow, you're cool aren't you?'

'Urhhh.'

'I think I need to come and see you to really understand you though.'

'Uhh.'

I should be certified.

It took a while and quite a few grunts to work out if Robert was giving a satsang any time soon and if I could go. He grunted yes, and through a series of more grunts and laughter I discovered he had a meeting in three nights' time, at six o'clock in the evening. I held the phone to my thumping chest and my heart was now trying to do the limbo under my ribs. Yes, I can do this, I thought. I looked down at my book to see I'd written *YES*, and *YES too!* If I was going to do this, somehow I had to cross America to get to where he lived, with a small baby, little money and all our crap. Fuck it. OK. I'll do it. What do I have to lose? Nothing! I put the phone back to my ear.

'I can do this, Robert! I'm going to come and see you. I have to bring my baby though because it's just the two of us.'

'Uhh.'

That sound was all I needed for my feet to be jumping up and down off the carpet in excitement.

I now knew where we were going next and hopefully he would have an answer as to where my home was! Ted really trusted this guy and spoke highly of him all the time; he said Robert had changed his life, given him clarity to understand what his life was about. I was desperate for my life to have clarity and be changed too.

Poppy started bouncing up and down on her bottom as I warbled down the phone about how excited I was that I was going to meet him. I told him how fabulous he was and how by simply speaking to him, I already felt better about life. I told him I'd call Ted to get his address, as it would take hours to go through the alphabet to understand where he lived in grunts, and a whole pile of them poured down the phone at me in response. I finally said, 'Thank you,' and put down the receiver.

That lounge room was now like the famous technicolour scene in the *Dumbo* movie: the scene where the birds pick up Dumbo's ears and with their help he discovers he can fly.

Chapter 47
Following a Star

Poppy was still happily entertaining herself when I put the phone down, so I picked it up to find a cheap flight to Arizona and a cheap car-hire there so I could drive to Sedona where Robert lived. I ran into our bedroom, grabbed my purse and spread all my money over the floor, counting it lots of times, grabbing it off of Poppy and hoping each time I counted that I'd made a mistake and a miracle might occur and more money might turn up. It didn't. I could afford two days' car hire, a cheap motel for a couple of nights and a plane ticket. I looked up above and prayed. I hadn't included money I needed for petrol and food and hoped God would somehow provide. He provided fish, didn't he?

'Hello,' I shouted to the ceiling. 'Can you please provide for us just one more time and I promise I'll start speaking to you when times are good too?'

I picked up the phone and booked everything. I had butterflies in my throat and stomach at the thought of what I was about to do. I dashed around making the house tidy again, and packed our bags so at least it looked like I attempted to leave this time. My head felt dizzy.

'*Surprise!*' I said to Ken as he came in the door, and then instantly entertained him with my story of how I was going to travel across America with a baby to see an enlightened man and how it took me today to organise it and tomorrow morning I'd leave because, 'I've booked the tickets!'

My energy had returned and I cooked them a final goodbye dinner. They were finally getting rid of me tomorrow morning and we had to celebrate; we were all smiling ... and the next morning, I left their key on the kitchen table and drove off to the airport.

The airport was busy; people were moving in thick packs like ants. There were no loudspeaker announcements and I had to keep looking at the flight information boards to find out when the plane was boarding. Planes were delayed. There were no vacant seats anywhere. People who sat on seats looked at me with a baby on my hip and looked the other way. This is how old people must feel on London transport, I thought. I sat on the floor with Poppy and lots of other people and together we all watched legs walking forwards and backwards, forwards and backwards. Poppy was very entertained by them. She sat in front of my crossed legs, staring at them as though she was watching a kid's cartoon and legs were the animated characters. My head was spaced out from untold nights of no sleep and I kept nodding off. I'd jolt forward with my arms automatically lurching forward, grabbing my daughter. I missed our flight to Arizona twice but the assistant behind the desk was caring and kept giving me new tickets.

We sat back down on the floor again and soon after, feeling dazed, I watched as Poppy stood up and toddled off. I gazed at her and she broke into a run. I guess the running stops her from falling over, I thought, and a woman sitting next to me brought me back to my senses by grabbing my arm and shouting in my face, 'Is that your child?' I jumped up and ran too.

My baby was now 11 months old and could walk!

On the flight all Poppy wanted to do was toddle up and down the aisle showing people how clever she was. The aisles of planes are perfect for toddlers. They are the perfect width, with arms on each side to grab hold of and plenty of smiles to confirm how well they are doing. I spent the whole flight walking hunched over, ready to catch a falling, ecstatic child.

We arrived in Phoenix, Arizona, rented a car and drove three hours across the desert into Sedona. As we arrived the sky turned black. A wizard's cape full of stars filled the night sky and I wondered how all the angels were doing up there and why on earth Poppy had chosen me for her mother.

The town of Sedona was small and I drove around it a few times looking for motel and hotel signs. Once I got my bearings I started inquiring at the cheapest looking accommodation first. But I then found myself having to enquire at the posh looking options as well. In every lobby I'd receive the same answer, 'I'm sorry, there are no rooms available.' I've just crossed the desert like a wise man guided by a star and now it looks like I'm going to have to find a barn to sleep in? But I wasn't as brave as any wise man and there was no fucking way I was going to look for a barn to sleep in, or sleep in the car alone with Poppy in the desert. I didn't like the dark; there were naughty boo-boo men in it. I kept driving, hoping to find somewhere to stay, but all I found that looked promising was a health food store. Hungry and tired with a very grumpy child strapped in the back seat, I drove into its car park.

I strapped Poppy to me in her sling and walked down the aisles looking at price tags and working out the cheapest option that would fill us both up. Poppy kept grabbing at all the pretty coloured boxes and I let her look more closely at a healthy cornflake carton. I wanted to open it up and cry into it. I walked the aisles again, this time more slowly. I didn't want to leave the shop; there were people in here and I didn't want to go out into the lonely darkness by myself. How many times can I get away with walking these aisles? It's a small shop, I still have nothing in my basket and people are going to think I am about to shoplift. I begrudgingly retraced my steps. I picked out the food I'd previously worked out was a good deal and ordered a brown bread sandwich with lots of sprouts in it from the deli counter. I'd watched someone else order one of them. It was huge. I'd looked at the blackboard pricelist behind the counter and they were nice and cheap. I asked if it cost more for extra mayo and thankfully the assistant said, 'No.' I got in the queue for the checkout.

Everyone in the shop looked wholesome and nice. Nice people go to health food shops, don't they? They wore bright coloured clothes that weren't conformist; they'd understand me, wouldn't they? I smiled at a few people in the queue, testing my theory, and they smiled back. No one looked weird. I must have, though: smiling so much, spinning my head around, I must have looked in need of medication. It was my turn at the checkout counter and the girl behind the till smiled at Poppy as she tapped away at her till and put my food into a brown paper bag. I opened up my purse and gave her my precious survival money and my heart smashed against my tits in sheer desperation. The exit door was close. I didn't want to go through it. There are boo-boo men out there. I saw a bench. It was at the end of the cash register. Next to the door. The darkness loomed at me with its scary arms beckoning me to come outside so it could kill us both. I rushed towards the bench and climbed on top of it, struggling with my baby and my brown paper bag. I stood up tall and looked down at everyone. My heart was now in my throat as I spoke out in my best English accent.

'HELLO EVERYONE,' I shouted.

People turned and stared up at me. I knew Americans liked English accents, so I made mine even stronger. 'PLEASE EXCUSE ME, BUT I WONDER IF YOU COULD HELP ME?' The checkout girl stopped working and was now staring at me too; people were cocking their heads to one side. 'I've just flown in to Phoenix airport and I rented a car and drove all the way here alone with my baby and I'm here for an important meeting that will happen tomorrow and I've looked everywhere in town for accommodation, but everything is full due to a New Age conference. I can pay someone. I have the money. What I am asking is, does anyone have a spare room I can rent for the night for me and my baby?' A woman dashed up to me. Grabbed my arm. Pulled me off the bench and ushered me outside. People smiled and waved goodbye.

Outside the woman told me that was a very dangerous thing to do, but she said I could stay with her. I thanked her and told her I did it because I thought it was more dangerous for us to sleep alone in the desert and I felt desperate. She told me she didn't have a spare room, but I could sleep on her couch and I'd be safe for the night.

'You can trust me,' she said. 'But you can't trust everyone.'

Her name was Lou and she told me she lived alone. She said now was too late, but in the morning she'd call her friends who sometimes had rooms to let.

Chapter 48
Alone

We got in our respective cars and I followed Lou. She parked outside a motel-looking door and I parked next to it. Lou opened the door and waited for me to get Poppy and our belongings out of the car and we walked inside. It was small and looked like a revamped motel room. Lou told me to put my bag by the couch and we sat on the floor around a small coffee table. We were all starving. We all had brown paper bags like homeless drunks and we shared our food together, munching and sitting on the floor. A couch supported my back. It was covered in a cheap polyester floral fabric. A double bed supported Lou's back and she got up and grabbed a cover from it and one of her pillows and a sheet from a small cupboard. She draped the sheet over the couch while I fed Poppy and told me this could be our bed for the night. Poppy fell asleep under my top and I lay her down on the couch as Lou put the kettle on. She got two mugs out of the cupboard to make some tea.

'What are you doing here?' she asked me, and I wanted to ask her the same thing.

I told her how I was travelling around the world with my baby looking for a home and I'd been on the road for eight months but still hadn't found one.

'And to be honest, Lou, I think I've been on the road all my life looking for it.' I told her I was now feeling desperate and I was in Sedona to see a man who might be able to help me. I told her about Robert and how I hoped he could shine some light on what the fuck I was up to.

She laughed. She said no man could ever make my life right for me and I told her I'd discovered that for myself, but maybe he could give me some guidance, as friends I knew well trusted him. She told me loads of people get drawn to Sedona looking for answers.

'And good luck, love, if you find what you are looking for. I'm still trying to work out what I'm meant to do with my own life.' She put the mugs down on the table.

Lou was about 40 or 50. She looked like she should be a mother. The lines on her face showed life hadn't been easy for her. Weirdly, my mum never had any lines on her face, and I used to study her face a lot when I was trying to come to terms with her behaviour.

Lou said, 'Tomorrow I'll go out and make some calls for you and help you find a room. I'll also help you find your Robert.'

I felt emotional thinking about my mum. And why was Lou alone here in this room? I wanted to ask her all about her life, but I felt something raw and hurting and I didn't want to go there. It might be like pulling back a messy bandage, and I didn't have the energy to patch someone up. I was tired of life as I sat on Lou's floor, sipping the hot comforting brew. We both became quiet.

I remembered quiet moments with my mum. One time I came back from the hairdressers after cutting off all my hair. 'Hello!' I heard her call out. I walked into the lounge and she was sitting on the couch smoking. Our thick heavy curtains were closed; she never opened them any more. The lamp was on and pictures of her family who never visited her sat around. Her children smiled out at her, all a lot younger then. With the innocence of youth we unconditionally loved our mum, but now we had grown up. I ran my fingers through my new short haircut. There was hardly any hair left. I felt I'd left my childhood on the hairdresser's floor. I was grown up like my brother and sister now. Mum put out her cigarette and snarled at me.

I avoided her look, sat down and kept looking at the pictures instead. There was a picture of her with George and Kay at a picnic. George was about 12 and Kay was by Mum's side. Both Kay and George needed her then and our mum looked beautiful. She wore a 1950s-style dress, tiny at the waist, and her hair was neatly piled on top of her head. I remembered how much pride she used to take in getting ready each day. She would spend hours at her dressing table applying the best face creams, massaging her face, carefully applying make-up and doing her hair. Mum would tell me the secret to looking good in old age was regular face massages.

There was another picture of George when he lived in the Bahamas. He was on a diving boat, smoking a cigarette. There were lots of pictures of Kay. One with her standing behind me, looking the tall, protective sister, and there was even a picture of Dax when he was a baby. Dad had flown to Las Vegas when Dax first went there. He wanted to make sure he would be safe. He came back with this picture. It was Dax next to a lion cub. I wasn't sure he would be safe. I missed all those family faces.

Mum wasn't saying anything, just staring. Her lips were clenched up and her hair was hanging limp and greasy around her face. She'd stopped styling it and often didn't wash it. 'What's the point?' she'd say. She hadn't bothered to get dressed today either. She was still in her dressing gown. She only got dressed nowadays to go shopping or to pick me up from school. She had nowhere to go, no friends, never spoke to her neighbours or even knew who they were. The only thing she looked forward to was when I came to stay with her. She'd say, 'You're the only thing worth living for, Jane,' and I wished she had a life apart from mothering me.

The only people she now hung with were the actors on the telly. I knew she'd been watching them all day long. She'd talk to them as if she knew them well and they helped to take her loneliness away: the flickering pictures hypnotised her for hours.

I looked at the ashtray. Smoking occupied her too, and cigarette butts poked out of a mountain of ash. There was an empty tea mug. A few crumpled cupcake wrappers. I knew she'd been looking forward to my return and now I presented her with my extreme haircut. I looked down, her guilty child, and the familiar I'm-not-good-enough feelings arose in me. I wasn't the daughter Mum needed. I wasn't a daughter Dad and Bunny wanted around either. I was a mistake. Mum always told me that: I was meant to be an abortion but the doctors got the date of her pregnancy wrong and by the time she went back for the operation, she was too far gone and she was stuck with me.

I'm a fucking mistake, I thought, but at least she's calm and not screaming at me. I wanted to be a good daughter.

'Mum, I bought a new skirt today, can you take it up for me please?'

She stubbed another cigarette deep into the pile of ash with her bony fingers and she brushed them off.

'Come into the kitchen,' she said and pulled her dressing gown around her and tottered off across the carpet, waving for me to follow. In the kitchen she pulled out the high foldaway stool and told me, 'Put on your skirt and stand on here. I'll go and get some pins.'

I undressed in the lounge and went back in the kitchen and stood on the stool facing our peeling wallpaper. I fucking hated this house. There were shrivelled, burnt cupcakes sitting on the kitchen counter; Mum couldn't even cook any more and I wondered if she would ever fix our peeling wallpaper. I doubted it. She'd taken to ripping off sheets of it that hung too low. She'd ripped off sheets in the lounge too and the upstairs bedroom. I used to think the falling wallpaper looked like ballerinas doing deep curtsies, and their skirts would flutter in a breeze. I often thought the whole house was performing a rendition of Swan Lake, and I shivered looking at the falling dancers.

Mum shuffled back in with the pins and started pinning up my skirt just below my knee. I looked down and asked, 'Can you make it shorter please?' She looked up and then shuffled around in a circle again. I looked down again as she finished pinning, 'Can you make my skirt just a bit shorter please?' She looked up at me again. I smiled. I knew I had to do this gradually. She snarled, and then shuffled around again. My skirt was now a miniskirt to upper-thigh. 'Can you make it just a teeny-weenie bit shorter Mum?' And she started pulling me about roughly and tucking the excess fabric into my waistband.

'*How the fuck is that?*' she asked.

'Perfect!' and she looked up at my head and then lunged at me with her pins. I fell off the stool and smashed into the wall as she stabbed at me. Blood ran down my leg as I pushed her off. She crashed into the fridge and slid down it, trying to hold onto something, her feet slipping. I football-charged out of there into the lounge and grabbed my stuff and turned. She was crumpled and unmoving on the kitchen floor. I rushed upstairs to shove more things in my bag and get out of there.

I wanted to get as far away from her as possible. I felt the bricks of the estate suffocating me as I ran out of the house. I knew Mum would be getting up by now. She would be fluttering. That's what she did when she got upset. She grew wings and flapped them high and low trying to take off from this world. Fuck, why was it so hard to love that woman? I got to the roadside and stuck out my thumb.

A desert chill started to seep under the crack in Lou's door and her cheap floral curtains fluttered against what must have been gaps in the windows. My eyes fluttered too and Lou said it was time for us both to crash out. She got into her bed with her one pillow and I squeezed onto the couch next to Poppy and put her other pillow underneath my head. As my eyes closed I thought back to the last time I saw my mum when I was a teenager.

Chapter 49

Sweet Sugar Candy

Surprisingly, I scraped enough qualifications to go to fashion college in Brighton. I'd hitchhike there and back every day, and in the first few weeks of college I was given a form asking for proof of ID. I started to sweat. I'd already left school at 15. Legally you weren't allowed to leave until you were 16, but my parents and I had been lying about my age since boarding school and no one had ever asked for proof of age until now. I told both my parents about the form. Dad told me to deal with it and Mum laughed. I tried leaving college, going to London and being a model, but I was too short and my life looked bleak as an unqualified dwarf. So I went back to college and told them the truth about my age. Mum was going to pick me up from the pub the day I heard the good news that I could stay at college; it was Monday, time to stay with her again. Autumn was whipping up the air but I was full of the joys of spring. I bounced into the pub to let Dad know, but he wasn't there as usual, so I called him instead. I called my sister and also my Nan and I was on the phone by the pub door when Mum drove into the car park.

'Gotta go, Nan, Mum's arrived to pick me up. I love you.'

I skipped outside with my knees high and my arms wide open, taking in the wind, and I threw open Mum's car door and put my head inside. 'Mum, I'm sorry, I'm not ready yet. I was late coming back from college. And guess what? I got some great news! Can you give me ten minutes to get my bag together and I'll tell you?'

'Come in the car now and tell me the news,' she said and I jumped in. I was so happy, I wanted to tell the world: I wasn't going to be a loser and not get qualified. I was going to be like my sister Kay.

'I'm allowed to stay at college!' I told Mum. She smiled and bent over to give me a congratulatory kiss, but for some reason, she went straight for my lips and held onto my shoulders so I couldn't refuse her. I then felt her tongue in my mouth and my whole world collapsed.

'What the fuck are you doing?' I sobbed, pulling away from her, falling out of the car onto the gravel, hardly seeing through my tears. I spat on the back of my hand and wiped it across my face. Gravel that had stuck to my hand carved me up. I looked at her. She was fumbling in her lap. 'I tell you I have great news and you stick your fucking tongue in my mouth?' Leaves were swirling in the air. Cold, stinking spit was all over my face and stinging me. I was back to the familiar confusion and hatred of my life. I didn't want to be part of it any more. It was just too fucking hard. The wind whipped my hair and I grabbed at it, not knowing what to do. I wanted to pull the madness out of my head and let the wind take me, take everything, away. I looked back at her. She lifted her hand from her lap and was now leaning over the passenger seat and reaching out her clenched fist towards me. The car park gravel was painful. She opened up her fingers and there was a sweet. A fucking sweet. What the fuck?

'Why are you showing me a fucking sweet?'

'Because I dropped it.'

'WHAT?'

'I tried to put it in your mouth. It's really nice and I thought you would like it. It's a soft toffee from Marks and Spencer's.'

'A toffee?'

She shook her head and smiled sweetly.

But her answer wasn't sweet and I felt sick. 'I'm not coming home with you. Go home. GO HOME.' I struggled to get up, crawling away from her. I slammed the car door shut and ran to the pub. The wind was at my back, making me go faster, and I got thrown against the door. I opened it. It slammed against the wall and I had to push against the force of the wind to close it again.

I stumbled into the pub, my mind and body confused. There was no strong wind pushing any more and in the pub it was calm. I ran and stood behind a wall so she couldn't see me. There were no customers yet. My breathing was heavy. The manager was behind the bar filling up the shelves with bottles for the evening shift. The smell of stale beer and cigarettes was in the air and my chest was rising and falling. I prayed to God that Mum would drive off and leave me. I ducked down and ran to another part of the pub. I crouched below a window where I knew she wouldn't look. I huddled on the cold stone floor and closed my eyes and willed her to leave. Go away. Go away. My brain was thumping. I quickly jumped up and peeked through the window and crouched back down again. She was still there in the car park. She hadn't moved. She was still sitting in the car looking at the part of the pub that I normally came out of. I turned and slumped down on the tiles and ice spread through my butt cheeks. I could smell the wood fire burning and could hear it crackling.

I used to think that big open fire in the pub was the pub's heart, but I felt its soul had left when my family had. I cried uncontrollably, tears hitting the tiles, and I bent over trying to stifle my sobs.

The pop and crackle of the fire floated through the air and mixed with the sound of clinking of bottles in the bar. I heard a car engine finally start up. I peeked out of the window again. She had turned the car and was now facing as if to leave the car park – but hadn't. There was no traffic. She could have gone. The car was not moving. Her head rose up to look out of her rear-view mirror. Mine ducked down. I heard a dog's nails on the tiles coming towards me and heavy dog breathing. The car engine grew louder and I froze as I heard it drive off.

The pub dogs were standing, panting, staring at me. I heard the manager go upstairs. I got up and ran to the pub toilets and rinsed out my mouth again and again. I gargled water and spat it out. I used soap on my face; it smelt of harsh disinfectant and stung me. I dried my face with rough paper hand towels and ran to the bar. I grabbed a half-pint beer glass and rammed it into the gin optic again and again. I filled the little space left with lime and carefully went upstairs with my hand covering the top, spillage leaking through my fingers. In my bathroom I took a humungous glug and it burnt like the cheap hand soap in the toilet. I filled the space in the glass with water and stirred it with my finger and I went and slumped down on the floor with the bed supporting my back. I gulped at my beer glass. This was medicinal drinking and I kept gulping until the glass was dry. The pain was so deep, I wanted to drown it, and I sobbed again. Sobs from a place so deep it felt my heart was ripping apart as I sat alone on that floor, bleeding from the inside, wanting someone to save me from my life. I fell into unconsciousness. When I woke there was an eerie silence in the pub.

The pub had opened for the evening shift, everybody had come, and they'd gone. The manager had gone to bed. My lights were still burning bright; he must have seen them as he passed by my room, but he hadn't knocked on the door to check on me. I felt sick and dragged myself on my hands and knees along the carpet, up the wall, stood up, hit the light switch. My lights went out.

Chapter 50
The Dance of Life

The sun rose early in Sedona and so did Lou. She left the room saying she was going to make some calls and she'd be back soon with some breakfast. I glugged on some water at the sink, it was dry in this desert, and Poppy woke up and I gave her a bottle of water too. I looked in Lou's fridge and it was empty. The room was empty; this was her life.

Lou returned with news of a room available. While packing my bags, I showed her the few pieces of jewellery I had left. She picked up a necklace, admiring it. 'It's yours, Lou, as a gift for letting me stay. It's to say thank you for everything.' She tried to give it back to me, saying the gift was too much, but I insisted she keep it.

'I have rich friends, Jane. I'll show them my necklace and tell them where you'll be staying so they can come and buy some from you.' I thanked her again. In the dark of the night I had felt calm in Lou's motel room, but now in the cool light of day I knew Lou wanted us out as quickly as possible. We jumped in our cars and drove in convoy to her friend's house.

The room I went to see was simple. It had sliding patio doors that led straight onto the desert and the walls of the room were painted white with one pretty picture. There was a large double mattress on the floor and a chest of drawers. 'I'll take it for a few days,' I said gratefully. The woman told me I could pay when I left. Lou placed a hand-drawn map of where Robert's house was on the chest of drawers.

'I'll be in touch by the phone here,' she said. I didn't know if I would actually see her again and I hugged her goodbye and thanked her for her kindness. If everyone did random acts of kindness like Lou, the world would be such a better place to live in.

I opened the patio doors and was grateful the room had air-conditioning. It was still early, but the desert heat was already taking hold. I stepped outside to see what Sedona was like in the daytime.

There were small bushes, small skinny trees, and they all looked in desperate need of water. I sat Poppy on the ground and placed some leaves in her hand. She kicked at the dry earth with her heels and grabbed it. It crumbled between her fingers and she found the sensation mesmerising. I stood up and looked out at the view. I was in awe. Majestic red mountains stood like giant gods in front of me, and my mouth dropped open. Lou had told me last night the mountains were what Sedona was famous for and now I was standing at their feet and feeling I should bow in respect. Lou told me the land in this area was famous like Glastonbury and Bali. Within the mountains lay energy vortexes. Evidently you could tell because trees nearby would have twisted trunks and branches as though they had grown in a whirlwind. Lou said if you stood in the energy vortexes it could intensify your own internal energies and help you to move forward and deal with unresolved issues. Or, Lou said, 'Maybe Sedona can make you accept your issues instead.'

That sweet my mum tried to shove in my mouth broke something in me that night. My mum, the woman who bore, fed, clothed and sheltered me, I now wanted to throw away like a sweet wrapper. I wanted to throw the life I knew in the bin too.

'Keep fighting for what you believe in, Kid. Keep pushing against your limits and keep going when you're exhausted and you'll go far in life. You'll end up a star like your old man.' My dad never gave me a lot of parenting, but whenever he did, I listened to him, and I started to dance.

Around obstacles, I didn't take no for an answer. 'One move after the other, baby steps. That's what you do when you fight,' my dad said. 'Don't think too far ahead of yourself or you might scare yourself and stop moving forward. Baby steps, Kid. Side step if you have to and never give up till the fight is over.' I kept taking steps and finally got to walk out of that pub with suitcases in my hands. I was 15 when I left the circus arena. I thought it had enough vaudeville acts in it without needing me as well. Dad bought me my suitcases. I moved into a shared house with a college friend, and his final words to me were, 'Get out there and explore the world, Jane. If you ever want to come back then at least you'll know what you're missing out on. Always be brave, Kid.' I fought with him not to see my mum again too and he told me, 'You're a good fighter, Kid. You can get whatever you want in this lifetime, just bullshit your way until you get it.'

Dad carried my bags out of his pub. He used to visit me in Brighton and paid my rent for a couple of years. I didn't see my mum for the next ten years. It was only when my sister became seriously ill with the same symptoms Mum had had at the beginning of her decline that I dashed back to help her again.

Chapter 51

It Wasn't the Cherry on the Top That Did It

Kay started feeling ill at about the same age Mum had. Kay tried not to see any similarities. Her sickness started with her being tired all the time. When Kay went to the doctors like Mum did in the early days, they prescribed vitamin pills and strengthening tonics, too. The pills and tonics didn't work for either of them.

Kay tried to justify her weak energy levels, but secretly she was scared because she remembered her mum having no energy in the early days. Kay had married her boyfriend Jim from university and when she became pregnant and her belly grew she experienced crippling stomach pains and bloating. She was told pregnancy nausea would only last a few months, but for her it lasted the whole pregnancy, and nausea and bloating then became her way of life.

Kay and Jim worked hard together to create a business; they had no family money, but they were smart and created a business with offices all over the world. It was the 1980s, everything was booming, but for Kay, tiredness, irritability, sadness and stomach pains were part of her daily life. The doctors said it was stress; Kay had a second child and the booming 1980s crashed into recession. Most mornings Kay cried at her dressing table because she didn't have the energy to lift up her hairdryer and style her hair. But she'd think, this is normal isn't it? I have a lot going on in my life and two young boys ... Her stomach pains, her wind, her emotions were all becoming very unstable now and she could hardly make it through the day. She fought against being like our mum; she kept going to different doctors trying to find the answer and they prescribed her more B vitamins, offered her anti-depressants and told her, 'These will all help with your anxieties ...'

I was travelling extensively around the world during Kay's sick years. I'd created that new life for myself I'd always dreamt of and I was in the fashion industry. I'd made a home in Bali and even though I knew Kay wasn't well, I had no idea of the severity of what she was going through. Nobody did. She was proud and didn't want to admit her weakness to anyone.

Kay would sob. She was on a bad path in life and she knew it. She was functioning on nervous energy and at the end of each day she'd plonk horizontal on her couch, looking like she was pregnant again – but she wasn't. Her mind would spin in odd directions and she flashed back to Mum: the same hospital trips, the pain, the blood pouring out of her bum. Kay had all the same symptoms ...

Kay called me in Bali when she was really bad. She said she wanted me to make her a promise and I said, 'Of course, I'll promise anything for you. What promise do you want me to make?'

'If anything happens to either one of us, Jane, and one of us ends up in hospital and not in control of their mind any more like Mum, we must promise to do something for the other. Will you promise?'

'Of course.'

My sister made me promise that if either one of us ever ended up in hospital out of her mind, the other sister must promise to wax off her moustache. We joked about keeping your dignity ... and as we laughed on the long distance call, I had no idea of the seriousness underlying my sister's request. Much later, Kay told me she had actually called me to ask for help, but she hadn't managed it. What she really wanted to ask me in that phone call was that if she ever lost the energy and will to keep trying to find the answer to her failing health, she wanted me to keep searching for her. She wanted me to promise I'd do everything to get her better.

But Kay also had Dad's fighting genes in her. She dragged herself out of bed, back into a hospital bed, and refused to leave until they had given her every possible test under the sun and found a real diagnosis: one that gave an explanation for *all* the symptoms she was suffering.

Kay was 34 years old when that hospital found out the truth about her failing health. Mum was 34 years old when Dad left her and her health rapidly declined too. Kay found out she had a disease that was genetic. It could run in families, and could lie dormant in the body for years, waiting to be triggered by trauma or shock.

When Kay was diagnosed with celiac disease, the good news was that the solution to regaining her health was simple. She simply had to give up eating gluten to become healthy again. Gluten is in foods such as wheat, rye, barley, soya sauce, gravy thickeners, cakes and breads. It's an elastin protein that holds things together in foods so they don't all fall apart, like bad crumbly cakes. Celiac disease makes your body attack itself and that's called having an autoimmune disease. Inside your intestines you have small finger-like protrusions called villi that sort through your food as it passes through your intestines. The villi collect up all the good things from your food, such as vitamins and nutrients, and let the rest pass through as poop. Celiac disease damages the villi and makes them lie down flat and stop working, which means your food stops getting filtered and you stop getting the nutrients your body needs. This can lead to malnutrition that will deplete organs and your nervous system and lead you into chronic illnesses, including depression.

When Kay was diagnosed, her family in England was on the verge of bankruptcy. Deep into the recession, Jim moved the whole family to Australia to try and salvage their last office there. In Australia, Kay stopped eating foods with gluten in them and her health slowly improved. It took her a couple of years to fully regain her heath and put her stressed-out family back together again. She studied everything she could about celiac disease, trying to make sense of what had happened to her. Then Mum came into her mind. Celiac disease is genetic. It can run in families. Maybe our mum had untreated celiac disease too? Doctors hardly knew about celiac disease when Kay got ill – doctors wouldn't have thought to test our mum for it.

Mum was now under the care of social workers in the UK and Kay contacted them. She informed them that she had celiac disease and it was genetic and asked if they could arrange to get Mum into hospital as soon as possible so she could be diagnosed too. Maybe this was the answer to all our mum's problems. Kay phoned me. She said I should get tested too.

We spoke to a celiac specialist in London dealing with mental health. He told us celiac disease can be fascinating. One of his patients was admitted into hospital because she said there was a television set on her head and all the programs were driving her mad. She also complained that she couldn't change the channels. The hospital put her on a diet of no wheat and no products with gluten in them, and discovered the patient actually craved these foods. But over the next weeks they slowly weaned her off foods containing gluten. As time went by the television set on her head shrank. The TV programs stopped annoying her. Eventually the TV disappeared altogether. The doctor told us his patient became totally sane again with not a sign of mental instability.

'So what happened to your patient after she regained her sanity?' we asked.

'Well, the problem can be,' he said, 'you need a patient with enough mental strength to stop eating gluten completely.' He told us that the patient was healthy when she left, but after some time she'd always return with the television set back on her head, playing the same annoying channels. Being a celiac is a bit like an alcoholic or drug addict: you have to want to change your life or no one can help you, and you have to be able to stop taking what is making you sick.

The doctor said he wished all patients in mental institutions could be checked for the disease as it was possible many more could be easily cured, but he still wasn't sure if this explained everything that was going wrong with the patient with the TV on her head.

After many calls to Mum's social workers, discussions and evaluations, they told us that to try and get our mum into hospital at this stage of her illness to check for the disease, we would basically need a long distance rifle with an elephant tranquilliser in it. They also told us our mum would not be a suitable case for treatment even if she did have the disease because her mind and body were now far too ill for the treatment to work. Kay argued the point. They argued back: 'You have to be realistic about this,' they said. 'If your mother is a celiac, it's too late to treat her.'

And that's when I returned to Mum's side again. I had to help her.

Chapter 52
A Cupcake Asylum

I flew back to England and drove back to the estate of my childhood. Mum had moved out of her house. There had been a terrible storm in England and it had turned a famous British landmark called Seven Oaks into five oak trees and at the same time it had blown off my mum's roof. The damp I'd lived among for all those years, that had created the ballerinas of my childhood, was obviously from the result of an unsound roof.

Mum stayed in the house with no roof for a while until the social services found her. They moved her into a monitored flat; at the bottom of the block of flats there was a social worker's office with someone always on duty. That's where I had planned a meeting. I was going to go and speak with Mum's social worker about her situation and then go and see my mum again.

I drove into Lewes, drove around the familiar roads and found the block of flats where Mum now lived. I stared at it from my car with my hands stuck on the steering wheel. I hadn't seen my mum since the sweet episode. My forehead was clammy. I had to do this somehow. I had to face my past and what I left behind all those years ago. I had to make things right. Feeling sweat all over me, I parked my car and got out.

I found the social worker's office in the entrance hall and there I was greeted with a smile and offered a cup of tea and a seat.

'Your mother's not well, Jane, but she is happy and stable in her own world,' the social worker told me. She told me she knew my mum very well, because she had worked with her for years, and she said I didn't need to be frightened of her because she wasn't violent. 'Jane, I think you should know her flat is very messy and it might shock you when you see it.' And she asked if I wanted her to come upstairs with me when I visited my mum.

I said, 'No, thank you.' I didn't want anyone from any institution being with me when I finally saw my mum again. I was over the people in white coats and I told the social worker, 'I'll come back to your office after I've seen her.'

'I've told your mum you're coming today so it won't be a shock for her,' she said, 'And I think she is looking forward to it.'

When the time came for me to leave the office and face my mum, I shook. The social worker saw and came over and hugged me. *I have to be strong. I have to be strong,* I kept telling myself, but as I left the office, I felt anything but. I pressed the lift button. I was taken up to her floor. I found her flat number and knocked on the door. I heard footsteps and flies buzzed in my stomach.

The door opened and a head peeked through a crack. 'Hello. What are you doing here?' Mum said.

'I've come to see you,' I said nervously.

'Well, you better come in for a cup of tea then.' Mum turned and waddled off down the hallway and I pushed the door open and poked my head in. I watched as she walked away from me and I could tell from her hunched-over back that she was heavier than I remembered her, but poking out of her old man's dressing gown were skinny, bony ankles and fingers. Her feet were in dirty checked slippers. I moved further into the flat to see her padding over old newspapers and rubbish up the hallway. She disappeared around a corner.

I was on autopilot and cautiously followed her. I walked over piles of newspapers and more nervous flies rose in my throat. I had to keep swallowing them down.

I entered a room and stopped. It was her living room, bedroom and kitchen all in one and I hadn't fully registered the amount of newspapers I walked over, but now I was standing on an ocean of rubbish. It spread from my feet to every corner of the room. Thick wads of newspapers, dirty clothes, bits of food, dead flowers, boxes from pre-packaged foods and plastic bags. An odd shoe here, one boot there. There was broken make-up, a hair-roller, toilet paper and empty alcohol bottles. I felt I'd fallen into a TV game show where I had to remember everything in front of me so I could tell my sister. But I didn't want any of this as a prize for my life. I froze as every sensory perception my mum had switched on for me as a kid absorbed my surroundings. A broken lamp, a child's toy, strange smells, old toast, tinfoil cupcake holders, old teabags looking like dried cushions for dolls' beds. I stared in disbelief and looked over at my mum.

She was sitting on a bed propped up by cushions that looked like sheep with dirty, fluffy guts coming out of them. Grubby floral polyester surrounded her; they were her bed covers. My eyes filled with tears; her bedding looked like it had been dragged out of discarded rubbish bins. 'Come and sit down,' she said, patting the bed.

'Do you mind if I open a window, it's a little stuffy in here?' I asked and turned so she couldn't see my crumpled up face.

There was a large window in her room and it gave me some relief. I walked over to it and looked out. My hands moved over it, trying to find a piece that would open because I needed to breathe again. A small part moved slightly and I took in a deep breath and looked at the familiar brickwork of the estate that had haunted my childhood. I wiped my eyes. I wanted to turn and face her again as the cool air made me feel better.

I turned. She'd built a fort around her bed – maybe it kept her safe from the outside world? – but the walls she'd built were unstable. They were made from empty bottles, cake boxes and newspapers. The cake boxes wobbled, piles of newspapers propped them up and the bottles provided some structural support. I wondered how my mum had reached her bed and I saw a pathway worn through the rubbish. My feet moved without my head instructing them and I took more steps towards her. Little aluminium cupcake holders scrunched underfoot and I wanted to hold them responsible for this mess. I reached the bed and sat on it. I had to grab at the polyester because I was melting into it and wanted to prevent myself from sinking further. Mum had sunk into her bed too and it was grimy under my touch.

'How are you then?' she asked.

We chatted nervously.

Strangely, we were like old friends who hadn't seen each other for a long time and it felt like no time had passed.

The flies in my tummy and throat disappeared. I listened to my mum speak and in return I'd say silly, nonsense things like, *You have a nice new flat, Mum, I like your window*, but all the time I was taking in her every detail, trying to make up for all the years I hadn't seen her. Is this what happens to someone when everyone stops caring about them?

Mum's hair was stuck to her head and it had grown into two long plaits that dripped down the front of her dressing gown. She was holding the dressing gown tightly around her and her belly had inflated so she looked like she was pregnant with twins. Her exposed skin was filthy. Mum had always been clean, maybe not tidy at the time I left her and not always dressed, but she had always been clean. The edges of the sleeves and collar of her gown were black. They matched her fingernails and the circles that ran around her neck like an African necklace. Weirdly, though, she looked stylish. Hanging from her neck, ears, wrists and fingers was every gold-coloured piece of jewellery that she must have found in the bins. She had a gypsy, rubbish-collecting look happening and a hairstyle to match. I looked closely at her face and, miraculously, she still didn't have a line on it. Underneath all the dirt, she still had beautiful skin. It was a shame Estée Lauder couldn't see this; all those years of massaging her face had worked. I looked into Mum's eyes, the part of her I knew so well. Her eyelashes were still long and thick and her eyes a deep brown, but there was something missing. Had her soul left when everything fell apart?

'I suppose you'd like a cuppa tea and a piece of cake then?' she said, trying to avoid my gaze.

'I'll make the tea,' I said, wanting to turn away from her again so she couldn't see my hurt. As I turned, empty cupcake holders looked at me accusingly.

I wanted to tidy them up, gather up all my feelings, the past, the rubbish, and put everything in a bin. I wanted to clean up my life and pretend none of this had happened. But it had and it was part of me and I had to face it. I awkwardly stood up and scrunched my way over towards the kitchen, but found myself at the window again and for the first time the bricks of my childhood were a comforting sight.

'Nice view,' I said.

'Watch out for the bastard spies,' Mum said.

'What are you talking about?'

'They're out there, fucking spying on us.' She cowered down behind her fragile wall and sank deeper in her polyester pillows. I looked out of the window and tried to work out what she was talking about.

'What spies, Mum?'

'I'll show you them fucking bastards,' she said and got up on her hands and knees. She fell off her bed, knocked a hole in her wall and crawled over the rubbish towards me. I looked down at her and she quickly jumped up and looked through the window and then ducked back down again. She looked up at me and told me where all the spies were. They were standing beside the lamppost, sitting on the walls, standing by cars and looking out of windows. She bounced up again.

'There! There!' She pointed all over the place with her dirty fingernails, jewellery banging against the glass. She crouched back down again. She looked up at me with her big brown eyes. 'They're fucking bastards, Jane. They're all fucking bastards out there,' and she turned and manoeuvred her way back behind her fragile wall again.

I turned and ran away.

Chapter 53

Aluminium Cupcake-Holders

Back at the social worker's office I broke down. 'Why can't I handle this?' I cried, and she told me she had been trained for years to do this job and not everyone had the ability to be around people like Mum.

'Why is Mum's apartment so full of rubbish?' I asked her.

'The situation now is the same as it has been for many years,' she told me. 'On paper your mum is able to look after herself, so legally she cannot be committed to an institution and now with government cuts there aren't any institutions where she could go anyway. The only way we can support her now is to help her function in her own world. Her apartment does get very messy and we did try getting the cleaners in regularly every week, but it didn't work. She's not very nice to people she doesn't know, she doesn't trust anyone, and she can be very uncooperative. Every few months now, we get the industrial cleaners in and they have a massive clean-up of her place. They bring in a skip and they hose down all the walls.'

'The walls?'

'Your mum can get very messy. But I assure you, she's happy in her own world, as long as you leave her alone.'

We talked about what the social workers had told my sister, how it would be impossible for Mum to follow any dietary restrictions now due to her mental state, and if we did manage to get her into hospital to diagnose her, all the doctors' and social workers' evaluations made it clear that Mum didn't have the mental capacity to continue treatment and to get well.

Mum's social worker now looked after Mum and all her finances. She was given money each week to survive and buy her basics. 'I can't give your mum too much money at one time because she spends it on alcohol and then upsets the other residents.'

I tried to accept everything that I was hearing.

'You also have to know, Jane, some days she will know who you are and other days she won't. If you visit her or not now, it won't make much difference to her. Trust me, I know your mother very well. I have been working with her for years.'

I drove away from that block of flats with my mind in a mess like my mum's floor. *Fucking cakes, fuck, fuck, fuck.* She became fucking addicted to what was making her fucking sick, like Bunny becoming addicted to alcohol.

I returned to Mum's flat again a few days later. I really wanted to try and help her. She opened the door to me and said, 'Oh, it's you again, Kay, come in for a cup of tea?' I walked down the hallway and this time she waved me off to the right. 'Make us some tea.' I walked towards the kitchen. The work surfaces were covered with rotten food, filthy crockery and rubbish. There was no washing-up liquid or tea towels to be found and the taps were black. I didn't want to touch anything. I found two chipped mugs in an open cupboard and what looked like blue cheese was growing in them. I opened up the fridge and closed it again as my stomach rose at the smell. But I had to start making this cup of tea somehow, and I dropped my bag and got out some rubber gloves and bin liners I'd brought with me. I had to help her. I grabbed at handfuls of rubbish on the kitchen benches and threw it into the rubbish bag. As I grabbed at more and more, I felt better. I was now helping, even in a small way, and as I worked I talked to her about the weather. I felt adventurous and I turned and grabbed a pile of rubbish off the floor. There was more underneath it. I grabbed again and it confused me because I didn't know where the floor was. Thick layers of papers dangled from my yellow, rubber-gloved hand and I could feel it was damp. Where I'd made a space on the floor, I found rotten food and I had to turn away and look out of the window to try and calm myself. As I looked out at the view and at my rubber gloves, I knew why this was a job for the industrial cleaners and not me.

I went over to Mum and gave her a bag of presents I had bought for her. She opened them. She liked the elastic-waisted skirt, the top, knickers and slippers; I'd bought them from Marks and Spencer's and I asked her if she would like to come out for a ride in my car with me next time I visited.

She nodded and said, 'Yes.'

'Where's your bathroom, Mum?'

'Down the hallway – but I'd save yourself.'

I went down the hallway and opened the only door on the left and fell back against the hall wall. There was shit all over the bathroom walls. It was smeared everywhere, like the childhood artist at my boarding school. I cried as I slammed that bathroom door and bent over trying to control myself. I didn't want her to hear me crying. This is what I used to do at boarding school: cry in the toilets like this with no noise coming out of me, just slime dropping out of my mouth and nose onto the floor.

I was suffocating again, I couldn't breathe, and I ran – again.

The social worker was waiting for me and I drowned her floor for a second time. She asked me, 'Jane, why are you really here?' And I explained how I wanted to help my mum. 'Are you here because you really want to be?'

As I delved deep, I answered her honestly. 'No.'

The social worker told me it was too late for my mum now. She told me she wouldn't be able to get better and they were taking the best care of her they could. She told me again that my mum was happy living in her own world and now it was time for me to make decisions about how I was going to live my life. Would I stay in the UK and look after my mum or carry on as I was before I came here: living in Bali and working in the business I had built up for myself?

'Your mum has this future, Jane, but you can make a different one, a brighter one. From what I hear you've been a good daughter and I think you've gone through enough trying to be one. This is now your time to enjoy your life, Jane. You deserve it. I think you've suffered enough. I don't know if we have another life after this one, but you have to choose how you are going to live yours. We can look after your mum. We're used to her and this kind of work; this is what I want to do in my life and I'm happy to do it. She's a nice person.' And the social worker held me like a baby. 'Jane, go off and live your life,' she said, 'This isn't what you are meant to do.' And I did …

Three years later, Mum set fire to herself, just after I'd given birth to Poppy. They found her dead body surrounded by small aluminium cupcake holders.

Chapter 54
Moving and Dancing or Walking

I felt weird as I looked at the Sedona mountains. It was strange that life had been moving me all over the planet and placing me in significant energy centres.

Some say the land of Bali is connected to the sex chakra of the world and for sure it opened up my sexual chakras and got me pregnant. Then I ended up in Glastonbury. The locals say the land is connected to the heart chakra of the world, and I felt my heart was protected there. Now I was in Sedona. Was this where I was going to deal with my internal shit? I looked around – is this all a big cosmic joke? It made sense now why there were no rooms available in town. Lou told me pilgrims flock to Sedona all the time, looking to shift something in themselves or to find something missing in their lives. I sat down on the earth with Poppy and sighed. What is going to happen to me here? I looked up at the mountains and Poppy giggled as a tiny lizard shot by, its bottom doing the mambo.

The dance of life and where it takes you can be a very strange thing. I held onto Poppy's hands and pulled her up and she stood and balanced. Then she wobbled forward, her nappy wagging. I grabbed her hands again and swung her back through the door and into the clean white room and then up onto my hip. I took hold of the piece of paper Lou had left for me on the chest of drawers and Poppy reached out for it too. It had Robert's address on it and a hand-drawn map of how to get there. There were pictures of the mountains on the map and I thought how kind Lou was to get all this information for me.

I felt a strange love deep inside of me as I looked at it. I felt that existence loved me and was looking after me. On this trip, it had looked after me time and time again and provided the perfect people to take care of me. I felt a deep gratitude for all the people who had come into my life and helped me to move along on my journey. Even when I ended up stranded in London with no money and no home, existence had sent me one of its angels, Rosemary.

As I looked at the map, I knew I had to start moving fast. The day was getting hotter. I was now living in the desert and I wanted to find Robert's house during the daytime before the black of the desert night made everything invisible again. Also I wanted to get up into those mountains and find some twisted tree-trunks and vortexes to sit on.

I drove to the health food store again and stocked up on some more food and water and I was grateful I didn't have to pay the rent yet. Then I drove up into those red mountains and the closer I got to them, the more stunning they became. I drove higher and followed lots of windy roads and hardly passed any traffic. Deep within them, I stopped, for no good reason other than I needed a pee. I opened the door and went to the back door to get Poppy out too. I looked up and saw an eagle circling overhead. The noise of its wings cut through the air and it soared effortlessly into the sapphire sky. Life was taking that bird higher and this bird was desperate for a pee from all the water I was drinking. I quickly unstrapped Poppy and wiped the rusk goo off her lacy summer dress and picked her up.

Even though I hadn't seen any cars on the road for ages, I still didn't want to get my knickers off in plain view and I also didn't want to leave Poppy in the car alone, so together we walked off into the bushes.

The mountains were still. Only our voices, the eagle's wings above us and our steps could be heard. Then I heard a girl laugh and I stopped dead.

Some distance in front of me I saw the edge of a picnic blanket. All the blood in my body rushed to my legs, ready to dash away, but then I felt embarrassed. The picnic blanket was a nice blanket. It didn't look like a blanket owned by a boo-boo man. I looked around me. I hadn't seen any other cars when I parked. I hadn't seen any on the road, either. Whoever was on the blanket must have heard us, though. I felt frightened again and started to panic, but then heard rustling and a girl laughing again. Oh my god, whoever was on the blanket was having sex! Now my fear had turned to edginess. I didn't want to come across as a pervert. Poppy was looking around like a bird peering out of her nest for danger; she could sense something was wrong too.

Okay, I told myself, be brave – they've heard you – they know you're here. Just walk forward – apologise – say you didn't realise anyone was here. Leave. With a pumping heart I bravely stepped into the clearing and the two people on the blanket roared with laughter.

'We saw the eagle and thought of you both and you're here!' they cried.

My head was now spinning. Poppy and I were in the middle of nowhere. Red rocks were looking down on us. Red earth spread out from us.

'*WHAT ARE YOU DOING HERE?*' I shouted and they continued to laugh as Poppy madly squirmed to get out of my arms and run to them.

'We drove here on the spur of the moment and thought we might run into you.'

It was Ted and Linguini. They had found out about Robert's satsang and thought they'd come too, but didn't know how to contact us. Ted threw Poppy up into the air with the eagle and she screeched with laughter as we all sat on the blanket together, catching up on news. Poppy kept getting up and running off and found it hysterical that someone always chased her and brought her back. But the sun was rising too fast and it was making us all wilt and we knew we had to find shelter from the day.

I looked up. The eagle had disappeared, but I knew that his appearance and Ted and Linguini's arrival meant something special was going to happen tonight at the satsang. We all left the clearing on different paths. Further ahead of my car, a small driveway split off the road on the left where Ted had parked his truck. That's why I hadn't seen it on the road. We planned to rest for the afternoon and meet again in the evening at Robert's house. As I drove off I thought life was funny.

There were many paths to a destination and it didn't matter which one you took, just as long you kept walking.

Chapter 55

Home

That evening I parked the car in front of the house where Robert Adams would be holding the satsang. Large cacti were silhouetted against the night sky. They looked like cowboys with their arms lifted up in the air, as if they were about to shoot.

Poppy was still awake, but she'd had a full day of exercise; she was worn out and I was well prepared. She had been bathed, fed and was now ready for her final milk feed. I entered the house early to find some people already sitting on the floor. There was a chair at the front. I guessed that was where Robert would sit and I was excited to be meeting him. I found a spot at the back and propped myself up against a wall. This time I'd brought toys, food, pens and paper. I put Poppy in my lap and proceeded to make a fort around us with all our supplies. Poppy was sleepy. I wrapped her up in a blanket and together we slowly watched the room fill with more people. Some came over to us; they would quietly say hello to Poppy and she'd put out her hand each time so they could hold it. There were no other babies in the room and I knew there was a good reason for that. Now was a child's bath time, getting-ready-for-bed time, not going-to-a-satsang time. I didn't want my child to have to go to any more either.

I hoped Robert would be able to end my journey. I wanted to go home so badly now – if only I knew where it was.

Ted and Linguini arrived. They came over and quietly kissed us both and then whispered they were going to sit at the front. I nodded and smiled and soon the room filled and slipped into a quiet meditation. That was the sign I was waiting for. I tucked Poppy further into her blanket, picked her up, covered her head and started to give her her final feed, but she kept pulling the blanket off her head. She wanted to look around the room. She made me nervous, but the look in her eyes was peaceful. Then Robert Adams entered.

Two helpers assisted him. They were on either side of him, holding his arms, and they guided him to the chair at the front. They sat him down and then sat either side of him like the lions in Trafalgar Square that sat protecting Nelson's Column. The two lions closed their eyes and I looked at Robert. He was no straight column. He had a little frail body that was dressed in white and he was bent over from his illness. His hair was white too. It was thin, cropped close to his head and his eyelids were closed, but flickered in his meditation. He was dribbling out of the corner of his mouth and I couldn't close my eyes because I was so fascinated by him. Indian bells rang. They announced the end of meditation and he opened his flickering eyes and looked at us.

He started to grunt.

I smiled.

He kept grunting.

I looked around to see if anyone else was going to laugh, but they were all very serious and I tried to be as well, but I had just crossed the desert with a baby to see this man and I was hoping he had the answer to my life, and here was a grunting cripple.

Robert was insistent on saying something and wasn't stopping. I had to put my head down and kiss Poppy's head to suppress my laughter. I travelled across America to listen to this? I won't ever take life seriously again! Poppy's eyes were fully open and she'd completely pulled the blanket off her head. She was intently looking at Robert, just like all the other people in the room. She was listening to him. Maybe he's speaking her language? She was taking this seriously and as I looked around, everyone else was too. Maybe I should. I straightened my back.

'Uhh, uh, uhhh,' he grunted and I looked around smiling; I couldn't help myself. Everyone was serious. Stop being a prat, I said to myself. Concentrate.

'Uhh, uuummgu, uhgmnh, uhh, umm,' and then – he stopped. I took another breath. He nodded at the lions at his feet and they started to translate for him.

To be honest, I can't remember a word they said, all I know was how I started to feel.

Maybe I was sitting on a Sedona energy vortex and it was going right up my arse, but I was becoming totally blissed as though on strong intravenous chamomile tea. Poppy kept staring mesmerised at Robert and was well behaved through the whole satsang. When it came to an end, we were told by the lions that whoever wanted to could come up to Robert for a blessing.

Poppy was 11 months old when I went up for him to bless her. 'I made it here,' I said to him quietly. 'I'm the girl on the phone and I've been on a very long journey.' He grunted at me and made a gesture with his hands. The lions by his side translated. They told me to put Poppy in his arms. I went closer to him and placed Poppy on his lap and he wrapped his arms around her to keep her safe. I knelt back down at his feet and she lay there looking up into his eyes and not moving. She never did that with anyone. He grunted as he looked into her eyes too.

'Robert wants her,' a lion translated for me.

'He can't have her,' I replied and Robert started grunting again.

'Robert wants you to leave her with him,' the lions continued. 'He said he can look after her.'

I wanted to cry. 'I would never leave my child. She's my family and I'm never giving her up.' Robert looked at me and started to laugh and held Poppy closer and leaned back as though to test my resolve and see if I really wanted her. I now laughed with him too, and I gestured to him that I wanted her back straight away. It was in that moment I knew my journey was over.

Robert's lions helped me to retrieve Poppy from his arms and they smiled at me. In Robert's eyes, I saw that he knew what had happened to me, and he nodded at me in acknowledgment. I nodded too and thanked him. I got up off my knees.

I turned and walked out of that house because it was time to take my baby home.

The stars winked as I looked for my car, but there were too many cars parked behind me and I couldn't leave. I sat down on the stone porch of the house and held Poppy wrapped in her blanket. I looked behind me.

The house was shining bright with people. They were now drinking chai and chatting and I could smell cinnamon in the air. I snuggled Poppy into my cross-legged lap, stroked her blonde hair and bent down to kiss her forehead.

'Honey, we don't have to keep searching for anything any more. I've found what I was looking for,' and I looked back at the brick house and knew it wasn't one of those.

I'd been on the road searching for such a long time, since I was a kid, and now, looking down at Poppy, I realised I had in my arms what I'd been looking for forever, and she was precious and falling asleep. Poppy had taught me so much about love since she had come into my life. She had taught me to never give up on it and to keep working at it even when you are exhausted. I felt so much love surrounding the two of us on that desert step. I looked up to the stars and hoped that somehow the Blond could hear me. I thanked him for coming into my life and giving me such a special gift.

I now knew where my home was. It was where my family was – wherever they were in the world, and my home right now was with Poppy and somehow I was going to get back to Australia to be with my sister too. I thought back to when I left Kay's house and felt silly I'd left; but sometimes it takes a journey to realise what you already have.

I giggled to myself and looked up to the sky and winked and I finally felt the fuse that had been burning up my bottom all these years, powering me forward like a dragon with no mercy for my life, go out. I sat on that cold stone porch and felt relieved and laughed again as I remembered another story I had constantly been telling Poppy during this journey. I looked at her closed eyes, her body was heavy, but I knew she was not completely asleep. I told her a story to take her to her dreams.

> One day a young girl went to a man sitting under a tree and asked him, 'Where is the Tree of Paradise?'
>
> 'If you are looking for the Tree of Paradise, you have to find a wise man, as only he will know.'

So the young girl went through the town and asked many people if they knew where a wise man lived. A fool very excitedly told her, 'I know where the wise man is! You have to go through the valley and over two mountains and there on the top of the mountain you will find another fool and he will know where the wise man is.'

She thanked him and went on her journey. She was on a mission. So she went through the valley, over a mountain, through streams and fields till she came to another mountain and there on top of a mountain she found another fool. 'Excuse me, do you know where the Tree of Paradise is?' she asked.

He told her he didn't know, but he knew of another fool who did, and sent her off in another direction.

Years passed, and many landscapes, fools and stories led her to yet more fools. But this girl was persistent and she didn't want to give up. One day a fool told her about a wise man who sat under a tree in a beautiful garden. It took her a long time to get to the garden, but as she walked through it, she beamed at everything around her, and at the very end of the garden she saw a tree with a man sitting underneath its branches. She walked slowly towards the tree and realised that this was the man she had first put her question to so many years before.

'Why didn't you tell me this was the Tree of Paradise?' she asked him.

'Because, if I had told you all those years ago,' the wise man said, 'you wouldn't have believed me anyway.'

Epilogue

What Happened to Everybody Afterwards

It took me a while to get back to Melbourne, Australia, but I made it there and made a home next to my sister Kay. We consider ourselves one big family. I went back to college so I could become an Australian resident and I studied counselling, so I could help other people. In Australia, when Poppy was seven, I met the man of my dreams. We got married and he adopted Poppy as his own child, but he had dreams too. Antony always wanted to work abroad, so for the past ten years our family have lived in China, where I became a writer.

Poppy is 18 and has left home in Shanghai to return to Australia to attend university. She has studied in some of the best schools in the world, travelled around the world more times than I could mention, and is one of the most caring, sensible people I know. A picture of her is on the back cover.

The Blond has never been part of our lives.

Kay went back to college and qualified as a homeopath. She specialised in helping children for a long time and then created a business helping adults who are too busy to look after themselves. Her business is called Mr Cornelius.

Rosemary, the sweet lady who rented me the cottage in Glastonbury, found the energy to move to Cornwall, where she'd always dreamed of living.

Helen has been a fantastic Nana Helen to Poppy and stayed in her life, keeping an eye on her, sending her presents and always calling to see how we are.

My brother Dax became a fighter pilot in the United States Air Force and Poppy and I were there to clap and cheer at his graduation. Dax fought in three wars for America and completed his contract before he realised he was a lover not a fighter and he resigned.

Sadly, Dax's graduation was the last time my brothers, sister and I were all in the same country together.

Ted continues to discover the joy in life, he is one of the happiest people I know. He is no longer with Linguine.

I sold my Bali house about ten years ago to a lovely woman who, in the contract of sale, agreed to always look after my Balinese family.

My brother George now lives in Spain with his wife and daughter.

Danny, my friend with one leg, found a woman who loved him. She helped him to get off the drugs. He is happily married with children.

Many of my other drug-taking friends died or have become mentally ill.

The Bunny died alone and an alcoholic.

My dad, at the age of 85, stopped seeing his sixth de facto wife, got another new girlfriend, and on the phone told me, 'Jane, you're never too old to try new things with your life!'

Thank you

To Antony, for telling me to 'Do it,' when I told him I wanted to give up work and write instead. The way you're constantly by my side supporting me whatever mad idea I come up with never ceases to amaze me.

To Poppy, for coming into my life and shining your radiance, for being proud of me giving up work to write a book and for styling the recent picture of you on the back cover.

To my UK family of friends: Nana Helen, Rosemary, Raymond, Dee, Guru Johnny, Komodo Mark and Chantelle, who helped me bring Poppy into the world – I cannot thank you enough.

To my sister, my rock. In so many ways, I wouldn't be here today and who I am without you.

To Antony, Jim, George and Dax for being the loving, inspirational men in my life.

To Ferg, Jack, Ellie, Jo and Sage, my special crew.

To my friends around the world who have stuck with me through all my transformations – you are gold.

To my writing groups in Hong Kong, thanks for your support, laughter and drunken nights wondering if we would ever get our books out into the world.

To Sussana, my first-ever writing teacher, who gave me the writing spark that never went out.

To Shannon Young, thank you for always sticking with me. Your edits on all my books have been magic and they gave me the confidence to put wings on them to make them fly. You're my editing angel.

Thank you to my Shanghai friends, Madeline Leary for taking the recent pictures of Poppy, Shafei Xia for the illustrations and Shen Gui Zhen for knitting me the cute slippers on the front cover.

To my agent Brian Cook who I adore, thanks for making me laugh, believing in me and getting me a publishing deal. To Foong Ling Kong who had the brilliant idea to combine the two books I wrote, *Cupcake Asylum* and *Baby and a Backpack*, into one. To my publishing team, the excellent Kay Scarlett, Julia Taylor, Linda Funnell, Juliet Chan, Nada Backovic and so many more at The Five Mile Press – you are so smart, what a joy to work with you. I'm so glad I didn't self-publish!

To my dad, who has entertained and made so many people happy in his life. You taught me unconditional love and so many lessons that have made me the strong woman I am today. Thank you for everything.

Work hard. Don't just dream your garden has plants in it. You have to put seeds in the earth, water them and look after them every day. And by caring about your vision, one day you'll discover a magnificent view in front of you.

Jane
A fellow gardener

If you would like to know more about Jane and see pictures from the *Baby and a Backpack* story please go to: www.janecornelius.com